JUST AND HOLY PRINCIPLES

PRINCIPLES

LATTER-DAY SAINT READINGS ON AMERICA AND THE CONSTITUTION

RALPH C. HANCOCK, EDITOR
BRIGHAM YOUNG UNIVERSITY

Pearson
Custom
Publishing

Cover photo: "Mormon Temple, Salt Lake City," courtesy of
The Church of Jesus Christ of Latter-Day Saints.

Printed in the United States of America

10

Please visit our web site at www.pearsoncustom.com

ISBN 0-536-01650-X

BA 990919 (College Edition)

ISBN 0–536–01693-3

BA 98476 (Trade Edition)

PEARSON CUSTOM PUBLISHING
75 Arlington Street, Boston, MA 02116
A Pearson Education Company

COPYRIGHT ACKNOWLEDGMENTS

Contents

Part Three

Acknowledgments

Thanks are due to the American Heritage program at Brigham Young University for its support in gathering and preparing the materials for this volume, and particularly to my colleagues Gary Daynes, Frank Fox, Clayne Pope, and Noel Reynolds for their valuable consultations—though the editor must claim full responsibility for any mistakes or oversights. I would also like to thank the able and diligent student assistants who have made this volume possible: Stephanie Swift, Jon Eskelsen, Jared Hancock, and Corbin Gordon.

The introduction is adapted and expanded from the editor's article "Constitution of the United States of America," in the *Encyclopedia of Mormonism* (New York: MacMillan, 1992). The biographical data used in introducing the authors was gathered largely from Lawrence Flake, *Mighty Men of Zion* (Salt Lake City, Utah: Karl D. Butler, 1974) and the *Deseret News Church Almanac* (Salt Lake City, serial).

Introduction

Ralph C. Hancock

Latter-day Saints have almost from the beginning attached special significance to the Constitution of the United States of America, a commitment that
is grounded firmly in LDS scripture. Beyond reinforcing the general Christian duty of "respect and deference" to civil laws and governments as "instituted of God for the benefit of man" (D&C 134:1, 6), the Doctrine and Covenants
states specifically that the Lord "established the Constitution of this land, by
the hands of wise men whom [He] raised up unto this very purpose" (D&C
101:80). The Prophet Joseph Smith once described himself as "the greatest advocate of the Constitution of the United States there is on the earth" (HC
6:56–7). All of his successors as President of the Church have reaffirmed the
doctrine of an inspired Constitution.[1] This consistent expression of loyalty is
particularly remarkable given the context of severe religious persecution and repeatedly unanswered appeals to justice.[2] From the standpoint of political theory, what is perhaps most notable in the tradition of LDS constitutionalism is
the reconciliation of apparently disparate ultimate principles of authority: the
unwavering loyalty of a Church based upon the governing authority of divine
revelation to a living prophet to a form of government founded upon natural,
rational, and equal rights.

The idea of an inspired Constitution is now rare in public discourse and
almost unheard of in contemporary constitutional and historical scholarship.
It was once common, however, to discern the hand of divinity in America's
beginnings, not only in popular and patriotic rhetoric, but among eminent
nineteenth-century historians such as George Bancroft. Perhaps even more
important is the repeated acknowledgment of divine aid by America's founding fathers. George Washington, most notably, frequently expressed gratitude
to God for the felicitous circumstances surrounding the rise of the United
States and chose the occasion of his first inaugural address to recognize the
providential character of the framing of the Constitution:

> *No people can be bound to acknowledge and adore the invisible hand which
> conducts the affairs of men, more than the People of the United States.
> Every step by which they have advanced to the character of an independent
> nation seems to have been distinguished by some token of providential*

agency. And in the important revolution just accomplished in the system of their united government, the tranquil deliberations and voluntary consent of so many distinct communities, from which the event has resulted, cannot be compared with the means by which most governments have been established, without some return of pious gratitude, along with an humble anticipation of future blessings which the past seem to presage.

The LDS teaching regarding an inspired Constitution is thus substantially in harmony with the self-understanding of the founding generation. Latter-day Saints believe that the Lord established the Constitution, not by communicating specific measures, but by raising up and inspiring wise men to this purpose. This emphasis on the extraordinary character of the American founders—and perhaps, more generally, on the founding generation as a whole—accords with assessments by contemporaries, as well as by later students of the period. Thomas Jefferson, then U. S. ambassador to France, described the Constitution Convention of 1787 as "an assembly of demigods." More than forty years later, Alexis de Tocqueville, the noted French observer of American society, included the American people as a whole in his praise of the founding:

> *That which is new in the history of societies is to see a great people, warned by its lawgivers that the wheels of government are stopping, turn its attention on itself without haste or fear, sound the depth of the ill, and then wait for two years to find the remedy at leisure, and then finally, when the remedy has been indicated, submit to it voluntarily without its costing humanity a single tear or drop of blood.*[3]

If the divine inspiration of the Constitution is mediated through the human wisdom of the founders and the founding generation, then it is natural to suppose that new needs and new circumstances might require the continued exercise of inspired human wisdom by statesmen and citizens alike. LDS leaders have indeed taught that the Constitution is not to be considered perfect and complete in every detail (as evidenced most clearly by its accommodation with slavery, contrary to modern scripture; e.g., D&C 101:79) but as subject to development and adaptation. It was part of the wisdom of the founders to forbear attempting too much; they therefore provided constitutional means for constitutional amendment. President Brigham Young thus affirmed that the Constitution "is a progressive—a gradual work"; the founders "laid the foundation, and it was for after generations to rear the superstructure upon it" (*Journal of Discourses* 7:13–15; below p. 17).

Given this developmental perspective, it is appropriate that tolerance and a reasonable diversity should exist in matters considered non-essential (B. H. Roberts, p. 61). Thus, where "political" or partisan questions are concerned, Church leaders have often proclaimed official neutrality and encouraged members to participate in the political process according to their best lights and to respect the right of others to do so (David O. McKay p. 87).

If the wisdom embodied in the Constitution is considered open to future development, so must it be understood as rooted deeply in the past. J. Reuben Clark, Jr., perhaps the most thorough expositor of the Constitution among past LDS Church leaders, emphasized the dependence of the founders' wisdom on "the wisdom of long generations that had gone before and which had been transmitted to them through tradition and the pages of history"[4] He saw the Constitution as the product especially of England's centuries-long struggle for self-government.[5] This historical perspective accords well with the account of the Book of Mormon, according to which the Lord guided the discovery, colonization, and struggle for independence of America (1 Ne. 13:12–13), in order to establish it as a "land of liberty" (2 Ne. 10:11).

Latter-day Saint teaching differs from the traditional providential view of the founding chiefly in embracing this liberty not only as blessing in itself but also, especially, as a condition for the restoration of the fulness of the gospel of Jesus Christ. Jeffrey R. Holland, in a panoramic essay that serves as the prologue to this collection, beautifully situates the American Founding in the broad sweep of sacred history, from Eden to the New Jerusalem. George Albert Smith, in an Independence Day speech of 1854 (p. 10), discerns the beginnings of the American Revolution behind the veil of this mortal existence. Orson Whitney (p. 55), and, fifty years later, Charles Nibley (p. 67) describe the Restoration of the Gospel as profoundly bound up with the coming forth of the American Republic in their common purpose of freeing all mankind to exercise moral agency. This point of view illuminates the significance of J. Reuben Clark's frequent affirmation that "this Constitution is part of my religion," (p. 100, 107), and it reveals the deep grounding in the LDS tradition of President Hugh B. Brown's 1963 statement in favor of full civil rights to all, regardless of race, color, or creed (p. 126).

This is not to say, of course, that American constitutionalism and the Kingdom of God are simply identical. Both Orson Pratt (p. 19) and Erastus Snow (p. 41) are clear that, however divinely ordained, the Constitution is imperfect and adapted to a sinful world. It deserves our loyalty because it is inspired of God as the best suited to the protection of human rights at this time. Elder L. Tom Perry makes in clear in 1976 that, even as the Church expands worldwide, the strength and goodness of the United States of America remains essential to the mission of the Restoration. The greatest significance of American republicanism for Latter-day Saints is, therefore, that it has served as the indispensable cradle of the Restoration—albeit at times a distinctly tumultuous one—and that it continues to provide a base of freedom and prosperity.

We have noted that LDS teaching about the wisdom of the Founding readily acknowledges that it was both conditioned by the past and open to the future. Still, there can be no question of completely reducing the Constitution to its historical conditions or of making it indefinitely open to re-interpretation. If the document framed in 1787 remains a touchstone today, this is because, in some admittedly imperfect way, it aims at "the rights and protection of all flesh, according to just and holy principles" (D&C 101:77). Thus J. Reuben Clark, though ever alert to the developmental character of the Constitution, emphatically warned the Saints in 1938 against the dangers of the new State, declaring that the "Great Fundamentals" must not be abandoned (p. 100, 101). Similarly, Levi Edgar Young had warned in 1937 that even small changes made in the name of "progress" might undermine constitutional liberties. President Heber J. Grant pleaded with members in 1944 never to depart from the inspired Constitution. And President David O. McKay affirmed plainly that "there are some fundamental principles of this republic which, like eternal truths, never get out of date . . . Such are the underlying principles of the Constitution."[6]

The scriptural reference to "just and holy principles" appears to locate these fundamentals in certain "rights." Section 98 of the Doctrine and Covenants recommends friendship to constitutional law based on the harmony between freedom under its law and freedom under God (D&C 98:6,8). Similarly, the Scripture links human "rights" with the opportunity to "act in doctrine and principle pertaining to futurity, according to the moral agency which I have given unto him, that every man may be accountable for his own sins in the day of judgment" (D&C 101:78). In this way, the reverence of Latter-day Saints for the Constitution is anchored in the fundamental doctrine of free agency, or the idea that God makes possible people's progress toward eternal life by exposing them to the consequences, good or bad, of their choices. LDS scholars who have examined the Constitution from the standpoint of this fundamental interest in moral freedom have exhibited its connection with the basic principles of the rule of law[7] and of the separation of powers[8], both of which concepts are connected with the ideal of limited government.

At the core of the LDS doctrine of an inspired Constitution there stands, then, a certain understanding of freedom as "moral agency." As the documents collected here demonstrate, throughout the history of the Church its authorities have consistently appealed to constitutional principles as supportive of this freedom. But these statements also tell a story of changing contexts and therefore of changing priorities and emphases. If, as James E. Talmage said in 1912, human beings tend to interpret rights in a one-sided way, favorable to their own interests, then a large part of constitutional wisdom would consist in leaning into prevailing winds of interpretation in a given historical context in order to reinforce neglected aspects of the whole of liberty. Thus, in the context of severe persecution, and speaking on behalf of a small minority whose rights were often utterly disregarded, Joesph Smith expresses the wish that the government had more power to enforce the Constitution (p. 5—(a wish that might be said to have been in a way fulfilled in the Supreme Court's application of the 14th amendment in the twentieth century); George Albert Smith, on the other hand, interprets the principles of the American Revolution so as to emphasize the Utah Mormons' *independence* from any central power (p. 11–12). Nineteenth-century LDS statements often partake of the age's belief in the progress of general enlightenment, a confidence that man's rational and natural rights must eventually overwhelm ancient prejudices; but later pronouncements reveal a concern that false understandings of progress—especially various European "isms" challenging American ideals—threaten sound constitutional principles.[9] Particularly striking is the strong emphasis on the threat of communism, a new atheistic tyranny, an emphasis that emerges at least as early as Rulon Wells' address of 1930 (p. 71) and is maintained throughout the whole middle third of the twentieth century. The importance of defending the Constitution against this organized threat as well as against the erosion of principles of limited government is a consistent theme in statements of Church authorities such as David O. McKay, J. Reuben Clark, and especially Ezra Taft Benson.

More recently, as the traditional moral consensus of American society has eroded and confidence in the inevitable progress of a simply rational constitutionalism has waned, Church leaders have articulated a new emphasis on the moral and religious sources of the morality on which the Constitution depends. In the last statements collected here, Elders Maxwell and Holland and President Hinckley remind us forcefully that constitutional freedom cannot endure without personal virtue. Elder Oaks (1992, p. 143) deplores the severing of rights from responsibilities, and defends the legitimacy of religious values in public policy debates. And Elders Ballard and Faust warn against the implicit establishment of secularism as a new state-sponsored religion.

The importance of the Constitution to Latter-day Saints has long been reinforced by a well-authenticated tradition deriving from a statement of Joseph Smith according to which the Constitution would one day "hang by a thread" and be rescued, if at all, only with the help of the Saints. Church President John Taylor seemed to go still further when he prophesied:

> *When the people shall have torn in shreds the Constitution of the United States the Elders of Israel will be found holding it up to the nations of the earth and proclaiming liberty and equal rights to all men* (Journal of Discourses 21:8).

The most recent warnings of Church authorities regarding the now imperiled bond between rights and moral responsibility suggest the need for continued reflection on the relationship between freedom and virtue as we renew our efforts to secure the political conditions for the fullest exercise of moral agency. If "moral agency" stands at the core of the doctrine of an inspired Constitution, then one might say that where LDS teaching in the nineteenth century emphasized the agency, Church leaders in the twentieth century have increasingly stressed the moral foundations of the Constitution, echoing the prophet Mosiah in the Book of Mormon: "If the time comes that the voice of the people doth choose iniquity, then is the time that the judgments of God will come upon you" (Mosiah 29:26–7; cf. Ether 2:8–12). To defend the principles of the Constitution under circumstances where the "iniquity" of the people has "torn it to shreds" might well require inspiration and wisdom equal to that of the generation raised up to found it.

NOTES

1. Beyond the sources provided here, one should consult on this point the comprehensive collection of statements by Church Presidents in Donald Q. Cannon, *Latter-day Prophets and the United States Constitution*. Provo, Utah, 1991.
2. This loyalty in the face of persecution is represented in many of the statements collected here, notably those by Joseph Smith (p. 3), George Q. Cannon (p. 35) and Erastus Snow (p. 41).
3. *Democracy in America*, ed. J. P. Mayer (Garden City, N.Y. Doubleday 1969), Vol 1. p. 113.
4. *Stand Fast By Our Constitution* (Salt Lake City, Deseret Books, 1978), p. 136. See also below, "Our Constitution—Divinely Inspired," p. [100], and the Independence Day speech of 1937 by Albert E. Bowen, p. 80.
5. See, below, "Constitutional Government," p. [92], on the Anglo-Saxon development of constitutionalism as opposed to Roman civil law.
6. See below, p. 88 [October 6, 1940].
7. See Noel B. Reynolds, "The Doctrine of an Inspired Constitution," in Ray C. Hilliam, ed., "*By the Hands of Wise Men": Essays on the U. S. Constitution* (Provo, Utah, Brigham Young University Press, 1979), pp. 1–28.
8. See Martin Hickman "J. Reuben Clark, Jr.: The Constitution and the Great Fundamentals," in Hillam, ed. pp. 39–57.
9. See, for example, James E. Talmage's early response to a "progressivism" that disparages the Constitution, p. 66.

Prologue

A Promised Land
Jeffrey R. Holland

Temporarily, we call it America. But it began with the single, primeval
continent of Genesis, and the miracle of millennial healing will bring that
unity again.

Some otherwise plain and rather ordinary places can become very special to
us. Our homes, a hillside, the hospitals where our children were born, the ceme-
teries where they are laid—these and many more have special meaning not so
much for the soil or brick itself but because of what has happened (or will yet
happen) there. That meaning has more importance as the events take on eternal as well as temporal significance.

"The place of Mormon, the waters of Mormon, the forest of Mormon,
how beautiful are they to the eyes of them who there came to the knowledge
of their Redeemer." (Mosiah 18:30.)

So sang the prophet who knew that a pool of water is no longer merely a pool of water once you have been baptized there. "From lowest place
when virtuous things proceed, the place is dignified in the doer's deed," said
Shakespeare. (*All's Well That Ends Well*. II. iii. 123–24.)

The most sacred of places, then, will always be these locations which
God has designated for holy and eternal purposes, locations where he is the
"doer of the deed." These places are revered forever by his faithful children
wherever they may be.

America is such a place, but of course it wasn't always called America
nor has it always been identified by a distinctive continental shape. Originally
it was simply a portion of that large, single land mass which God in his creative process called "Earth" and which, when completed, was pronounced
"good." (Gen. 1:10.) Whatever its name and geographical configuration,
however, it was from the beginning a land of divinity as well as a land of
destiny.

The choicest part of this earthly creation was a garden "eastward in
Eden" where God placed our first parents, Adam and Eve. This resplendent

place filled with paradisiacal glory was located on that part of the land mass where the city Zion, or the New Jerusalem of the earth's last days, would eventually be built. (See D&C 57:1–3, D&C 84:1–3; and Joseph Fielding Smith, *Doctrines of Salvation*, 3:74.) After Adam and Eve were driven out of the Garden, they dwelt at a place called Adam-ondi-Ahman, located in what is now Daviess County, Missouri. In that region this first family lived out their days, tilling the soil, tending the flocks, offering sacrifices, and learning the gospel of Jesus Christ from on high. There Adam prophesied concerning all the families of the earth and, three years before his death, called together the righteous remnant of his posterity and bestowed upon them his last blessing. The Lord appeared unto this faithful group and Adam's family rose up "and blessed Adam, and called him Michael, the prince, the archangel.

"And the Lord administered comfort unto Adam, and said unto him: I have set thee to be at the head; a multitude of nations shall come of thee, and thou art a prince over them forever.

"And Adam stood up in the midst of the congregation; and, notwithstanding he was bowed down with age, being full of the Holy Ghost, predicted whatsoever should befall his posterity unto the latest generation." (D&C 107:54–56.)

Never before had one spot of earth been favored with such a meeting, nor provided the stage for such sacred scenes from the drama of man's ultimate destiny.

But even as such sacred manifestations and proclamations were recorded, the land was being polluted with unrighteousness. The willful Cain had already made his covenant with Satan and taken the life of his younger brother, Abel. Others were joining in the work of darkness until shortly God "cursed the earth with a sore curse, and was angry with the wicked, . . . for they would not hearken unto his voice, nor believe on his Only Begotten Son." (Moses 5:56–57.) The righteous Enoch helped save a city but the heaven wept over the wickedness of his generation, shedding their tears "as the rain upon the mountains." (Moses 7:28.) Indeed, the earth itself groaned against the defilement of God's sacred soil, crying: "I am weary, because of the wickedness of my children. When shall I rest, and be cleansed from the filthiness which is gone forth out of me? When will my Creator sanctify me, that I may rest, and righteousness for a season abide upon my face?" (Moses 7:48.)

Two generations later the Lord was so pained by that generation "without affection" (Moses 7:33) that he opened the windows of heaven and cleansed the entire earth with water. Thus, the "everlasting decree" (Eth. 2:10) was first taught that he who will not obey the Lord in righteousness will be swept from his sacred land. The lesson would be tragically retaught in dispensations yet to come.

Holy scripture records that "after the waters had receded from off the face of this land it became a choice land above all other lands, a chosen land of the Lord; wherefore the Lord would have that all men should serve him who dwell upon the face thereof." (Eth. 13:2.) Such a special place needed now to be kept apart from other regions, free from the indiscriminate traveler as well as the soldier of fortune. To guarantee such sanctity the very surface of the earth was rent. In response to God's decree, the great continents separated and the ocean rushed in to surround them. The promised place was set apart. Without habitation it waited for the fulfillment of God's special purposes.

With care and selectivity, the Lord began almost at once to repeople the promised land. The Jaredites came first, with stories of the great flood fresh in their memories and the Lord's solemn declaration ringing in their ears: "Whoso should possess this land of promise, from that time henceforth and forever, should serve him, the true and only God, or they should be swept off when the fulness of his wrath should come upon them." (Eth. 2:8.)

Despite such counsel, however, the Jaredite civilization steadily degenerated into a violent society which forced a man to keep "the hilt of his sword in his right hand" (Eth. 14:2)—until finally he "ate and slept, and prepared for death on the morrow." (Eth. 15:26.)

But even as the last light flickered on Jaredite civilization, a bold new sun rose to illuminate a thousand years of Nephite-Lamanite experience on the same soil. Despite periods of war and rebellion, these people nevertheless had great moments of power and purity, including the personal ministry of the resurrected Christ, who walked and talked and prayed with these New World inhabitants for three indescribable days. There in the meridian of time the land enjoyed three generations of peace and perfection, which it would not know again until the Master's millennial reign.

But the lessons of history, if not learned well, are certain to be taught again, and a lone father with his son lived to see the self-destruction of these people of promise. The Nephite-Lamanite morality descended from "sorceries, and witchcrafts, and magics" (Morm. 1:19) into rape, murder, and cannibalism (see Moro. 9:7–10), creating a vision so repulsive that it was "impossible for the tongue to describe, or for man to write," a scene of greater wickedness than had ever been seen "even among all the house of Israel" (Morm. 4:11, 12). A thousand years after God had given such choice land to their fathers and a thousand years before he would attempt to do it again. Mormon wrote to his son Moroni:

"O the depravity of my people! They are without order and without mercy. . . .

"They delight in everything save that which is good: and the suffering of our women and our children . . . doth exceed everything. . . .

"Thou knowest that they are without principle, and past feeling. . . .

"Behold, my son, I cannot recommend them unto God lest he should smite me." (Moro. 9:18–20.)

This favored branch allowed to run over the wall had reached that forewarned "fulness of iniquity" and was dwindling into disorder, darkness, and death.

Then in the allegorical prophecy made of these events, "the Lord of the vineyard" looked at the waste of his creation—and wept. "What could I have done more for my vineyard?" was his painful cry. No answer could be given. "Have I slackened mine hand, that I have not nourished it? Nay, I have nourished it, and I have digged about it, and I have pruned it, and I have dunged it; and I have stretched forth mine hand almost all the day long, and the end draweth nigh." (Jac. 5:41, 47.) In spite of such grief and despair the Lord of the vineyard determined to "spare it a little longer" (Jac. 5:50)—long enough for one final attempt, long enough for one more dispensation, long enough for one final experiment focused on the promised land.

So, after a thousand years of preparation, the Spirit of God rested upon a young Italian sailing under the flag of Spain, and, as Nephi had seen in vision, "he went forth upon the many waters, even unto the seed of my brethren, who were in the promised land." (1 Ne. 13:12.) This "Christian of almost maniacal devoutness" as Alistair Cooke calls him, this man with the zeal of Galileo, Don Quixote, and John the Baptist combined, was not to be denied. (Alistir Cooke, *America*, New York: Alfred Knopf, 1973, p. 30.) "Our Lord with provident hand unlocked my mind," said Columbus, "sent me upon the seas, and gave me fire for the deed. Those who heard of my enterprise called it foolish, mocked me, and laughed. But who can doubt but that the Holy Ghost inspired me?" (Jacob Wasserman, *Columbus, Don Quixote of the Seas*, New Brunswick: Rutgers Univ. Press, 1959, p. 20.) Columbus stood on the captain's deck, but the all-seeing eye of the Lord was on the compass, and the hopes of every dispensation filled the sails. The prophet Nephi had also seen in vision what followed: colonization, war, and the birth of a new nation.

"And it came to pass that I, Nephi, beheld that the Gentiles who had gone forth out of captivity did humble themselves before the Lord: and the power of the Lord was with them.

"And I beheld that their mother Gentiles were gathered together upon the waters, and upon the land also, to battle against them.

"And I beheld that the power of God was with them, and also that the wrath of God was upon all those that were gathered together against them to battle. And I, Nephi, beheld that the Gentiles that had gone out of captivity were delivered by the power of God out of the hands of all other nations." (1 Ne. 13:16–19.)

Once again, after meticulous preparation and precise timing, the Lord had begun to build on his promised land a congregation that had compacted to pursue "the glory of God and the advancement of the Christian faith." The cultural freedom of the Renaissance and religious freedom of the Reformation underscored the strong sense of personal freedom espoused in the Enlightenment to provide the ideal attitudes and environments for the beginning of this "first new nation." George Washington, six years before he was inaugurated as the initial president of the Grand Experiment, wrote of America's moment in history:

"The foundation of our empire was not laid in the gloomy age of ignorance and superstition, but in an epoch when the rights of mankind were better understood and more clearly defined than at any former period. The researchers of the human mind after social happiness have been earned to a greater extent, the treasures of knowledge . . . are laid open for our use and their collected wisdom may be happily applied in the establishment of our forms of government." (Henry Steele Commager. "America and the Enlightenment," in *The Development of a Revolutionary Mentality*, Washington, D. C.: Library of Congress, 1972, p. 14.)

Thomas Paine also sensed the propitiousness of the times. "The case and circumstance of America present themselves as in the beginning of a world," he wrote. "We have no occasion to roam for information into obscure fields of antiquity, nor hazard ourselves upon conjecture. We are brought at once to the point of seeing government begin, as if we had lived in the beginning of time." (Commager, p. 19.)

Neither Washington nor Paine knew, however, the full import of their work or their time. Indeed it was a beginning, but it was a beginning of the end. The work of pilgrims and Puritans, patriots and politicians had been to prepare the way for prophets of the living God. With what Washington called "the singular interpositions of Providence" a political path had been prepared that would allow the "restitution of all things." (Acts 3:21.) Less than a score of years after the Constitutional Convention had concluded its work and freedoms of conscience, speech, press, and worship had been guaranteed in a historic Bill of Rights, the Prophet Joseph Smith was born in clear, graceful Vermont, home of Ethan Allen and his Green Mountain Boys. As Elder Paul H. Dunn recently declared to a Church-wide audience.

"[Joseph] grew up toward adolescence just like the new land. He fitted it. He was young, clean, unspoiled—a lad without a past, kneeling in a grove. This pristine land—this innocent young man—and thus the Lord reached out and kept his promise. He established his conditions over centuries; you see, God has time. His plan made it possible for the holy priesthood and the Church to be restored upon the earth—the restoration of the gospel of Jesus Christ—but only in America. . . .

"The purpose of America was to provide a setting wherein that was possible. All else takes its power from that one great, central purpose." (*Ensign*, Nov. 1975, p. 54.)

Thus in one final moment worthy men and righteous principles came together for the restoration of heavenly things. With his center stake in America, God began stretching the cords of his tabernacle to all the world, lengthening the habitation of Israel and establishing Zion wherever the pure in heart dwell. When that great global mission is complete and the angels declare "there shall be time no longer" (D&C 88:110), then the king and master of heaven and earth shall return to his temple and reign for a thousand years on a renewed and paradisiacal earth.

"He shall command the great deep, and it shall be driven back into the north countries, and the islands shall become one land;

"And the land of Jerusalem and the land of Zion shall be turned back into their own place, and the earth shall be like as it was in the days before it was divided." (D&C 133:23–24.)

These two cities, Zion (the New Jerusalem) and the ancient city of Jerusalem, will be those capitals out of which both the word and law of the Lord shall go forth and to which all nations shall flow. (See Isa. 2:2–3.)

It is good that the historical celebration of the United States bicentennial allows us to focus on a land in which God has done so much of his work. It has not always looked the same geographically nor has it always been governed the same politically. But that all seems appropriate since the meaning of America, in its most theological sense, is something more than borders and boundaries, something above nativism and nationalism. It is an ideal, a thing of the spirit. Benjamin Franklin told his colleagues, "Our cause is the cause of all mankind," and Patrick Henry spoke much more than he knew when he said America had "lighted a candle to all the world." (Henry Steele Commager, "The Revolution as World Ideal," *Saturday Review*, Dec. 13, 1975, pp. 13–18, 110.) The significance of that cause and that candle will not be misunderstood by Latter-day Saints wherever they may live. As with temple sites, missionary service, and area general conferences, gospel experience transcends the borders—and, if necessary, the flames—of nationalism.

A Frenchman, a contemporary of the colonial Founding Fathers, sketched the clearest meaning of America for those of other nations. Although the twenty-year-old Marquis de Lafayette had been ordered by Louis XVI of France to give up his expedition to aid the rebellious Americans, he defied the command and embarked for the New World. On board his ship *The Victory* Lafayette wrote back to his beautiful and concerned wife, Adrienne: "Out of love for me, become 'a good American'. . . . The welfare of America is closely bound up with the welfare of all mankind."

(Maurice de la Fuye and Emile Baubeau, *The Apostle of Liberty: A Life of LaFayette*, New York: Thomas Yoseloff, 1956, p. 30.) So it has been and so it yet will be. And so it is—but in ways which only those who embrace the Restored Gospel of Jesus Christ can fully understand or appreciate.

PART ONE

Church Authorities in the Nineteenth Century

Joseph Smith

Joseph Smith, born December 23, 1805 in Sharon Windsor County, Vermont, was the founder and first President of the Church of Jesus Christ of Latter-Day Saints. He received the Melchizedek Priesthood and was ordained an Apostle in May 1829 under the hands of Peter, James, and John; was sustained as First Elder of the church April 6, 1830, at the age of 24; ordained a high priest June 3, 1831; and sustained as President of the high priesthood January 25, 1832. He was martyred June 27, 1844, at Carthage Jail, Hancock County, Illinois, at the age of 38. During his lifetime he had 48 lawsuits filed against him, being acquitted of all but one. He was a general in the Illinois State militia and commander of the Nauvoo legion. He served as Mayor of Nauvoo in 1842, and announced his candidacy for the President of the United States in 1844. The third item included here was published in connection with this candidacy.

March 25, 1839, Liberty Jail

Godly principles give scope and liberality to the mind, and guarantee the rights of all. The Constitution is a glorious standard. Though we are denied its protection we uphold its truth, along with that of the Bible, the Book of Mormon, etc.

We ought always to be aware of those prejudices which sometimes so strangely present themselves, and are so congenial to human nature, against our friends, neighbors, and brethren of the world, who choose to differ from us in opinion and in matters of faith. Our religion is between us and our God. Their religion is between them and their God.

There is a love from God that should be exercised toward those of our faith, who walk uprightly, which is peculiar to itself, but it is without prejudice; it also gives scope to the mind, which enables us to conduct ourselves with greater liberality towards all that are not of our faith, than what they exercise towards one another. These principles approximate nearer to the mind of God, because it is like God, or Godlike.

Here is a principle also, which we are bound to be exercised with, that is, in common with all men, such as governments, and laws, and regulations in the civil concerns of life. This principle guarantees to all parties, sects, and denominations, and classes of religion, equal, coherent, and indefeasible rights, they are things that pertain to this life; therefore all are alike interested; they make our responsibilities one towards another in matters of corruptible things, while the former principles do not destroy the latter, but bind us stronger, and make our responsibilities not only one to another, but unto God also. Hence we say, that the Constitution of the United States is a glorious standard; it is founded in the wisdom of God. It is a heavenly banner; it is to all those who are privileged with the sweets of its liberty, like the cooling shades and refreshing waters of a great rock in a thirsty and weary land. It is like a great tree under whose branches men from every clime can be shielded from the burning rays of the sun.

We, brethren, are deprived of the protection of its glorious principles, by the cruelty of the cruel, by those who only look for the time being, for pasturage like the beasts of the field, only to fill themselves; and forget that the "Mormons," as well as the Presbyterians, and those of every other class and description, have equal rights to partake of the fruits of the great tree of our national liberty. But notwithstanding we see what we see, and feel what we feel, and know what we know, yet that fruit is no less precious and delicious to our taste; we cannot be weaned from the milk, neither can we be driven from the breast; neither will we deny our religion because of the hand of oppression; but we will hold on until death.

We say that God is true; that the Constitution of the United States is true; that the Bible is true; that the Book of Mormon is true; that the Book of Covenants is true; that Christ is true; that the ministering angels sent forth from God are true, and that we know that we have an house not made with hands eternal in the heavens, whose builder and maker is God.

October 15, 1843

I am the greatest advocate of the Constitution there is, but it does not adequately provide the means of enforcing its good sentiments. An officer of the Government who refuses to extend the protection guaranteed by the Constitution should be subject to capital punishment.

I am the greatest advocate of the Constitution of the United Steates there is on the earth. In my feelings I am always ready to die for the protection of the weak and oppressed in their just rights. The only fault I find with the Constitution is, it is not broad enough to cover the whole ground.

Although it provides that all men shall enjoy religious freedom, yet it does not provide the manner by which that freedom can be preserved, nor for the punishment of Government officers who refuse to protect the people in their religious rights, or punish those mobs, states, or communities who interfere with the rights of the people on account of their religion. Its sentiments are good, but it provides no means of enforcing them. It has but this one fault. Under its provision, a man or a people who are able to protect themselves can get along well enough; but those who have the misfortune to be weak or unpopular are left to the merciless rage of popular fury.

The Constitution should contain a provision that every officer of the Government who should neglect or refuse to extend the protection guaranteed in the Constitution should be subject to capital punishment; and then the president of the United States would not say, "Your cause is just, but I can do nothing for you."

February 7, 1844
"Views of the Powers and Policy of the Government of the United States"

I am troubled by the condition of this land which declares the equal rights of man but allows the enslavement of millions and the unjust punishment of others. The officers of this noble nation should seek to ameliorate the condition of all, black or white, bond or free. The preamble to the Constitution means what it says without reference to color or condition.

On Monday, January 29, 1844, Joseph Smith, his counselor Hyrum Smith, and the Twelve Apostles met "to take into consideration the proper course for this people to pursue in relation to the coming Presidential election." They decided that they would be unable to support either of the presidential candidates of the major parties, Martin Van Buren and Henry Clay for causes which they stated. It was then moved by Willard Richards and voted unanimously—"That we will have an independent electorial ticket, and that Joseph Smith be a candidate for the next Presidency; and that we use all honorable means in our power to secure his election." Joseph Smith in accepting this nomination by the General Authorities of the Church outlined a campaign that would cover the nation. He also began that day the dictation to his secretary, W. W. Phelps, of an outline for his "Views on the Powers and Policy of the Government of the United States" which was to be his presidential platform. The next evening, February 7, 1844, the same group again met in Joseph Smith's office where he completed and signed his "Views" or platform. The following evening, February 8, 1844, a political meeting was held and Joseph Smith's "Views" were publicly read for the first time by W. W. Phelps. Joseph Smith then addressed the meeting giving his reasons for becoming a candidate for President of the United States. On October 15 the Times and Seasons *published an article entitled "Who Shall Be Our Next President?" and Joseph Smith's campaign for President of the United States was launched.*

For additional background see: DHC 6:187–233, 243, 334–340, 386–397; CHC 2:202–209; CHMR 2:368–373; RCH 1:421–455; also Andrew Love Neff, *History of Utah, 1940*, pp. 24–28.

My cogitations, like Daniel's, have for a long time troubled me, when I viewed the condition of men throughout the world, and more especially in this boasted realm, where the Declaration of Independence "holds these truths to be self-evident, that all men are created equal; that they are endowed by their Creator with certain unalienable rights; that among these are life, liberty, and the pursuit of happiness;" but at the same time some two or three millions of people are held as slaves for life, because the spirit in them is covered with a darker skin than ours; and hundreds of our own kindred for an infraction, or supposed infraction, of some over-wise statute, have to be incarcerated in dungeon gloom, or penitentiaries, while the duellist, the debauchee, and the defaulter for millions, and criminals, take the uppermost rooms at feasts, or, like the bird of passage, find a more congenial clime by flight.

The wisdom which ought to characterize the freest, wisest, and most noble nation of the nineteenth century, should, like the sun in his meridian splendor, warm every object beneath its rays; and the main efforts of her officers, who are nothing more nor less than the servants of the people, ought to be directed to ameliorate the condition of all, black or white, bond or free; for the best of books says, "God hath made of one blood all nations of men for to dwell on all the face of the earth."

Our common country presents to all men the same advantages, the facilities, the same prospects, the same honors, and the same rewards; and without hypocrisy, the Constitution, when it says, "We, the people of the United States, in order to form a more perfect union, establish justice, ensure domestic tranquility, provide for the common defense, promote the general welfare, and secure the blessings of liberty to ourselves and our posterity, do ordain and establish this Constitution for the United States of America," meant just what it said without reference to color or condition, *ad infinitum*.

The aspirations and expectations of a virtuous people, environed with so wise, so liberal, so deep, so broad, and so high a charter of *equal rights* as appears in said Constitution, ought to be treated by those to whom the administration of the laws is entrusted with as much sanctity as the prayers of the Saints are treated in heaven, that love, confidence, and union, like the sun, moon, and stars, should bear witness,

> *"For ever singing as they shine,*
> *The hand that made us is divine!"*

Unity is power; and when I reflect on the importance of it to the stability of all governments, I am astounded at the silly moves of persons and parties to foment discord in order to ride into power on the current of popular excitement; nor am I less surprised at the stretches of power or restrictions of right which too often appear as acts of legislators to pave the way to some favorite political scheme as destitute of intrinsic merit as a wolf's heart is of the milk of human kindness. . . .

George Albert Smith

George Albert Smith was born June 26, 1817 in Potsdam, St. Lawrence County, New York. He was baptized a member of the church on September 10, 1832 and at the young age of 22 was ordained an apostle of the Lord Jesus Christ on April 26, 1839. He was admitted as a member of the bar of the Supreme Court of the Territory of Utah and received his certificate as an attorney, counselor-at-large and solicitor in chancery. He was elected a member of the convention that drafted the Constitution of Utah, and, along with Elder John Taylor, represented the Church before Congress in its petition for statehood. Elder Smith was elected a member of the first legislature of Utah and reelected every year until his absence from the states in 1870. He was recognized as the father of the southern settlements, the chief of which, St. George, was named in his honor. At the time of his talk Elder Smith was an apostle; the saints had been in the Salt Lake valley for almost exactly seven years.

*In this address, Elder Smith teaches that the American Revolution
began behind the veil and argues that the principle of Independence continues in its progress. He looks forward to the day when the Saints might
enjoy independence in regulating their own affairs.*

*July 4, 1854
Celebration of the Fourth of July
An address delivered in the Tabernacle,
Great Salt Lake City*

The causes which produced the American Revolution were so far behind the
veil, that the writers of American history and the orators who expatiate on the
subject on occasions like this, and on other occasions, have not acknowledged
that it was the Almighty—the invisible and omnipotent hand of Him who
made the heavens and the earth and the fountains of waters, who worked the
secret wires, and opened up the revolutionary scene, to lay a foundation and prepare a people, with a system of government, among whom his work of the last
days could be commenced upon this earth.

Persons present to-day may consider that no other country in the world
would have allowed the persecutions and oppressions that have fallen upon
the work of God in this land, of which many of you have been partakers. But
in this you are mistaken; for there is no nation under heaven among whom
the kingdom of God could have been established and rolled forth with as little opposition as it has received in the United States. Every species of oppression and opposition, which has aimed at the destruction of the lives and liberties of the members of this Church, has been in open violation of the laws
of the country; while, among other nations, the links of the chain of government are so formed that the very constitution and laws of the country would
oppose the government of God. This is the case almost without an exception.

I will say, then, the American Revolution had its beginning behind the
veil. The invisible providence of the Almighty, by his Spirit, inspired the
hearts of the Revolutionary Fathers to resist the Government of England and
the oppressions they had submitted to for ages. When ground to dust, as it
were, in their mother country, the first settlers in this land looked to the West.
They fled from oppression, and planted their standard upon American soil,
which was then a wilderness in the possession of savages. The climate, pro-
ductions, extent, and nature of the country was then unknown to distant
nations. It appeared, however, to offer an asylum for the oppressed, even at
that early day.

A party escaped from oppression, and landed in Massachusetts; another party, for a similar cause, left the mother country, and landed in
Connecticut; and so a number of the early States were formed by settlers who

fled from their native country through religious oppression. The young colonies grew until they became somewhat formidable, and began to realize that they were entitled to some common national privileges; that they had a right to the protection of certain laws by which their ancestors were protected; and also that they had a right to an equal voice in the making of those laws.

What was the greatest trouble? The right of making their own laws was denied them by the King and Parliament; and if they made laws, the King claimed the right of abrogating those laws at pleasure, and also appointed officers who could dissolve the National Assembly and levy taxes without the consent of the inhabitants of the Colonies.

These were the main causes of the Revolution. God caused these causes to operate upon the minds of the colonists, until they nobly resisted the power of the mother country. At that time Great Britain stood pre-eminent among the nations of Europe, and had just finished the wars against several of them combined. God inspired our fathers to make the Declaration of Independence, and sustained them in their struggles for liberty until they conquered. Thus they separated themselves from the parent stock; and, as an historian of that age quaintly said, when they signed that Declaration, if they did not all hang together, they would be sure to all *hang* separately. Union is strength.

But how does this Revolution progress? That is the question. Has the great principle that colonies, territories, states, and nations have the right to make their own laws, yet become established in the world? I think if some of our lawyers would peruse the the musty statutes at large, they would find that there are several colonies of the United States who have seen proper, under the limited provisions then given them, to enact laws for their own convenience; but they suffered the mortification of having them vetoed by the General Congress. Look, for instance, at the statutes in relation to the Territory of Florida, and see the number of laws enacted by that people, and repealed by act of Congress.

It is curious to me that the progress of the Revolution has been so small, referring to that which is produced in the minds of the whole American people. Every organized Territory, wherever it exists, has the same right that the early revolutionary fathers claimed of Great Britain, and bled to obtain,—that is, of making its own laws and being represented in the General Assembly as a confederate power.

This Revolution may possibly increase in the future, and is, no doubt, progressing at the present time. One individual in particular, during the present session of Congress, has become so enlightened as to say in the House, "*You have no business with the domestic relations of Utah*;" and, consequently, I think the principle is making headway.

I want to see the Revolution progress, so that the great head of the American nation can say to every separate colony, "Make your own laws, and cleave to the principles of the Constitution which gives that right."

But the Revolution is progressing, and the time is not far distant when Territories will enjoy privileges that have been held back for the purpose of pandering to a relict of that monarchy which oppressed the American people. Is it reasonable that people dwelling thousands of miles from the parent Government should not have the same privilege of regulating their own affairs as those who live in its vicinity? It is the same kind of oppression and restraint that was placed upon our Revolutionary Fathers by the King and his Parliament. The American Government has fallen into the same errors, touching this point, as the British Government did at the commencement of the Revolution.

This is what I have to say on the rise and progress of the American Revolution. It is progressing slowly. While the nation is extending itself, and increasing in power, wisdom, and wealth, it seems, at the same time, to remain, in some respects, on the old ground occupied by the mother country in the early settlement of this land. I raise my voice against it, for I love American Independence: the principle is dear to my heart. When I have been in foreign countries, I have felt proud of the American flag, and have desired that they could have the enjoyment of as much liberty as the American people.

At the same time, *we* have a right to more liberty; we have a right to elect our own officers and have a voice in Congress in the management of the affairs of the nation. The time is coming when we shall have it. The Revolution will by-and-by spread far and wide, and extend the hand of liberty and the principles of protection to all nations who are willing to place themselves under the broad folds of its banner.

Brigham Young

Brigham Young, the second president of the Church of Jesus Christ of Latter-Day Saints, was born June 1, 1801, in Wittingham, Windham County, Vermont. His father, John Young, fought in the Revolutionary War, and his grandfather in the French and Indian War. His family relations on both sides were among the staunchest supporters of freedom in the American Colonies. Brigham was baptized on April 14, 1832, and named to the first quorum of Twelve apostles of this dispensation on February 14, 1835. He was one of the most vocal opponents to Sidney Rigdon's claim to be guardian of the church after the Prophet Joseph's death. At a conference held October 8, 1848, he was unanimously sustained as President of the Church.

    This talk was given just seven years after he led the saints to the Salt Lake Valley, at the time the author was the governor of Utah territory. President Young states that the revolution may be said to be "progressing," but in the wrong direction and, furthermore, that the Constitution is a developing or progressive work. He argues it should be altered to promote the election and retention of good men in office.

July 4, 1854
Celebration of the Fourth of July
A discourse delivered in the Tabernacle,
Great Salt Lake City

The revolutions made by the Government of the United States, with regard to real progression generally, are small indeed; so small that it is impossible to perceive any advancement. It is true the Constitution has been revised by the voice of the people; but wherein is it bettered? Some say it is bettered; but as to the light and knowledge that now exist with regard to the true spirit of republicanism, the revolution is on the retrograde motion. No one will question for a moment that many resolutions in the United States have become in a great degree popular, notwithstanding they have been in many instances unconstitutional and in open violation of the statute laws, and have been winked at by the most influential officers of the Government. There has been a progressive revolution since the close of the war, but not in virtue, justice, uprightness, and truth. It has become quite a custom, and by custom it has the force of law, for one party to mob another, to tear down and destroy Catholic churches, drive citizens from the ballot box, disallowing them the right of franchise, and persecute, and kill a great people. Revolution in the United States is progressing; but to the true spirit of Democracy and the science of government, the Revolution I refer to is strictly opposed.

One of them is a monster having many heads, and the other is a monster with no head at all. The impulse that is given to the Government is like that of the animal creation: when they are hungry, they are impelled to eat, and to drink when they are thirsty. When this necessity presses upon them, all the sensitive powers are on the alert to search for food. All their natural impulses to action originate in the appetite: they receive them from the demands the interior of the animal makes upon the creature. It then becomes the duty of the head to search out a method to supply these demands with food suitable to the nature of the animal, which administers health, strength, vigour, growth, and beauty to the whole body.

What ought to be the Government of the United States? And what are Whiggery and Democracy as they now exist? Nothing, and a little less.

The question, What is a true Republican government?, is easily answered. It is a government or institution that is perfect—perfect in its laws and ordinances, having for its object the perfection of mankind in righteousness. This is true Democracy. But Democracy as it is now is another thing. True Democracy or Republicanism, if it were rightly understood, ought to be the Government of the United States. They might have had that government long ago; but as it was said by my predecessor in the stand, "Whom the Lord would destroy, he makes mad;" consequently, he must take away the wisdom of that man, or of that people. No man or people possessing wisdom will give vent to wrath, for that is calculated to weaken, to destroy, to blot out of existence.

When the Supreme Ruler of the universe wishes to destroy a nation, he takes away their wisdom in the first place, and they become insensible to their own interests, and they are filled with wrath; they give way to their anger, and thus lay the foundation of their own destruction. To him who seeks to save, he gives wisdom, which enables any people, nation, or individual to lay the foundation for strength, increase, and power. When we look abroad upon the nations, we can see this truth verified; and when we look at home in our own nation, it is no less verified. We see that wisdom is actually departing from the lawgiver, and the knowledge and the discretion the judge possessed years ago have vanished. We discern that the very policy adopted by the nations to fortify them in strength is calculated to sap their foundations. The axe is laid at the root of the tree, and all nations are filling up the cup of their guilt.

Suppose I were speaking to the assembled millions of the inhabitants of the United States, what counsel or advice could be given to them that they might regain what they have lost? Can any temporal means be adopted to save them from the vortex of ruin into which they are fast approaching—a doom which they never can avert without sincere repentance? Yes, there is seemingly a human policy, if adopted, that would snatch them from destruction. What is it? Let the people rise *en masse* to lay the foundation of a wholesome, independent, free, Democratic (as the people call it), Republican government—a government which, if carried out, will be perfect in itself.

Let the people see to it that they get righteous men to be their leaders, who will labour with their hands and administer to their own necessities, sit in judgment, legislate, and govern in righteousness; and officers that are filled with peace; and see to it that every man that goes forth among the people as a travelling officer is full of the fear of the Lord, and would rather do right as a sacrifice than do wrong for a reward.

What would be the result, if this course was adopted by the people of the United States? It would destroy the golden prospects of those who were seeking for gain alone, and men would be sought for, in the nation, State, or Territory, who were for the people, and would seek earnestly for their welfare, benefit, and salvation. We want men to rule the nation who care more for and love better the nation's welfare than gold and silver, fame, or popularity.

Let the people lay the foundation for carrying out the Republican Government which was instituted by our fathers, instead of maintaining a government of anarchy, confusion, and strife. Were this people here an independent people, and had the privilege of selecting their own officers, and I should be chosen to dictate them in their selections, I would watch and guard faithfully their rights, and see that they selected men who had not the dimes in view. The motto should be—"If you do not labour for the good of the people, irrespective of the dimes, we do not want your services; for if you labour for the money, you seek to benefit yourselves at the people's expense." I make this application and turn it eastward, which you know is the way the world rolls. If the Government knew what the wants of the people were, they would take away the salaries of political demagogues, and stop their running and their stump preaching, from one end of the land to the other, to make proselytes to their cause. This would have a tendency to put an end to party names, to party jealousies, and to party conflicts for ever. And the people should concentrate their feelings, their influence, and their faith, to select the best man they can find to be their President, if he has nothing more to eat than potatoes and salt—a man who will not aspire to become greater than the people who appoint him, but be contented to live as they live, be clothed as they are clothed, and in every good thing be one with them.

It is yet in the power of the people of the United States to lay a foundation to redeem themselves from the growing consequences of past errors. What would be the result, were the United States to take this course—viz., to strike out that clause in the Constitution that limits the services of a President to four years, or the term of service of any good man, and continue to revise the Constitution and laws as they become familiar with their defects; then reduce the salaries of all officers in all the departments? Would not such a course revolutionize any kingdom or government, and be very likely to produce union and prosperity?

Are there any more improvements that might be made? Yes. If we are what we profess to be—a Republican Government, there is no State in the Union but what should be amenable to the General Government holding to the old English rights in Rhode Island. Then Congress, with the President at their head, could meet and veto every act made by any department of the Government, if it was necessary. So let Congress come together when any of the States transcend the bounds of right, and hold them amenable for their actions. The General Government should never give any portion of the nation license to say they are free and independent. This should only apply to the nation as a whole. We have a little experience in this kind of independence. For instance, the Government of the United States were willing to take my money for lands in Missouri, which were in the market; but the people in that sovereign, that free, and independent State rose up and mobbed me, drove me from my possessions, and confiscated my property to themselves; and the General Government has no power to redress my wrongs. This is only one instance among many of the kind which I might enumerate to show the impolicy and downright mockery of such boasted independence. While such outrages remain unredressed, this nation never should defile the sacred term by saying they have a REPUBLICAN GOVERNMENT.

The General Constitution of our country is good, and a wholesome government could be framed upon it, for it was dictated by the invisible operations of the Almighty; he moved upon Columbus to launch forth upon the trackless deep to discover the American Continent; he moved upon the signers of the Declaration of Independence; and he moved upon Washington to fight and conquer, in the same way as he moved upon ancient and modern Prophets, each being inspired to accomplish the particular work he was called to perform in the times, seasons, and dispensations of the Almighty. God's purpose, in raising up these men and inspiring them with daring sufficient to surmount every opposing power, was to prepare the way for the formation of a true Republican government. They laid its foundation; but when others came to build upon it, they reared a superstructure far short of their privileges, if they had walked uprightly as they should have done.

What shall be done? Let the people, the whole American people, rise up and say they will have these abuses regulated, and no longer suffer political demagogues to gamble away their money, but turn them out of office to attend to their own business. Let the people make a whip, if not of good tough raw hide, of small cords at least, and walk into the temple of the nation, and cleanse it thoroughly out, and put in men who will legislate for their good, instead of gambling away their money and trifling with the sacred interests of the nation which have been entrusted to their keeping.

I would not speak so plainly, were it not that statesmen use the same privilege, and that, too, in the halls of Legislatures. We can never get a true Republican government upon any other principle. The object those have in view who look and long for the gaudy trash of this world should be removed, that men may occupy the high and responsible seats of the nation who will care for the welfare of the people, and cannot be bought with money, or that which it can purchase.

Can the Constitution be altered? It can; and when we get a President that answers our wishes to occupy the executive chair, there let him sit to the day of his death, and pray that he may live as long as Methuselah; and, whenever we have good officers, strive to retain them, and to fill up vacancies with good men, until there are none who would let the nation sink for a can of oysters and a lewd woman.

The signers of the Declaration of Independence and the framers of the Constitution were inspired from on high to do that work. But was that which was given to them perfect, not admitting of any addition whatever? No; for if men know anything, they must know that the Almighty has never yet found a man in mortality that was capable, at the first intimation, at the first impulse, to receive anything in a state of entire perfection. They laid the foundation, and it was for after generations to rear the superstructure upon it. It is a progressive—a gradual work. If the framers of the Constitution and the inhabitants of the United States had walked humbly before God, who defended them and fought their battles when Washington was on the stage of action, the nation would now have been free from a multitude of place-hunters who live upon its vitals. The country would not have been overrun with murderers and thieves, and our cities filled with houses of ill-fame, as now; and men could have walked the streets of cities, or travelled on conveyances through the country, without being insulted, plundered, and perhaps murdered; and an honest, sober, industrious, enterprising, and righteous people would now have been found from one end of the United States to the other.

The whole body is deranged; and the head, which ought to be the seat of sense and the temple of wisdom, is insensible to the wants of the body, and to the fact that, if the body sinks, the head must sink also.

The progress of revolution is quite considerable in every government of the world. But is the revolution for the constitutional rights of the people in progress? No; it is on the retrograde. I know how they can be brought back to the people, and the Government be redeemed and become one of the most powerful and best on the earth. It was instituted in the beginning by the Almighty. He operated upon the hearts of the Revolutionary Fathers to rebel against the English King and his Parliament, as he does upon me to preach "Mormonism." Both are inspired by him; but the work unto which they are called is dissimilar. The one was inspired to fight, and the other to preach the peaceable things of the kingdom of God. He operated upon that pusillanimous king to excite the colonists to rebellion; and he is still operating with this nation, and taking away their wisdom, until by-and-by they will get mad and rush to certain destruction.

Will the Constitution be destroyed? No: it will be held inviolate by this people; and, as Joseph Smith said, "The time will come when the destiny of the nation will hang upon a single thread. At that critical juncture, this people will step forth and save it from the threatened destruction." It will be so.

With regard to the doings of our fathers and the Constitution of the United States, I have to say, they present to us a glorious prospect in the future, but one we cannot attain to until the present abuses in the Government are corrected.

Orson Pratt

Orson Pratt was born September 19, 1811, in Hartford, Washington County, New York. He was baptized on September 19, 1830 at the age of nineteen. He received, through the prophet, the revelation found in the Doctrine and Covenants, section 34, calling him on a mission. He was a member of Zion's camp and was ordained an Apostle in Kirtland April 26, 1835.

In this speech Elder Pratt affirms that the Constitution is from God, but that it is necessarily adapted to human imperfections. Eventually all Governments will be replaced by the Kingdom of God.

July 8, 1855
The Kingdom of God
A discourse delivered in the Bowery,
Great Salt Lake City

The subject of the coming of the kingdom of God, and its organization upon the earth, is one of vast importance to the present generation, as well as to all past generations, who are equally concerned with the present. Ever since the day that men were organized upon the earth they have been equally concerned in regard to that period—that eventful period when God's kingdom should be established upon the earth. That day or period has been looked forward to as the day of the perfection of their glory and exaltation.

And when that time comes, all governments, and systems of government, that have been organized upon this little creation of the Almighty, contrary to the order of heaven, or in other words—all governments that have not been theocratical in their nature, but that have been organized in a greater or less degree by man's wisdom, will be done away.

The Almighty in some degree controls among mankind, as far as they will let Him. He controls the destinies of the nations, so far as they will permit Him; yet He does not control them so far as to destroy the agency of the human family, consequently they, through their own corrupt notions, have departed from the great principles of government given by the Lord to man in the beginning. Mankind have felt a disposition to seek after some kind of government of their own; they have all seemed to manifest a feeling to have a different government from the one established by the Almighty; and hence, they have all rebelled against His government, and they have introduced creeds and systems of their own manufacturing.

If there had been a government upon the face of the earth, from the creation of man to the present time, according to the mind and will of God; you would not have seen in the present age, and in generations that are past, different nations, different classes of people, having different governments, as we now behold them, but there would have been a oneness of nationality—a unity existing over all the earth. But mankind have existed for ages past in a divided state—in a broken condition, because of their rebellion against the laws and government of heaven.

If God made this earth, and all things that pertain unto it, and if all were created for His honor and glory, He has the right to govern and control them by His own laws; and He has a right to enforce that government, and show Himself able to control the works of His hands, and it is the duty of all men to render obedience to His requirements. The government of heaven would not have been separated from the government of men, or in other words, there would not have been two kinds, one called ecclesiastical, and the other a civil government; but inasmuch as they have rebelled, and become corrupt and wicked, governments have been introduced of a different character; and the Lord has, in some measure, sanctioned those governments, so far as there were good principles existing among them.

All good principles and laws have emanated from the Almighty, and have come to man by inspiration from Him. For instance, the government of the United States, or the Constitution, came from Him; it was given, we believe, by inspiration, and there are many things connected with the various institutions of men that are very good. There are many good laws and good institutions in the government of the United States, as well as among many other governments, but the government of the United States is one of the best that has been organized among men upon the face of the earth for many generations.

"Did the Lord have a hand in the organization of the United States government?" asks the enquirer. Yes, the Lord had a hand in framing its Constitution. Why did not the Lord, at that time, introduce a perfect government—a theocracy? It was simply because the people were not prepared for it—they were too corrupt; and although they had more integrity, more virtue, more honesty, and more sympathy and feeling for that which is just and upright and good, than any other portion of the inhabitants of the earth, and probably more than a great many now have, yet they were far from being prepared for the government of God, which is a government of union.

They were far from that, consequently the Lord inspired them to introduce a government that He knew would be just suited to their capacity, and hence it was that He inspired Jefferson, Washington, Franklin, and others to introduce those measures which they did, and to carry them out, and they were such as were just suited to the conditions and circumstances of the people; hence the government of the United States we, as a people, venerate and defend.

Why do we do this? We do it because God had His hand in the organization of it; His hand in the organization of it; He controlled it so far as He could do so without interfering with the agency of man.

We have seen plainly and clearly that had it not been for the organization of this government, as has wisely and justly been said, where would have been the liberty of the Latter-Day Saints?

This government, then, was organized to suit the people and the circumstances in which they were placed, until they were prepared to receive a more perfect one.

But will the government of the United States continue for ever? No, it is not sufficiently perfect; and, notwithstanding it has been sanctioned by the Lord at a time when it was suited to the circumstances of the people, yet the day will come, (I will say it on my own responsibility and not that of this people,) the day will come when the United States government, and all others, will be uprooted, and the kingdoms of this world will be united in one, and the kingdom of our God will govern the whole earth, and bear universal sway; and no power beneath the heavens can prevent this taking place, if the Bible be true, and we know it to be true.

The Lord will govern all things that He has made and created, for it is entered upon the records of heaven that all nations shall bow to His authority; and, consequently, we respect the government of the United States, because it has good principles in it, and not that we think it will endure for ever.

Many great and glorious principles are contained within the Constitution of our country, not to say that it is perfect, but it is perfect so far as it pertains to the rights and privileges of the children of men. But there is a nucleus of a government, formed since that of the United States, which is perfect in its nature. It is perfect, having emanated from a Being who is perfect.

But some may enquire, is it right—is it lawful for another government to be organized within the United States, of a theocratical nature? Yes, perfectly so! Does not the Constitution of our country guarantee to all religious societies the right of forming any ecclesiastical government they like? Certainly it does, and every intelligent man knows this to be the fact.

The nucleus of such a government is formed, and its laws have emanated from the throne of God, and it is perfect, having come from a pure fountain; but does this make us independent of the laws of the United States? No, this new government does not come in contact with the government of the United States. In keeping our covenants, and observing our religious laws and ceremonies, or the laws that God has given to the children of men, we are not required to violate the principles of right that are contained in the Constitution and laws of the United States.

Had not the government of the United States been framed, where would have been safety for this people? I answer, nowhere. If this Republican government had not been organized upon this continent, the kingdom of our God could not have been protected; but the hand of the Lord has been in it, and superintended its organization, and no one can hinder its progress.

If this government had been formed in any other kingdom or nation upon the earth except the United States, where would have been the privileges and liberties of this people? Without the interference of the Almighty, and the manifestation of His miraculous power for our protection, we should have been rooted out of the earth.

God foresaw this—He knew what would take place long beforehand, and He saw that it was not only necessary to have a day set for the preparation, and also for the beginning of the Latter-day work, but it was likewise important for the different kingdoms and nations which were in existence, and that had been organized by man, to go to work and start up some religious reform, and for the people to struggle against their mother church, and

to fight against her tyranny and oppressions, that religious liberty and freedom, and the right of a free exercise of their religious opinions, might be guaranteed to the human family, not all at once, but gradually. We find that at the
Reformation, when the great struggle for freedom and religious liberty took
place, some of them were wrought upon to come to this new continent for the
purpose of securing to themselves religious freedom and religious right; and
inspired by the Almighty, as was Columbus who discovered this land, they
planted their feet upon the American soil.

They were an humble people and God began to work in their minds,
and they continued to increase, for a while, in union and love, having obtained
privileges which before they were deprived of; and no doubt they imagined to
themselves that universal freedom was about to be ushered in, but it was not
exactly so, neither was that degree of liberty and freedom to suffice which they
had then secured, but it was like John the Baptist's mission, merely to prepare
the way. It was said of John, that among all that were born of women there
were none greater than he, and yet the least in the kingdom of heaven was
greater than he; and of all governments that had arisen among men, there
were none so great and good, as the government of the United States, and yet
the government of God in its very infancy was greater than it.

And why was this? Because its laws emanated from a more perfect
Being.

It was for this purpose, then, that a republic was organized upon this
continent to prepare the way for a kingdom which shall have dominion over
all the earth to the ends thereof.

Hence, the Prophet Daniel has told us, that the kingdom of God should
be cut out of the mountains without hands; in other words, when the kingdom of God should be taken from the mountains, it should be taken by the
power of the Almighty, and not by human hands; it should be organized by
the Lord, and governed by His laws. God, who interests Himself in the affairs
of men, was to speak from the heavens, and inspire His servants to give laws
and revelations to His people, informing them that His kingdom was to be
taken from the mountains in His own due time, and that it should increase
until it should become a great mountain and fill the whole earth.

David has said, in speaking of that time, that when the wicked rulers,
and corrupt kings of the earth, should come up to Zion, they should, while yet
afar off, be seized with fear and trembling, and hasten away; for it will be no
place for wicked and corrupt characters; but there will be millions of others
who will come up to Zion, besides the Saints of God; they will come to behold
the glory of God which will rest upon Zion. They will come in such numerous hosts that the gates of Zion will have to be open day and night to receive
them; they will come as a multitude of nations, swarming in day and night.

Kings, nobles, and great men, from all the principal nations of the earth, will come flocking to Zion with their armies, and their servants to view the grandeur of Zion; and they will have to be obedient to the mandates of the great King who shall issue forth His laws from Zion, or it will be no place for them to abide in.

We need not think that we can get into any place where we will not be associated with the Gentiles; for the Lord intends that we shall be among them all through this mortal state, and even in the Millenium we find that there will be two classes of beings upon the earth. And if there are corrupt individuals found, they will be visited with punishment according to the deeds they are guilty of.

Then, I rejoice; I look forward to the day of glory, when the glory of Zion shall be like a light upon a hill, which will illuminate the whole world; and the great men of the earth will come to see the glory of God, and be taught in the holy commandments that will proceed forth from our midst; and they will look upon Zion, and wonder, and be astonished.

May the Lord bless us, and may the Spirit of the Lord abide with, and continue to surround and overshadow us, and may we not be fearful because of the oppressor and the wicked, but trust int he living God, an He will continue to protect us all the day long, and no power can prevail against us. If we were not one tenth as numerous as we are, what would it matter; if God be on our side, He can use up the wicked, and protect us.

And as has been said by the First Presidency, all that we have to fear is our own wickedness, and corruptions, and liability to depart from the true faith. If we will be true and righteous, and if we will have faith in God, this is all that is required.

If we are faithful to our covenants, the fury of the oppressor will not harm us, and where will be the strong arm of man? It will be like the flax in the flame, like a moth-eaten garment, the wicked shall vanish away, and there will be no place found for them.

Then hearken to the counsel that proceeds from the First Presidency, and hold up your heads, and do not let them droop, and in this way, we shall prosper, and obtain a holy dwelling place in the presence of our God for ever. May God grant these blessings for His Son's sake. Amen.

John Taylor

John Taylor was the third President of the Church of Jesus Christ of Latter-Day Saints. He was born November 1, 1808, at Milnthorpe, Westmoreland County, England. He was baptized in 1836, and called as an Apostle on July 8, 1838. In October 1841, he and Elias Higbee were appointed a committee to petition Congress for a redress of the wrongs heaped upon the Saints in Missouri. Elder Taylor was in the Carthage jail when the Prophet Joseph and his brother Hyrum were martyred; his life was miraculously saved from a bullet by a vest pocket watch. Elder Taylor was many times a member of the Utah legislature, and Speaker of the House. He was sustained as President of the Church in October 1880. In this speech, given in 1865, Elder Taylor says that while the Saints look forward to the full reign of the Kingdom of God, we are to remain loyal to the Constitution of the United States, despite our enemies' gross abuses of power.

Sunday, Mar. 5, 1865
Religious Ideas of the World Contrasted with Those of the Saints—Loyalty of
the Saints to the Constitution—
Persecutions They Have Endured—Prophecy in the Church
Remarks made in the Tabernacle,
Great Salt Lake City

Reported by E. L. Sloan

We believe in God, and therefore we fear him; we believe he has established his kingdom upon the earth, and therefore we cling to it; we believe that he is designing to turn, and overturn, and revolutionize the nations of the earth, and to establish a government that shall be under his rule, his dominion, and authority, and shall emphatically be called the government of God, or, in other words, the kingdom of God. There is nothing strange, however, in this; for a great many parties, both in the United States and in the governments of the old world, have believed in the kingdom of God being established in the last days; it has been a favorite doctrine, both among Socialists and Christians, and much has been said and written about it, theoretically. The difference between them and us is, they talk about something to come; we say that it has commenced, and that this is that kingdom.

Well, but do you not hold allegiance to the government of the United States also? Do you not believe in the laws and institutions thereof? Yes, we have always sustained and upheld them; and although we have had many very heavy provocations to make us feel rebellious and opposed to that government, yet we have always sustained it under all circumstances and in every position. When they tried to cut our throats, we rather objected to that, you know. We had some slight objection to have our heads cut off and be trampled under foot; we did not think it was either constitutional or legal. But when they took their swords away from our necks and said that we might enjoy the rights of American citizens, that was all we wanted.

There is, however, a kind of political heresy that we have always adopted. We have always maintained that we had a right to worship God as we thought proper under the constitution of the United States, and that we would vote as we pleased. But some people took a notion to say "they would be damned if we should." We told them, however, that was a matter of their own taste; that we would seek to be saved and yet we would do it. It has always been a principle with us, and in fact is given in one of our revelations, "that he who will observe the laws of God need not transgress the laws of the land." It has always been a principle inculcated by the authorities of this Church, and taught by our Elders, never to interfere with the political affairs of any nation where they might be—that is, as Elders. They go forth with the Gospel of peace, to preach to the people, and not to interfere with their political institutions. If a mission of that kind should be given at any future time, all well and good. I have always so represented our belief, and acted accordingly, wherever I have been, and so have my brethren in England, in France, in Germany, and in all nations where I have been. I have always adhered to the laws of the nation where I sojourned. In the United States we stand in a political capacity, in this Territory, as part and parcel of the United States. We occupy that position; we are obliged to do so; we cannot help ourselves if we wish it, but we do not wish it. We are a number of men here—a multitude of people, men, women, and children, occupying quite an extensive Territory, with settlements extending over a distance of 500 miles in length. What the amount of population is I am not prepared to say; but I am prepared to say that, as a population, as a people, as a Territory, we have always been loyal to the institutions of our government, and I am at the defiance of the world to prove anything to the contrary. When we left—I was going to say the United States—what did we leave for? Why did we leave that country? Was it because its institutions were not good? No. Was it because its constitution was not one of the best that was ever framed? No. Was it because the laws of the United States, or of the States where we sojourned, were not good? No. Why was it? It was because there was not sufficient virtue found in the Executive to sustain their own laws. That was the reason, gentlemen. Is this anything to be proud of? It is a thing that should make every honorable American hide his head in shame; and all reflecting, intelligent, and honorable men feel thus.

It is well understood that executive officers, whether State or Federal, are bound by the most solemn oath, to sustain the constitution and laws of the United States and of the States where they reside; and where these concerned aided in, or permitted, the expulsion of forty thousand American citizens from their homes, they stood perjured before their country and God; and this huge suicidal act of ostracism proclaimed them enemies of republican institutions and of humanity; traitors to their country, and recreant alike to its laws, constitution, and institutions. "But it was only the damned Mormons. It was only the damned Mormons. It was only them, was it not?" Who were these "damned Mormons?" We cannot help thinking about these things just the same as we do about religious matters. Why, these "damned Mormons" were American citizens; and the constitution and laws of the United States, and of the several States, guaranteed, just as far as guarantee is worth anything, to these "damned Mormons" just the same rights and privileges that they did to the blessed Christians. But we came here. Now, what is the use of trying to hoodwink us and tell us that we have been very well treated? They know we cannot believe them, and that no rational, intelligent, honorable man would expect us to believe them; such assertions are an outrage at variance alike with common sense and our own experience. But did we rebel? No, we did not act as the Southern States have done. We came here, and, in the absence of any other government, we organized a provisional state government, just the same as Oregon did before us. Thus, in the midst of this abuse heaped upon us, we showed our adherence to the institutions and constitution of our country. If bad men bore rule, if corrupt men held sway—men who had neither the virtue nor the fortitude to maintain the right and protect the institutions and constitution of this, shall I say, our once glorious country,—if men could not be found who possessed sufficient integrity to maintain their oaths and their own institutions, there was a people here found of sufficient integrity to the constitution and institutions of the United States not to abandon them. That has been our feeling all the time, and it is based, also, upon that belief considered by a majority of the people of this and other nations as erroneous and false. Again when, after these things had transpired, we petitioned the United States to give us either a territorial or a state government, did that show anything inimical to the institutions of our Government? Verily, no; the very fact of our doing this proclaimed our loyalty and attachment to the institutions of the country. We got then, and had given unto us, a territorial government. We were recognized once more as citizens of the United States. We had sent among us Governors, appointed by the United States; Judges, a Secretary, Marshal, and all the adjuncts, powers, and officers with the territorial government. By them, in many instances, we have been belied, traduced, abused, outraged, and imposed upon. Have we retorted against the United States? No, we have not. Is it the duty of Federal officers, governors, judges, and other officers coming into our midst, secretaries, Indian agents, etc., to conspire against the people they come among? Is it their duty to traduce, abuse, vilify, and misrepresent them? In other places such men would be summarily dealt with. We have borne these things from time to time. They were not very much calculated to strengthen the attachment that we had so often and so strongly manifested to the government of which we form a part. Still, we have been true to our trust, to our integrity, and to the institutions and constitution of our country all the time in the midst of these things.

Through some of these misrepresentations and a corrupt administration, a pretext was found to send an army out here. We heard the report sounding along from those plains that they were coming to destroy and lay waste. What, a government destroy its own offspring? An army raised against an infant Territory? The cannon and the sword, the rifle and the pistol, brought to spread death and desolation among a peaceful people. Is that republicanism? Are those the blessings of a paternal government? Is that the genius of those institutions that were framed to protect man in the enjoyment of all his rights, and to guarantee equal rights to all men? Would that country be an asylum for the oppressed? Would it be a place of refuge or protection to any one? What was left for us to do under those circumstances but to act as men and American citizens? To fall back on our reserved rights, and say to those political gamblers who would stake the lives of the citizens of a Territory in their damning games. Back with your hosts, touch not God's anointed, and do his prophets no harm. Was there anything wrong in that? No; I would do it ten thousand times over under the circumstances, under this government or any other on the face of the earth, with God to help me. No man, no government has the right, at the instigation of traitors, to destroy innocent men, women, and children. God never gave them such a right, and the people never gave it to them, and they never had it. True, after a while, some peace-commissioners came along; why did they not come before and inquire into matters? Because of the lack of virtue and integrity among those who professed to rule the nation, and because of a desire to make political capital out of our destruction. Does that alter the institutions of our country or interfere with the Constitution of the country? Verily no. And our hearts beat as fervent in favor of those principles to-day as they ever did. But we feel indignant at the rascals who would try to betray those principles bequeathed to the nation. We cannot help it. We reason upon these principles the same as we do upon other things.

But we frequently hear, "You are not loyal." Who is it that talks of loyalty? Those who are stabbing the country to its very vitals. Are they the men that are loyal? Those who are sowing the seeds of discord; those who are perjuring themselves before high Heaven and the country they profess to serve? Are these the loyal men? If so, God preserve me and this people from such loyalty from this time, henceforth, and for ever. We look at these things from another stand-point, and view them in a different light entirely from most others.

Sometimes people think we are acting almost hypocritically when we talk of loyalty to the Constitution of the United States. We will stand by that Constitution and uphold the flag of our country when everybody else forsakes it. We cannot shut our eyes to things transpiring around us. We have our reason, and God has revealed unto us many things; but never has he revealed anything in opposition to those institutions and that Constitution, no, never; and, another thing, he never will.

But did not Joseph Smith prophecy that there would be a rebellion in the United States? He did, and so have I scores and hundreds of times; and what of that? Could I help that? Could Joseph Smith help knowing that a rebellion would take place in the United States? Could he help knowing it would commence in South Carolina? You could not blame him for that. He was in his grave at the time it commenced; you killed him long ago; but you did not do away with the fact that this state of things should exist. If the Lord—we all talk about the Lord, you know, Christians as well as "Mormons," and about the providences of God, and the interposition of the

Almighty—if the Lord has a design to accomplish, if there is a fate, if you like the word any better—and some infidels as well as Christians believe strongly in the doctrine of fate—if there is a fate in these things, who ordered it? Who can change its course? Who can stop it? Who can alter it? Joseph Smith did not instigate the rebellion in South Carolina, for he was not there.

We look at things through a different medium than some do, and we feel perfectly calm, perfectly tranquil with regard to our status and what is to come religiously, politically, and every other way.

I am not surprised at men marvelling at our proceedings and wondering at the course we pursue, and in relation to our views. It cannot be expected that they can do anything else. Jesus said to Nicodemus, when he came to talk with Him concerning the things of the kingdom of God. "Except a man be born again, he cannot see the kingdom of God." And if he cannot see it, how can he comprehend it? How can a man comprehend a thing which he cannot see? So it is with the truth, because no man knows the things of God but by the Spirit of God. "Then you place yourselves on a more elevated platform than anybody else?" This we have the arrogance to do; but we have the honesty to acknowledge that it is from God we receive all, and not through ourselves; and that is why the world will not acknowledge nor believe in the philosophy of the heavens and the earth, of time and eternity; that all things are within the grasp of the intelligence of that mind that is lighted up by the light of the Spirit of God. But how vague and uncertain are the ideas of those who have not that Spirit! Look at the arguments, not only of the divines of the present day but of past ages, in regard to their religious views; look also at the difference of opinion of the best philosophers in regard to the science of life. There is nothing tangible, nothing real, nothing certain. Nothing but the Spirit of God can enlighten mens' minds. Standing on this platform, we view all things of a political and religious nature associated with the earth we are living on as being very uncertain, intangible, and unphilosophical. We expect to see the nations waste, crumble, and decay. We expect to see a universal chaos of religious and political sentiment, and an uncertainty much more serious than anything that exists at the present time. We look forward to the time; and try to help it on, when God will assert his own right with regard to the government of the earth; when, as in religious matters so in political matters, he will enlighten the minds of those that bear rule, he will teach the kings wisdom and instruct the senators by the Spirit of eternal truth; when to him "every knee shall bow and every tongue confess that Jesus is the Christ." Then "shall the earth be full of knowledge like as the waters cover the sea." Then shall the mists of darkness be swept away by the light of eternal truth. Then will the intelligence of Heaven beam forth on the human mind, and by it they will comprehend everything that is great, and good, and glorious.

In the meantime, it is for us to plod along in the course God has dictated, yielding obedience to his divine laws, and be co-workers with him in establishing righteousness on the earth; and with feelings of charity towards all mankind, let our motto always be, "Peace on earth and good will to men."

May God help us to do so, in the name of Jesus. Amen.

Wilford Woodruff

Wilford Woodruff was born March 1, 1807, at Avon, Hartford County, Connecticut. He was ordained an Apostle April 26, 1839, at the age of 32, and was sustained as President of the church April 7, 1889, at the age of 82. He was a member of Zion's camp, part of the first company to reach the Salt Lake Valley, and served several terms in the Territorial legislature. He is most known for his extensive record keeping; his journals provide much of the early history of the church. The first talk included was given while Elder Woodruff was an Apostle; the second was given as President of the Church. Both testify to his experience with the founding fathers in the St. George temple.

September 16, 1877

We have labored in the St. George Temple since January, and we have done all we could there; and the Lord has stirred up our minds, and many things have been revealed to us concerning the dead. President Young has said to us, and it is verily so, if the dead could they would speak in language loud as ten thousand thunders, calling upon the servants of God to rise up and build Temples, magnify their calling and redeem their dead. This doubtless sounds strange to those present who believe not the faith and doctrine of the Latter-day Saints; but when we get to the spirit-world we will find out that all that God has revealed is true. We will find, too, that everything there is reality, and that God has a body, parts and passions, and the erroneous ideas that exist now with regard to him will have passed away. I feel to say little else to the latter-day Saints wherever and whenever I have the opportunity of speaking to them, than to call upon them to build these Temples now under way, to hurry them up to completion. The dead will be after you, they will seek after you as they have after us in St. George. They called upon us, knowing that we held the keys and power to redeem them.

I will here say, before closing, that two weeks before I left St. George, the spirits of the dead gathered around me, wanting to know why we did not redeem them. Said they, "You have had the use of the Endowment House for a number of years, and yet nothing has ever been done for us. We laid the foundation of the government you now enjoy, and we never apostatized from it, but we remained true to it and were faithful to God." These were the signers of the Declaration of Independence, and they waited on me for two days and two nights. I thought it very singular, that notwithstanding so much work had been done, and yet nothing had been done for them. The thought never entered my heart, from the fact, I suppose, that heretofore our minds were reaching after our more immediate friends and relatives. I straightway went into the baptismal font and called upon brother McCallister to baptize me for the signers of the Declaration of Independence, and fifty other eminent men, making one hundred in all, including John Wesley, Columbus, and others. I then baptized him for every President of the United States, except three; and when their cause is just, somebody will do the work for them.

I have felt to rejoice exceedingly in this work of redeeming the dead. I do not wonder at President Young saying he felt moved upon to call upon the Latter-day Saints to hurry up the building of these Temples. He felt the importance of the work; but now he has gone, it rests with us to continue it, and God will bless our labors and we will have joy therein. This is a preparation necessary for the second advent of the Savior; and when we shall have built the Temples now contemplated, we will then begin to see the necessity of building others, for in proportion to the diligence of our labors in this direction, will we comprehend the extent of the work to be done, and the present is only a beginning. When the Savior comes, a thousand years will be devoted to this work of redemption; and Temples will appear all over this land of Joseph—North and South America—and also in Europe and elsewhere; and all the descendants of Shem, Ham, and Japheth who received not the Gospel in the flesh, must be officiated for in the Temples of God, before the Savior can present the kingdom to the Father, saying, "it is finished."

May God continue to bless us, and guide and direct our labors, is my prayer, in the name of Jesus.

Amen.

April 1888

I am going to bear my testimony to this assembly, if I never do it again in my life, that those men who laid the foundation of this American government and signed the Declaration of Independence were the best spirits the God of heaven could find on the face of the earth. They were choice spirits, not wicked men. General Washington and all the men that labored for the purpose were inspired of the Lord.

Another thing I am going to say here, because I have a right to say it. Every one of those men that signed the Declaration of Independence, with General Washington, called upon me, as an Apostle of the Lord Jesus Christ, in the Temple at St. George, two consecutive nights, and demanded at my hands that I should go forth and attend to the ordinance of the House of God for them. Men are here, I believe, that know of this, Brothers J. D. T. McAllister, David H. Cannon and James G. Bleak. Brother McAllister baptized me for all those men, and then I told those brethren that it was their duty to go into the Temple and labor until they had got endowments for all of them. They did it. Would those spirits have called upon me, as an Elder in Israel, to perform that work if they had not been noble spirits before God? They would not.

I bear this testimony, because it is true. The Spirit of God bore record to myself and the brethren while we were laboring in that way.

What has been said with regard to this nation and to our position is coming to pass. All the powers of earth and hell will not stay the hand of Almighty God in the fulfillment of those great prophecies that have to come to pass to prepare the way for the coming of the Son of Man. You who have gathered here are my witnesses of this. I feel as though the day has come when every Elder and every Latter-day Saint ought to stop and consider the position he is in and the covenants he has entered into. Is there anything on the face of the earth that will pay you to depart from the oracles of God and from

the Gospel of Christ? Is there anything that will pay you to lose the principles of salvation, to lose a part in the first resurrection with the privilege of
standing in the morning of the resurrection clothed with glory, immortality
and eternal life at the head of your father's house? No, there is nothing. I feel
sorry many times when I see men who have the Priesthood forget almost that
they have any interest in the work of God.

The stenographic work in taking the account of the proceedings was
done by Arthur Winter.

JOHN NICHOLSON
Clerk of Conference

George Q. Cannon

George Q. Cannon was born January 11, 1827, in Liverpool, Lancashire, England. He was ordained an Apostle August 26, 1860. He was sent on a special mission to Washington to help clear up many of the misconceptions that had abounded due to the Johnston's army incident. While serving in this capacity he worked closely with senators and representatives. Elder Cannon was then chosen as a delegate to present the constitution to Congress and work for Utah's administration as a State. He was elected four consecutive times to be Utah's delegate to Congress; however, he was denied his seat in his last election due to the Edmund's Act. At the time of this talk, which urges the members to be loyal to the Constitution of the United States despite persecutions, he was a member of the First Presidency.

General Conference, Salt Lake City, April 3, 1881

While the missionaries were thus engaged [abroad], the work at home did not cease. Persecution at home was not arrested. Mobs continued to gather together as they had done before the Elders crossed the ocean; and it was not then the cry that "these Mormons were introducing patriarchal marriage, which we think hurtful to our civilization"; that was not the charge. In the early days the charges urged against the Saints when they went out West to the limits of the Republic, were, that they believed in anointing and in laying hands upon the sick; that they believed in revelation; that they believed in prophets; that they listened to the counsels and teachings of those prophets. Was not this very dangerous? But this was not all. It sounds very queer in these days to think that one of the gravest charges made against the Latter-day Saints by the mob that drove them from their homes in Jackson County was that they were Yankees and abolitionists! Designing men, seeking for pretexts that would answer the purpose of inflaming the minds of ignorant people, seized and used this as a good ground upon which to base designs for expulsion. Missouri was a slave State, and the Latter-day Saints were in the main New England people; they who were not were from New York, Pennsylvania and other middle States. But they were known as Yankees, and, as their enemies asserted, abolitionists—a suitable people to be pounced upon and driven out. . . . Now, during all these years, and subsequently, when we were being mobbed, plundered, and driven, the Latter-day Saints had an abiding faith, based upon the revelations that God had given through brother Joseph Smith, that the day would come when we should be a great people, when our virtues would be recognized, when our patriotism would be vindicated, when our loyalty to truth and to the principles of virtue and of good government, of pure republicanism would be established and the work of God with which we are connected become universal. Brother Joseph had predicted this. The Elders, the Saints, the people old and young believed it with all their hearts. The hatred of mobs, the burning of houses, the destruction of property, the expulsion from homes never weakened their confidence in the truth of these predictions, and their eventual fulfillment. That feeling had been implanted there by the Almighty; the Spirit of God had borne testimony to it in their hearts, and they never doubted it. Hated by a township, they foresaw the time when they would be hated by a county; hated by a county, they foresaw the time when they would be hated by a State; hated by a State, they foresaw the time when they would be hated by men who constituted a party who, it might be said, were the representatives of the nation; hated by a nation, they foresaw the time when the would be hated by other nations, until, as I have said, their loyalty to truth, to virtue, to good government, to good order and everything that is pure, holy and God-like, would be vindicated and established in the eyes of all men—by the nations at large, as well as their fellow-citizens.

How unlikely a thing to have been when there were but six persons composing this church! Yet the revelations given previous to that organization, the word of God as it has come down to us embalmed in that sacred book which contains the revelations given through the Prophet Joseph Smith, foretells in plainness just such results as these that I have alluded to. The spirit of this work, its character, the results which should follow it were plainly mapped out beforehand as though all the events connected with it had already taken place and were written by the pen of the historian, instead of that of the prophet. The historian can delineate with no greater accuracy (though he may give more details) when he writes the history of this people and the results of the labors of the elders of this Church, than it has been written for half a century.

The inhabitants of the earth, contrary to their will, and despite their wishes, are contributing to establish the prophetic calling of Brother Joseph Smith, and to fulfill the revelations of God given through him. . . .

Here is a feeble people in these mountains who have come here fleeing from persecution, carrying with them when they left their native States and launched forth into an untrodden and unknown wilderness, a love for the principles of liberty for which their fathers, many of them, had fought. Notwithstanding their persecutions and the vile treatment they had received at the hands of their fellow-citizens, they did not allow that feeling to dominate to their hearts; but loving the flag, the stars and stripes; loving the republic; loving the institutions of freedom, loving the Constitution, loving the laws, and carrying with them that love into the heart of the wilderness, and there laying the foundation of a great commonwealth they sought for admission as a State, and to have in that State every human right fully guarded and civil and religious liberty secured for people of every creed, and of no creeds, not seeking for alliance with Mexico, whose land they occupied, not seeking alliance with Great Britain, who was their neighbor on the north; not seeking alliance with the wild races, or endeavoring, or seeking to set up an independent republic, but their hearts going back fondly to the home of their fathers, to the land which their fathers had helped to redeem and make free, to the Constitution upon which the government of the land was founded, to the flag for which their fathers had fought and bled, they showed to the world that persecuted as they might be, hated as they might be, despised as they might be, and driven as they might be, they could not extinguish within them the love of liberty, the love of true republicanism. This was the testimony which this people bore to the inhabitants of the earth; and it might be thought, as I have said, that the people who had done this, working with unceasing toil to reclaim the waste places and make them habitable and beau-

tiful and a fit abode for themselves and their children; sending out missionaries at untold sacrifice to the nations of the earth to proclaim the Gospel and
gather in the honest from their own land and from the remotest nations of
the earth; doing this for years, until gradually, as we see, the stately structure
of a great commonwealth rises up around us; law executed; liberty preserved;
the utmost freedom extended to every human being throughout the length
and breadth of these mountain valleys; life and property as secure here as they
ever were in any of the States of the Union; strangers coming in here before
the railroad was built, weary and foot-sore, received with hospitable kindness.
This tabernacle, after it was erected, and before this was erected, the old
tabernacle, and before that was erected, the bowery, opened to preachers of
every denomination, men of every creed united to proclaim their tenets, to
give us their views; women protected throughout this land with such sacred-
ness that they, old or young, beautiful or homely, could traverse every valley
and pass through every town north and south, night or day, without hearing
a word that would be improper, without ever witnessing a gesture that would
annoy them; emigrants with their wagons coming in and leaving them in
town unguarded, and not a thing harmed or taken.

God has spoken concerning this work; this is the last work that the
Prophets or the Apostles have called the dispensation of the fullness of times.
There was to be a time when Satan should have to recede inch by inch, step
by step. That time has come. The column of the righteous, of the true is press-
ing onward; there is an irresistible power behind it. It will go forward gathering into its ranks the honest and virtuous from every nation; just as sure as we
live this will be the case. It will gather people from every nation. It seems like
a very strange thing to say, but on all proper occasions I say it with a great deal
of pleasure, at home and from home, that I have been taught from early life
that the day would come when republican institutions would be in danger in
this nation and upon this continent, when, in fact, the republic would be so
rent asunder by factions that there would be no stable government outside of
the Latter-day Saints; and that it is their destiny as a people, to uphold constitutional government upon this land. Now, a great many people think this is
a chimera of the brain; they think it folly to indulge in such an idea; but the
day will come nevertheless. There are those in this congregation who will witness the time that the maintenance of true constitutional government upon
this continent will be dependent upon this people, when it will have to be
upheld by us.

We are battling all the time for human rights. We did so in the States
before we were driven out; we have done so throughout these mountains, and
are doing so to-day, contending for our rights. Even before the great tribunal
of our nation, Congress, the contest is going on; for attempts are constantly
being made to wrest from us our liberties, as citizens; and we are standing our

ground as best we can, pleading for our rights, pleading for liberty of conscience, pleading for that freedom which belongs to the country, which God
has guaranteed through the Constitution; not for ourselves alone, but for
every creed, for every member of the human family. We do not want liberty
for ourselves alone; we desire every man to have it; liberty for Ingersoll, and
all who believe as he does; liberty for the followers of Mohammed and all who
believe in the Koran; liberty for Beecher and for those of his way of thinking;
and even Talmage who has talked so badly about us, we would have him enjoy
liberty; yes, and permit him to say what he pleases about us, to take what view
he pleases of our belief and practices, and to tell everybody what he thinks
about them. We would give him the utmost liberty to do this, and every other
man, to say what they please about us or about anybody else, as long as they
do not interfere with the rights and the liberties of the people against whom
they are opposed, protesting always, however, that men in criticising others,
should confine themselves strictly to the truth, or be held responsible to the
laws for slanders and falsehood. All sects and all people should have this liberty, that is, liberty of conscience, liberty of speech and liberty of the press, as
long as it does not degenerate into license, and interfere with the rights of
others. We claim this for ourselves; we contend for it, and we shall contend
for it until it is gained.

Erastus Snow

Elder Erastus Snow was born November 9, 1819, at St. Johnsbury, Cale-donia County, Vermont. He was converted at the age of fourteen and bap-tized on February 3, 1833. He was called and ordained into the Quorum of the Twelve Apostles on February 12, 1849. Elder Snow became an "exile for hardships' sake" when the anti-polygamy crusade commenced. This talk was given just three years prior to his death and during the crisis surrounding plural marriage. In this talk, Elder Snow teaches that though the Consti-tution is necessarily imperfect because of sin, one must remain loyal to it even when others abuse its powers. He further expresses his admiration for the extension of the franchise to women and former slaves.

April 6, 1883
Delivered in the Tabernacle
Great Salt Lake City

God our heavenly Father had moved upon the nations and sent out from the nations of the old world streams of emigration to the new world, who were panting for freedom and liberty, and who struggled to burst the bands with which they were bound, and the yoke from off their necks, and were striving to learn how to be free. And in penetrating the new world and its wilds, and in grappling with and overcoming the difficulties attending the forming of new settlements and planting colonies in the new world, they learned the value of freedom, and therefore studied to preserve it; and they labored to establish a form of government under which it might be maintained. In all these works and labors we discern an overruling providence, and manifestations of the mercy and loving kindness of God to His people, and the revelations of His Spirit imparted, to a greater or less degree, unto the wise and patriotic fathers of our country, who were thus enabled to unite upon the best form of government existing among men, or which, perhaps, ever has existed, unless it has been those which God himself directly revealed through the Patriarchs and Prophets of older times. But so far as any political organizations of government upon this earth, the Republican or Democratic form of government established in these United States—(the foundations of which were laid by our fathers over a hundred years ago), is the best calculated to promote the objects sought, and to maintain the rights of man, and the guarantees of religious and political freedom, of any form of government known to mankind. But that it or any other form, in this imperfect and sinful world, is altogether perfect is not to be expected, and therefore cannot endure for ever. But we regard the present form of government of this nation as embodying the greatest amount of virtue and principles best calculated to maintain and preserve the rights of man.

In the early history of this Church a revelation was given through the Prophet Joseph in which the people are commanded to observe the Constitutional laws of the land, and to uphold by their votes and sustain upright and honorable men to administer them; which also stated that He had inspired the fathers to establish this form of government for the good and benefit of man.

I deem it of much importance that these principles should be well understood and thoroughly impressed upon the minds of the Latter-day Saints throughout the world, and especially those dwelling upon this American Continent and within the pale of this government, that they may implant in the hearts of our children a love of freedom and human rights, and a desire to preserve them, and to aid in maintaining and defending them in all lawful and proper ways; and to study the constitutional laws of the land, and make others acquainted with them; knowing the principles contained therein, and of learning how to apply them to ourselves, to our children, and to our fellowmen who are willing to be governed thereby; study them that we may also learn how to use them in suppressing tyranny, misrule and other evils that affect mankind; for God has ordained this form of government in this age of the world, and has chosen His own instruments to further His great purposes on the earth—the organization of his Church, the proclamation of the everlasting Gospel, the establishment of His Zion, and bringing to pass His wonderful works which He predicted by the mouths of the ancient Prophets. And this political system and order of government is a power in His hands established, preserved and defended thus far by Him, which He will continue to use as long as the people are worthy of it, as long as they will maintain their integrity, uprightness and virtue; and at no time will the Latter-day Saints, as a people, ever stand approval before God in violating those principles or slackening their efforts to maintain and defend them. They are closely allied to the teachings of the ancient Prophets and Apostles, to the doctrines, practices and teachings of the Savior and His disciples, and they are the best means and aids of extending and promoting those principles on the earth. Whatever some may have thought of the mal-administration in our government and of the efforts of individuals and sometimes of large factions, to abridge the rights of the people, and of their blind zeal and efforts to reach the Latter-day Saints, and to stamp out the religion we profess—whatever may have been thought of the efforts of such individuals, cliques, or factions, and of their warfare against us; and who in that warfare trample under foot constitutional provisions of our Government—undermine the foundations upon which it rests—we must never in our feelings charge any of these things to this system of government, or to the principles enunciated in the Constitution, which we are commanded to observe and keep. We must charge it always where it belongs—to the bigotry, the ignorance, the selfishness, ambition and blind zeal of ignorant and corrupt politicians, their aiders and abettors, and all this should only serve to make us try more earnestly, anxiously and faithfully to combat such efforts upon constitutional grounds, calling upon God to help us therein.

We were told this morning by Brother Woodruff—quoting the word of the Lord given through the Prophet Joseph Smith concerning the promise He has made to His people—that inasmuch as we will be true to ourselves, true to God, true to our covenants and to our holy religion, that He will fight our battles, defend and maintain our cause, make it triumph and flourish, so that the wicked shall have no power to prevail against us. These promises have often been repeated to us, and last October we had a renewal of this assurance and this promise in the word of the Lord given unto us through His servant President John Taylor, and at a time and period, too, when many in our midst were weakening and their knees were beginning to tremble a little, and there

45

were others who were inclined to falter and doubt, and fear was upon some. Our enemies—especially the bigot, the hypocrite, the demagogue, the political quacks of the country—rejoiced, thinking that they were succeeding in their efforts to weave webs around us, to forge fetters for our feet and yokes to place upon our necks, and to lash us into obedience to them. But the great majority of the Latter-day Saints were calm in their feelings as a summer's morning, trusting as they have ever done in the promises of God, inspired with faith and hope in his overruling providence; and while we were doing what we might do properly under the Constitution and institutions of our country for the maintenance of our freedom and liberty, leaving the rest with God, exercising faith in His promise, continuing to pray for His blessing to attend our efforts and to hedge up the ways of our enemies, yet we have waited calmly for the result of the promises of God, and the answer to our prayers and the fulfillment of those things that have been spoken to us; and how signally have we seen them fulfilled. We have seen the very means which the enemies of this people have devised and intended for their enslavement become before us as chaff, as thorns crackling under the pot, as a broken yoke to be used to kindle the fires of freedom and liberty. In former times the efforts that have been made in Congress and out of Congress to press the representatives of the people to hostile and unconstitutional legislation as a means to help religious bigots to suppress the doctrines of Christ, the ordinances of life and salvation, the rule and reign of righteousness among the people of God—I say, in their efforts to reach our religious principles and faith, and the exercise of those principles under that faith, and to crush it out from the earth—in their efforts to do so, they have moved upon statesmen to violate the Constitution of our country and the principles of human freedom on which our government has been founded in order to accomplish this purpose. But all those who have thus stultified themselves before the world, and before the heavens, and have done violence to their oath of office and to the Constitution, to the rights of man, and to the principles of freedom and liberty, have weakened, have gone down, the sceptre of their power has fallen from their grasp, they have been dishonored before the heavens and before their people as a rule, and sooner or later we will witness others going down into the pit of forgetfulness as their predecessors have done. For the Lord has decreed it. And to-day the young men of Israel who are assembling in their Improvement Associations in all the Stakes of Zion, in all the Wards and settlements of the people throughout the land, and in their quorum meetings, and in their political assemblies, are all learning and cultivating these principles of liberty in their minds, introducing and extending them among the rising generation, the sons of Zion, and not only the sons, but the daughters that are coupled with the sons, the wives that are coupled with the husbands, in this labor of love, the struggle for the maintenance of freedom and liberty. It is a source of satisfaction to me that the Lord has moved upon His servants and the Legislature of our Territory to be among the first to lead the van of human progress in the extension of the elective franchise to women as well as men, and to recognize the freedom and liberty which belongs to the fairer sex as well as the sterner; for the Gospel teaches that all things are to be done among us by common consent, and the Prophet Joseph commanded and introduced in our midst the custom we are following to-day, that of presenting to all the congregations of Israel, at our General Conferences, and our local or Stake Conferences, the General Authorities of the Church, to be justified or condemned by the voice of the people, to be upheld and sustained by the confidence, faith and prayers of the people; or otherwise to be reproved by the votes of the people for their misdeeds or mal-administration. These are things continually before the people, as well as the revelations which God has given unto us, and which are written and taught in our Sabbath schools and public gatherings, and to all who come within the scope of these instructions, viz., a love of freedom and liberty.

We have come to the understanding that every soul of man, both male and female, high and low, is the offspring of God, that their spirits are immortal, eternal, intelligent beings, and that their entity depends upon their agency and independent action, which is neither tramelled by God himself nor allowed to be restrained by any of His creatures with His sanction and approval; that the whole theory of God's rule and government in heaven and on earth is founded upon this principle of agency—self, independent action. And it is upon the free and independent exercise of this agency that the decree of God is founded, that all men shall be judged according to the deeds done in the body, none having it in his power to say that he was not at liberty to exercise this agency untramelled.

So far as relates to the administration of government and the exercise of political power, or the exercise of any manner of influence—political, religious or social—every man and every woman will be held accountable to God for the manner in which they exercise it. Kings and emperors, presidents and statesmen, judges and all officers of the law, will be held responsible for the administration of the power reposed in them. And if, while acting officially, they disregard their oath of office and violate the principles that should govern them, they become guilty of mal-administration, and will be held accountable unto God, and should be strictly accountable to the people who place them in power. But every individual, in an individual capacity, will be held answerable to God for all his acts of whatsoever character, and so far as, in the exercise of that agency, men trespass upon the rights of their fellowmen they must be held answerable to their fellow-men for such trespass and wrong. And for this purpose human government is instituted, approved by the people, to hold each other responsible unto each other or unto the community, for the abuse of their freedom and liberty, and for this purpose laws are enacted and judges provided to judge according to the law, and to administer the law when it becomes necessary to punish transgressors.

I testify unto all Israel, and unto all the world, that God has called us, and required us to observe and practice these things; and that it is not the work of man, and that the institutions of this Church are not the institutions of man. And when we speak of the institutions of our common country, we say in the main, though God has used man in instituting this form of government, and in establishing its institutions and maintaining freedom upon this land, they are nevertheless the institutions of heaven; and God has revealed unto us that He did establish them by the hands of wise men, whom He raised up for that special purpose, and redeemed the land by the shedding of blood. It is therefore part of His great work, as much so as the part of revealing the keys of the Priesthood to Joseph, and the ordinances thereof, for the salvation of His people. For the political organization upon the land was designed by heaven to be a protection to the righteous. "But," says one, "is it not designed to protect the wicked?" No, not in wicked acts, but in their freedom and liberty, to think and to speak and to act, and to choose for themselves; for in those rights all must be protected. God has always protected them, both in heaven and on earth. And he designed that all men should protect one another, and if necessary be united for the protection and welfare of all flesh. Not that the laws of the land or the laws of God will protect the wicked in doing wickedly, but on the contrary, will condemn and judge them. They are left to choose for themselves their course of life in exercising their agency in all things pertaining to themselves and the service of their God, and to use freedom and liberty in doing good, that which is right; but there is no such thing as liberty to do wrong and be justified in that wrong, neither on earth nor in heaven, neither by the laws of God, nor the just laws of man.

Now, the Supreme Court of the United States, in its great zeal to establish and maintain monogamy upon this American continent, and to strike a blow at the patriarchal order of marriage, believed in by the Latter-day Saints, in its decision in the Reynolds' case announced the doctrine that religion consists in thought and matters of faith and concerning matters of faith, and not actions, and the government is restrained by the terms of the Constitution from any efforts to curtail this freedom and liberty. Wonderful doctrine! A wonderful strain of judicial thought to announce to the world, this wonderful doctrine that the government should not attempt to restrain the exercise of thought, or the exercise of faith! I would like somebody, that knows how to defend this doctrine, to tell me how any one man, or any set of men on the earth could go to work and catch a thought and chain it up and imprison it, or stop its flight, or root it out of the heart, or restrain it, or do away with it. Let them go to and try to chain the lightning, stop the sun from shining, stop the rains from descending and the mist from arising from the ocean, and when they have done this, they may talk about restraining men's faith, and exercising control over the thoughts and faith of the people. The fathers who framed our Constitution were not such dunces, I am happy to say, as Attorney-General Devens, who put that nonsensical language and doctrine into the mouths of the chief justices of the Supreme Court of the United States—the fathers who framed our Constitution, I say, were not such dunces, they did not attempt to place constitutional restrictions upon the law-making power, to restrain them from interference with faith and thought and the exercise of religious opinion; but they did attempt, and they did it in plain language, to restrain the law-making power from any effort at making law for the establishment of religion, or prohibiting the free exercise thereof. And the exercise of religion implies something more than mere faith and thought. I may think about being baptized for the remission of my sins, I may believe it is right I should do it, I may be convinced that God has required it of me, and I may think I ought to do it, and think I will; but all this faith and all this thought don't amount to as much as you can put in your eye, until I arise and go forth to be baptized, and when I do this, then I exercise the faith which is in me, and it produces the works. This principle may be equally true of everything else pertaining to the exercise of religion. I may believe it is right for me to be enrolled with a religious community that meets to worship, and I may believe it is right and a religious duty to meet with them from time to time to celebrate the supper of the Lord and partake of bread and wine, and when I partake of the bread and of the wine in commemoration of the sacrifice of the Lord Jesus, it is but the exercise of that faith which is in me. I may believe that God meant what he said when He gave that general commandments to His children to multiply and replenish the earth, and I may think about it; but it is my duty, if I want to raise potatoes, to plant the seed; if I desire to raise fruit I must go to and plant the fruit trees; if I desire to cultivate the earth I must use the proper means necessary to cultivate and improve it before I can gather the fruits of it. And then to do the other thing, to form a union as God has enjoined in the holy bond of matrimony, we must enter into that bond for the purpose of multiplying our species and thus bring forth the fruits of our bodies. I may believe this doctrine, as contained in the revelations of God; but what will this amount to unless I exercise myself in it. I shall remain a bachelor, worse than a hermit—a parasite in the commonwealth—unless I rise up and put my faith in practice and exercise myself in my religious belief.

Charles W. Penrose

Charles Penrose served as Assistant Church Historian from 1896 to 1899. He was born February 4, 1832 at Camberwell, London, England. He joined the church on May 14, 1850, being the only member of his family who ever embraced the gospel. He served on the Ogden City Council and was later elected to be a delegate from Weber County to the constitutional convention of 1872. He was editor-in-chief of the Deseret News, and also served in the territorial legislature in 1879 and again in 1882. At General Conference, April 4, 1896, he was sustained as assistant Church Historian. In this talk, brother Penrose says that the first amendment protects religious exercise as well as religious belief. This address was given in the midst of the crisis surrounding plural marriage.

July 26, 1884
Delivered in the Tabernacle, Salt Lake City,

Reported by John Irvine

Some people seen to imagine because we have embraced a doctrine which is not popular in the world, because we have embraced a faith which is contrary to the generally received notions in regard to religion, that we ought to have no rights whatever as citizens of our common country. We do not look upon the matter in that light. We consider that we have the right under the Constitution of the United States to believe anything which seems right to us, and not only to believe it, but to carry it out in our practice, so far as we can do so without interfering with the rights of other people. The first amendment to the Constitution of the United States says: "Congress shall pass no law respecting an establishment of religion, or prohibiting the free exercise thereof." We understand that amendment as it is written. We do not wish to interpet it, or to give to it any meaning other than the plain language conveys. The language is, "That Congress shall pass no law respecting an establishment of religion, then, Congress has nothing to do. Congress cannot set up a religion, nor can it pass any law respecting an establishment of religion." With the establishment of religion—that is, to prevent its free exercise. There are some people in these latter times who interpret that amendment to mean that people may *believe* what they please, but it carries with it no freedom of practice. People may beileve what seems right to them, but they must not carry it out if it happens to be contrary to the views of the great majority. Now, it appears to me that that is a very narrow interpretation of the meaning of that Amendment to the Constitution. It appears to us, as it must to the great bulk of the people of the country—the sovereign people—that without any constitutional amendment, or the passage of any law, people everywhere are of themselves free to believe. We do not think a law can interfere with belief, even if one were passed for the purpose fo interfering with it. A man's belief cannot be controlled by any Act of Congress or of Parliament. No edict of a government or any other law-making body can interfere with my freedom of belief. When a proposition is placed before my mind, and I reflect upon it, and it appears to be correct, my mind receives it and I believe it. Sometimes persons believe in spite of themselves. Sometimes a man will believe a thing in spite of his own desires not to believe. Then this faith cannot be controlled by any person outside of the man himself, and sometimes he cannot control it himself. No edict or law, or any power of man on the earth can alter a man's belief, or prevent him from believing. A law can be enacted to prevent the carrying of that belief into practice; but it cannot interfere with belief, and it needs no amendment to the Constitution, no enactment of Congress or of any law making body on earth, to protect a man in mere belief. Then it is clear to us that the intention was, that a man should have not only the right to believe, but that he should be protected in the free exercise of that belief. As the language states, Congress is not to pass any law respecting an establishment of religion, nor prohibit the free exercise thereof. What is the exercise of belief in religion? Why, it is certain acts men perform prompted by their belief, prompted by their religion. Suppose a man believes it is right to be baptized in water—buried in water for the remission of sins—how can he evidence his belief in that principle? He can only do it in the way specified by the Apostle James. He says: Show me thy faith without thy works and I will show thee my faith by my works." "But wilt thou know, O vain man, that faith without works is dead." That is the only way in which faith can be truly shown—by works. If I believe that baptism is right I evidence my belief by being baptized, and if I am not baptized it either shows that my faith is very weak or that it does not exist: that I have not the courage of my faith, or else that I do not believe at all.

Now, we consider that we have a perfect right under the Constitution of our country to believe what seems right to us, and then to carry it out. "Well," some one may say, "do you think there should be no restriction to this? Are people to be protected in any kind of religion they may have? Suppose a man were to come here from India who believed it a religious duty, under some circumstances, to strangle a man, would he have the right under the Constitution of the United States, to strangle? Again, there are people who believe it is right, in India, to burn a widow on the funeral pile, that her spirit may be sent to keep company with her husband in the other world. Would that person, or those persons have the right, under the Constitution of the United States, to carry out their belief in this country?" We say no. We say that the Thug has no right here to practice his faith. We say the Sattee could not be established in this country. "Why not? You believe it is right under some circumstances for a man to have more wives than one, and that those who thus believe are protected by the Constitution in the practice of their religion. Why should not those who believe it right to strangle, or to burn widows, have the right to practice their religion under the Constitution of the United States?" The dividing line is very simple, as truth generally is. It is very easy to be drawn. It is to be drawn in consonance with the spirit of the Declaration of Independence, and with the principles that underlie our government. In the Declaration of Independence it is laid down that there are certain rights that cannot be alienated, that are natural, that are inherent, that are not imparted by governments: they do not belong to politics, but they are inherent in the individual—the right to life, the right to liberty, the right to property, and the right to the pursuit of happiness. These rights are inalienable. They belong to every individual. They are not conferred by law. They belong to us. They are born in us. They belong to every person who breathes the breath of life. Then, an act of any individual or any government which infringes upon these natural rights is wrong in and of itself. If any individual interferes with the rights of his fellow men he may be restrained by the secular law. The right to life, and to liberty, and to the pursuit of happiness, and to property belong to all individuals alike. One body of people professing one faith must not interfere with the rights of any other body of people professing another faith. The Latter-day Saints, as well as the Latter-day sinners, the Methodist as well as the Catholic, the Jew as well as the Gentile—all people alike in this great country must be protected equally in these natural rights which belong to them.

Here, then, is where the line must be drawn. Anything that persons profess to do under the name of religion, which interferes with the rights of others is wrong, and the secular law may step in and protect the citizens and restrain or punish those people who attempt to do this under the plea of religion. If I do anything which interferes with the life, the liberty, the happiness, or the property of my neighbor, the law has a right to step in and protect my neighbor and restrain me. But if my religion—that which I believe to be true, and which I try to carry out as a part of my faith—does not interfere with human rights, does not infringe in any degree upon the rights of my fellow man, neither Congress, nor any other law-making power on the face of the earth, has the right to interfere with me under the Constitution of the country. I have a right to the exercise of my religion so long as it does not infringe upon the rights of other people. There is where we draw the line, and we think it is the right place. And we are standing up, not only for our own rights in this respect, but for the rights of all people upon the face of this land.

You cannot violate a principle of truth without receiving very bad consequences. Those who attempt to do that will be sure to reap the fruit of their labors at some time or other. And when the Congress of the United States commences to move away the foundation stones of the system that the fathers of this nation built up, they are working on very dangerous ground, and the consequences thereof will not be confined to the few people against whom these measures are made. It is the duty of every patriot, of every man who loves his country, and of every woman who loves her country, to do their part in preventing the passage of such enactments as these, and in vindicating the principles and doctrines which enter into the Constitution of our beloved country. So we are standing up not only for our own rights, but for the rights of others, and this is one of the duties enjoined upon us by our Heavenly Father.

This Church, this system, this organization to which we belong has not been set up by the wisdom of man, but has been set up by the power of God, by the command of the Almighty, and has been sustained by him up to the present time. All the efforts which are made to break it down will only tend to build it up. Every law the United States may pass with the intent to disintegrate this work, to divide the people, to crush the power that exists in the midst of the Latter-day Saints, will only tend to consolidate the people, to bind them closer together, to make their faith more intense, their convictions more certain, and to make their determination more persistent. That will be the effect.

We want to attain to the celestial kingdom. We want to fit ourselves for the society of the holy ones, the society of the best that ever lived upon the face of the earth, and for that we are Latter-day Saints. If men could prove to us that we are wrong, then they might have some chance of converting us. But when they trample upon our inalienable rights, upon our constitutional privileges, upon our religious liberty, why, then, we feel like resisting. But we are not going to fight. We naturally repel the assaults against us, but it is in the way of defence. Our motto, like that of the volunteers in London, is, "Defence, not Defiance." We defend our rights and privileges against all attacks, and in doing so we are standing up for the rights of all the people of this great country. For if you tear away the underpinning from the structure the fathers established, the whole institution may come down with a crash. I tell you we have got to watch for these things, and this is part of our mission. We must preach the Gospel and build up the Kingdom of God, and contend for our constitutional rights, because they are given of the Lord. The Constitution of our country was revealed of God. God has made known to us that He inspired the framers of the Constitution, and caused that instrument to be brought forth, so that all people might be protected in their rights. We claim the same rights as other folks, and no more.

Orson F. Whitney

Orson Whitney was born on July 1, 1855, in Salt Lake City. At the age of twenty-three he was called to be Bishop of the Eighteenth Ward. A year later, he married. Brother Whitney served as a delegate to the Constitutional Convention for the State of Utah, and took a leading stance in favor of Women's Suffrage. Elder Whitney was ordained an Apostle on April 9, 1906. This talk was given during the crisis surrounding plural marriage; many of the leaders of the church had been forced to go underground at this time.

April 19, 1885
Delivered in the Tabernacle
Great Salt Lake City

The earth upon which we dwell is only one among the many creations of God. The stars that glitter in the heavens at night and give light unto the earth are His creations, redeemed worlds, perhaps, or worlds that are passing through the course of their redemption, being saved, purified, glorified and exalted by obedience to the principles of truth which we are now struggling to obey. Thus is the work of our Father made perpetual, and as fast as one world and its inhabitants are disposed of, He will create another earth, He will people it with His offspring, the offspring of the Gods in eternity, and they will pass through probations such as we are now passing through, that they may prove their integrity by their works; that they may give an assurance to the Almighty that they are worthy to be exalted through obedience to those principles, that unchangeable plan of salvation which has been revealed to us.

These simple truths, most of which are plainly spoken of in this holy word of God, the Bible, are distorted by the enemies of the Saints to indicate that they are treasonable to the government under which they live. They say we are traitors because we speak of the Kingdom of God; that a kingdom cannot exist within a republic; that it is *imperium in imperio*; that there is no room in this broad land for the Kingdom of our God. They might as well say there is no room in Christianity for the love of God. Why, this great government was established for the very purpose of introducing this work. Inspired men like Washington and Jefferson were raised up to frame a Constitution liberal in its provisions, extending the utmost freedom to all men, Christian or heathen, who desired to make this glorious land their home; that they might have the unrestricted right to worship God according to the dictates of their consciences. We believe that God raised up George Washington, that He raised up Thomas Jefferson, that He raised up Benjamin Franklin and those other patriots who carved out with their swords and with their pens the character and stability of this great government which they hoped would stand forever, an asylum for the oppressed of all nations, where no man's religion would be questioned, no man would be limited in his honest service to his Maker, so long as he did not infringe upon the rights of his fellow men. We believe those men were inspired to do their work, as we do that Joseph Smith was inspired to begin this work; just as Galileo, Columbus, and other mighty men of old, whom I have no time to mention, were inspired to gradually pave the way leading to this dispensation; sentinels, standing at different periods down the centuries, playing their parts as they were inspired of God; gradually freeing the human mind from error, gradually dispelling the darkness as they were

58

empowered by their Creator so to do, that in culmination of the grand scheme of schemes, this great nation, the Republic of the United States, might be established upon this land as an asylum for the oppressed; a resting place, it might be said, for the Ark of the covenant, where the temple of our God might be built; where the plan of salvation might be introduced and practiced in freedom, and not a dog would wag his tongue in opposition to the purposes of the Almighty. We believe that this was His object in creating the Republic of the United States; the only land where his work could be commenced or the feet of his people find rest. No other land had such liberal institutions, had adopted so broad a platform upon which all men might stand. We give glory to those patriots for the noble work they did; but we give the first glory to God, our Father and their Father, who inspired them. We take them by the hand as brothers. We believe they did nobly their work, even as we would fain do ours, faithfully and well, that we might not be recreant in the eyes of God, for failing to perform the mission to which He has appointed us.

This is the "treason" of the Latter-Day Saints. They preach the coming of the King of Kings, whom all Christians ought to worship; whom all Christians ought to welcome; and instead of passing laws to prohibit, and prevent, if possible, the growth of this work, which has as its object the blessing of all mankind, they should join hands with the Latter-day Saints in consummating it; for as sure as there is a God in heaven it is His work, and He will accomplish it. Hauling men before magistrates; immuring them in dungeons; driving them from city to city, or shedding their blood, will no more stamp out this work than it will blot out the glory of the sun. They who take up the sword to fight against Zion will perish by the sword before she perishes; they who leave God out of the question in dealing with the "Mormon problem" will find before they get through that it is suicide to run against Jehovah's buckler.

The old fable which Æsop tells of the woodman who went into the forest to get a handle for his axe, describes accurately the position in which we find ourselves. The woodman went and consulted the trees of the forest, asking them to give him a handle for his axe. The other trees, the stronger ones, arrogating to themselves authority and ignoring the rights of others, thought that they could dispose of them as they pleased. They conferred together and decided to grant the request, and they gave to the woodman the ash. The ash fell; but the woodman had no sooner fitted the handle to his axe, than he began upon the other trees. He did not stop with the ash, but he hewed down the oaks and the cedars, and the great and mighty monarchs of the forest who had surrendered in their pride, the rights of the humble ash. An old oak was heard to complain to a neighboring cedar, "if we had not given away the rights of the ash we might have stood forever; but we have surrendered to the destroyer the rights of one, and now we are suffering from the same evil ourselves."

This nation may think that it is strong enough—powerful enough—to treat the people of Utah as they please. They are; we do not pretend to compare with them so far as that is concerned. But if there is any truth in eternal justice; if there is such a thing as retribution, woe be unto this forest of States if they surrender into the hands of tyranny the rights of the Utah ash! It cannot be done with safety. If they trample upon the rights of their fellow men, there must come a time in the eternal revolutions of the wheels of justice when their own necks will be beneath the tyrant's heel. They will suffer themselves from the laws they have passed against the maligned, misunderstood, down-trodden people of Utah. I hope to God, as an American patriot, that this never need come. I hope the eyes of this nation will be opened, that they may see the danger in which they stand from afar; but if I were a prophet I would prophesy in the name of God that if they give away our rights, if they trample upon our liberties, and surrender us as a sacrifice to popular clamor, the day will come when their own necks will feel the galling yoke; the laws they pass now to deprive us of our rights as American citizens, will deprive them of their rights, and they will drink the cup heaped up, pressed down, and running over. I hope this never need be; but I dare predict it on that condition, in all humanity, with no spirit of treason, or of ill will to my country; but with a feeling of sorrow that some of our fellow-citizens have it in their hearts to treat us in this cruel manner.

This is the treason which we preach. We desire to benefit our country; benefit our fellow-citizens; benefit our fellow-men. We believe this world is the Lord's, and that He is coming to reign upon it as it is His right to reign. I care not how soon it is accomplished. The reign of Christ will rob no man of his rights; no righteous government need fear it; neither the United States, nor the nations of Europe; if their consciences are clear, need dread the coming of the King of Kings. They must acknowledge if they are Christian nations, that they owe their allegiance to Him whose right it is to reign. They should be proud to lay their crowns and sceptres at His feet, and acknowledge Him to be Lord of Lords, and crown Him King of Kings.

This is a glance at the mission of the Latter-day Saints. These are some of the views we cherish and which we cannot recede from; we would be unworthy of our lineage as the sons and daughters of Abraham, the sons and daughters of Liberty, if we should forsake the things for which our forefathers lived and died, and suffered all manner of persecution. We leave the issue with God. Let the world persecute us, if they desire to assume that responsibility; we will seek to return good for evil. When they come with the sword we will meet them with the olive branch. We will say peace on earth when they have war on earth. We will do our duty as God shall give us strength, and leave the result with Him who over-rules the acts of all men and all nations for the ultimate redemption of the human family, of which we are some of the humble representatives.

PART TWO

Church Authorities in the Twentieth Century

B. H. Roberts

B. H. Roberts was born March 13, 1857 in Warrington England. He was ordained a Seventy on March 8, 1877, and later a President of the Seventy on October 7, 1888. He was elected to the Constitutional Convention which framed the organic law of the State of Utah. Elder Roberts was later elected to the fifty-sixth United States Congress, but was not permitted to take his seat. Elder Roberts is known for his many volumes of historical, biographical, and doctrinal works. In this address, given in 1912, Elder Roberts points out that the Book of Mosiah teaches a political principle equal to the greatest in American political thought: the great doctrine of a direct, moral responsibility to God of a free people. This was the basis of the Lord's inspiration of the Founding of this Republic.

General Conference, Salt Lake City, October 1912

The Latter-day Saints are a blest people. There *does* exist—I was about to say there can exist, but I would rather say there *does* exist—perfect unity in relation to all these essentials: in regard to the faith we have received, in regard to the dispensation of the fulness of times which God has revealed in these days unto us. And so I rejoice in these blessings, and can look forward with perfect confidence that in all these great and essential things, touching the salvation of men, the Church of Christ will remain absolutely united. Belief in and acceptance of these things are essential to the unity and integrity and the very existence of the Church.

Now, when you contemplate that other division, the non-essentials, here you have a field wherein liberty should exist; wherein should exist tolerance; tolerance in our social relations and activities, in our commercial affairs, and in industrial pursuits; in the sphere of civil government. These things in which the judgment of men may be exercised, and where it is merely a question, perhaps, of policy, or of administration. If only we can infuse into this sphere of the non-essentials, where one man's judgment may be as good as another's, if in that field we can only bring in the principle of charity, and of tolerance and the recognition of the liberty of all men, it seems to me then we shall have good reason to believe that in this sphere of non-essentials, we shall get along quite as happily as we may in the field where we are united in reference to absolute essentials. I believe that we are entitled to take an optimistic view with reference to these matters that make up the sphere of non-essentials; and especially in relation to the sphere of civil government. There is a passage in the Book of Mormon that to me has been very instructive, and also very encouraging. I think I will read to you this passage, since some of you may possibly have missed it. It occurs in the Book of Mosiah, where there is described a transition from a monarchial form of government to a reign of judges, which in reality was a sort of republic, or rule by the people. The value of this passage that I shall read is in that it expresses confidence in the ability of the people to rule, to govern themselves; and this inspired man. Mosiah, calls upon them to exercise that duty, and to do it in the fear of God. In recommending the changes in the form of the Nephite government, he said:

> *Therefore choose you by the voice of this people judges, that ye may be judged according to the laws which have been given you by our Fathers, which are correct, and which were given them by the hand of the Lord. Now, it is not common that the voice of the people desireth anything contrary to that which is right; but it is common for the lesser part of the people to desire that which is not right. Therefore this shall ye observe, and make it your law, to do your business by the voice of the people. And if the time comes that the voice of the people doth choose iniquity, then is the time that the*

judgments of God will come upon you, then is the time He will visit you with great destruction even as he hath hitherto visited this land. * * * And I command you to do these things in the fear of the Lord, and I command you to do these things, and that ye have no kings; that if this people commit sins and iniquities they shall be answered upon their own heads, for behold I say unto you, the sins of many people have been caused by the iniquities of their kings. Therefore their iniquities are answered upon the heads of their kings. And now I desire that this iniquity should be no more in this land, especially among this my people; but I desire that this land be a land of liberty, and every man may enjoy his rights and privileges alike, so long as the Lord sees fit that we may live and inherit the land, yea, even as long as any of our posterity remains upon the face of the land.

To my mind Joseph Smith, in bringing forth that principle through the Book of Mormon—the principle of personal, moral, responsibility to God for the government that obtains in free republics—has contributed one of the mightiest thoughts to the political life of the age in which he lived, that any man has brought forth in all the contributions that have been made to political thought in America. Patrick Henry's idea that men had an inherent right to rebel against insufferable tyranny is not equal to it. Jefferson's great doctrine of the Declaration of Independence, that all men are created equal, and that they are endowed with the inalienable rights of life and liberty and the pursuit of happiness, is not greater than this Book of Mormon doctrine. Webster's great contribution of "nationalism," viz., that this nation was an indestructible union of indestructible states, is not superior to it. And Lincoln's great thought, that the principle of the Declaration of Independence, that all men are of right free, must hold good as to the colored race as well as to the white race, does not surpass it. Because this great Book of Mormon thought is this: that while governments derive their just powers from the consent of the governed, there goes with that the awful, moral responsibility, direct to God, of every man and woman participating as sovereigns in a free government, for the kind of government that obtains in such country. The great doctrine of direct, moral responsibility of God of a free people is indeed a soul-inspiring utterance, but it is also an awe-inspiring condition, and on its face bears evidence of the divine source whence it comes.

It was upon this principle of confidence in the ability of the people to govern themselves that the Lord inspired those whom we call the "fathers of our republic," the founders of the constitution—it was upon this great principle of belief in the ability in the people for self-government, that the cornerstones of this republic were laid. Governments were announced in the Declaration of Independence to be the creatures of the people; and indeed it was further announced in the Declaration of Independence—and you must remember that the Declaration of Independence is the preface to the

Constitution, the Constitution merely organized agencies for carrying out the principles of liberty announced in the document known as the Declaration of Independence—it is announced, I say, that if governments become destructive of the liberties and rights of the people, it is the right of the people to alter or even abolish them, and institue new form that shall, in their judgment, tend better to preserve their rights and their liberties.

The signers of the Declaration of Independece and the framers of the Constitution were inspired from on high to do that work. But was that which was given to them perfect, not admitting of any addition whatever? No; for if men know anything they must know that the Almighty never yet found a man in mortality that was capable at the first intimation, at the first impulse, to receive anything in a state of culire perfection. They laid the foundation, and it was for after generations to rear the superstructure it. It is a progressive and gradual work.

I think it is divine wisdom manifested in the Constitution of our country that provision is made for its amendment, from time to time, as experience and larger views and changing conditions may warrant. However, upon this subject of change in the Constitution, I believe that the conservative spirit should prevail; that care and very great concern ought to be exercised with reference to change in the fundamental law of our government; but let us not think because we believe in the great truth that the Constitution of our country was the product of divine inspiration., that new conditions and a constantly changing status would not warrant, from time to time, changes in the fundamental law of the land.

Now, in relation in all these matters, we are operating in the realm of the non-essentials, that is, the realm where human judgment may be exercised; and where men may not be able to come to absolute unity of understanding in relation in matters and in that event, let us remember that it is the realm where liberty and tolerance prevail and it is proper that charity also should abound.

I thank the Lord and the brethren for this opportunity of saying so much in relation to these questions that are occupying the attention of the people. I rejoice that in the great field of the things which are essential, that the Lord has spoken, and that there is ground for absolute unity existing among us; and I sincerely trust that for this other field, in the realm of non-essentials, there will be liberty, and tolerance and in both—in the exercise and administration of both essentials and in the realm of liberty—which is the pure love of God—may abound.

James E. Talmage

James E. Talmage was born September 21, 1862, at Hungerford, Berkshire, England. He was baptized on June 15, 1873, and ordained an apostle December 7, 1911. He is known for his many volumes of scientific and theological works, the most famous being Jesus the Christ. This following speech was given just one year after his ordination to the Apostleship. He warns against giving in to the human tendency to interpret liberty in a narrow, one-sided way, thus neglecting freedom and rights of others. Reacting to a tendency in progressive thought to disparage the Constitution, he reaffirms its inspired founding.

General Conference, Salt Lake City, October 1912

I believe that we are too apt to apply the rules of liberty and of freedom in one-sided way. There are men who say that they have the right to smoke tobacco if they want to, and in this State if they be of age they have that right legally and I know they exercise it (laughter), but I long to see the day when I shall have some rights too in that matter, and when I shall not be forced to breathe the foul emanations that come from smokers' mouths. I hope to see the day when women will no longer be offended as they board or leave street cars or as they pass along the streets, by having clouds of tobacco smoke blown into their faces. I believe we shall improve in the matter of liberty and come to see that there are rights that others have as well as rights that we claim for ourselves. The spirit of the Gospel safeguards the right of no man to the injury of another, but provides for the liberties of all; and I hope that I will never become so lifted up in egotism that I shall feel that I am the people and that I know it all. I hope that I shall ever be led to seek for those to whom I feel I can look with confidence for advice, for counsel, for guidance, and if I choose to follow the counsel and advice of those in whom I have respect. I claim that I have the right so to do as a citizen and a free man.

I trust that the spirit of charity will manifest itself in our souls and that we will be willing to allow unto others those privileges and rights that we ask for ourselves; that we may in very truth be worthy of the measure of liberty which belongs to the Church of Jesus Christ, for if it be what it professes to be, the repository of truth, there must be in it the elements of true liberty and not that false freedom of the spurious kind which is being put forth in an uncensing stream from the devil's factories. We have to scrutinize very carefully the goods that are offered in the markets today lest we be deceived. I rejoice in the fact that this people stand for the Constitution of the nation. . . .We stand for the Constitution and do not believe in any false notions of advancement and enlightenment and progressivism such as seeks to undermine that foundation of our liberties, for as a document we know that it was inspired and we believe that the men who framed it were raised up, as truly as was ever prophet raised up in Israel in ancient or modern times, to frame that instrument and thereby provide for the fulfillment of prophetic utterances regarding the freedom and the liberty that should prevail in this choice land.

Charles Nibley

Charles Nibley was born February 5, 1849, at Hunterfield, Scotland. He rose from very modest circumstances to be named the director of the Western Pacific Railroad. He was ordained as the Presiding Bishop of the Church in December 1907 and was later called to serve as Second Counselor in the First Presidency under President Grant on May 25, 1925. In this talk, President Nibley argues against all forms of slavery and says that the Constitution is for the benefit of all men. He further argues that the principles of the Constitution are inseparably connected with the Restoration of the Gospel. He finally admonishes the members of the church to teach their children Constitutional principles.

General Conference, Salt Lake City, April 1925

This last revelation (D&C 101:77–80) was given just after the Saints had been driven from their homes in Missouri. Yet the Lord's words to his people were that the Constitution of the United States is that which "I established." This divinely conceived Constitution is, we are told, for the benefit of all mankind. The Lord said that its underlying principles are for the benefit of all flesh, not made for this country alone, but intended to govern the whole world.

Why is it that the elders are not permitted to preach the gospel in Russia today, where there are a hundred and eighty million people who have scarcely heard of the gospel? It is because of the moral agency that the Lord speaks of in the revelation known as section 101. These people are denied their free agency. The rulers of this people have a wrong conception of the rights and privileges which the Lord says pertain to all mankind.

In the 109th section of the Doctrine and Covenants is a prayer, given by revelation to Joseph the Seer, which was repeated in the Kirtland temple at the time of its dedication on March 27, 1836. I shall not undertake to read it, but shall quote only the 54th paragraph:

> *Have mercy, O Lord, upon all the nations of the earth; have mercy upon the rulers of our land; may those principles which were so honorably and nobly defended, namely, the Constitution of our land, by our fathers, be established forever.*

These words were uttered as a part of the dedicatory prayer, notwithstanding the persecution the Saints had suffered prior to 1836, persecution suffered at the hands of people who were prejudiced, people who were ignorant as to what the Latter-day Saints stood for, ignorant as to their beliefs and their aims. Notwithstanding all this, and clearly showing the broad and liberal spirit of this great latter-day work where such matters are concerned, the words last quoted were uttered as a part of the dedicatory prayer.

The revelations found in the Doctrine and Covenants, sections 98 and 101, which I have quoted, and in which the Lord has said that no man should be in bondage to another, were given at a time when millions of Negroes were in bondage in the southern part of the United States. At that time there existed a great question as to whether or not slavery should be perpetuated, and it seemed that the decision might be in favor of continuing to hold this black-skinned race under bondage to the white men who owned them. This question was settled a few years later, when the Supreme Court rendered its decision in the Dred Scott case. Dred Scott was a Negro who escaped from serfdom and went into one of the eastern states. His owner followed him and replevined him, claiming he was after his own property, just as he would go for a mule or an ox or a cow. Under the law the slave was his property. Chief Justice Taney, then at the head of the Supreme Court, delivered the decision that this was the law, the constitutional law. This decision was the law of the land; but in the justice and mercy of Almighty God, even a law which became a constitutional law, had to be overthrown, and the Lord raised up Abraham Lincoln and others to see that the law laid down by Him—that one man should not be in bondage to another—was set right and true freedom established in this land.

From that day on, millions more of slaves have been freed in Russia and other lands. In these latter-days, thrones have tottered and fallen, and in place of these has come a representative form of government, a government of the people, a government which gives the people their moral agency, spoken of in the revelations I have read, and which the Lord says is pertinent to all mankind.

It is true that there might be a constitution similar to ours in such countries as Mexico or Russia, and the results would not be at all the same, for the people of these countries are not as intelligent as are the people of this nation. But even in such countries, our Constitution could not help but produce a better government, for in that Constitution are the underlying principles which will, in time, teach these people to govern themselves intelligently. In order that the various peoples of the earth may at sometime reach the point at which they can intelligently govern themselves, the Lord in his mercy has in the past overthrown nations comprised of millions of people who have been subjected to unrighteous domination.

Now, coming to our own land, our own Constitution, I think we hardly appreciate sufficiently, what this Constitution means to us and to the work of the Lord. It is my belief that this Constitution, which the Lord declared he established, is for the benefit of all mankind. Verse 77, Section 101, reads as follows: "According to the laws and constitution of the people, which I have suffered to be established, and should be maintained for the rights and protection of all flesh, according to just and holy principles." Certainly, the fundamental, governing principles which the Lord has established on the earth under the name of the Constitution of the United States, were meant for all men, everywhere. These principles, with their accompanying freedom and liberty, are inseparably connected with our great latter-day work, it seems to me; for the Lord tells us that this freedom, this liberty, was brought about through the hands of wise men whom he raised up. Without this great Government of ours, this God-given Constitution, the gospel of Jesus Christ could never have found an abiding place in the earth. They are connected, correlated, interlocked one with the other; for the Constitution, like the gospel itself, is for the benefit of all flesh, for all mankind.

The Book of Mormon tells us that so long as the people of this nation are willing to acknowledge Jesus Christ as the God of this land, or as the ruler of this nation, so long shall his mercies be extended unto them.

Notwithstanding the weaknesses of our people, and of other people, I believe that today there is a greater desire in the minds of millions of people of this nation to acknowledge God and to acknowledge Jesus Christ and to live righteous lives than there has ever been before. While in some ways wickedness may be increasing, yet there is an earnest desire in the hearts of millions of people in this nation to acknowledge God and serve him.

Only a month ago President Coolidge delivered his inaugural address, and he closed it with the name of God upon his lips. These are the closing words of that address:

> *America seeks no earthly empire built on blood and force. No ambition, no temptation, lures her to the thought of foreign dominion. The legions which she sends forth are armed, not with the sword, but with the cross. The higher state to which she seeks allegiance of all mankind is not of human, but of divine, origin. She cherishes no purpose save to merit the favor of Almighty God.*

Here is a direct acknowledgement, most direct, coming from the very head of the nation, showing that the nation believes in God, believes in his divine providence, and asks for nothing save the favor of God.

I believe that it is my duty and your duty to teach our children concerning this great God-inspired Constitution, this great law of liberty which he has given to this world, and which was never given before to any nation in any land. Never before has there been a representative government of this kind. Republics have been tried, hundreds of times, thousands of years ago, but never was there anything like this Government.

Rulon S. Wells

Rulon Wells was born July 7, 1854, in Salt Lake City Utah. In November 1900, he was elected to the Lower House of the legislature of the State of Utah. He was set apart as one of the First Quorum of Seventy in April 1893. In this General Conference talk given in 1930, Elder Wells establishes that a purpose of the plan of salvation is to liberate man from bondage, both temporally and spiritually. It is the enemies of God, such as the atheistic tyrants of Soviet Russia, who seek to destroy the agency of man.

October 1930
Of the First Council of Seventy

The work of the Lord had its beginning before the foundations of this earth were laid. It has been one great struggle between good and evil, a great struggle for the liberty of the children of God. This work contemplates an exercise of free agency, of liberty. It is for the purpose of making men free and securing unto them their inalienable rights, which they, of necessity, must exercise in order to obtain eternal life. There can be no salvation in compulsion. There can be no reward through compelled obedience. But when men elect in the free exercise of their agency to serve God instead of serving mammon, thereby do they comply with the conditions of salvation.

This Gospel is a plan of liberating mankind from bondage. "The whole world lieth in sin, and groaneth under darkness and under the bondage of sin" (D&C 84:49), but the truth from heaven has a mission to perform, namely, to liberate us and make us free. It is no wonder that the Latter-day Saints have espoused the great cause of human liberty, that they regard this great government of which we form a part as having been inspired of Almighty God, that they regard the Constitution of our land and that instrument that preceded it, known as the Declaration of Independence, as being inspired of the Almighty for the salvation and the protection of the children of God. We rejoice in being citizens of this great republic, the freest country in all the world. Its principles, the very foundation upon which it has been established, are set forth in that Declaration of Independence, wherein it is stated that "all men are created equal and that they have been endowed by their Creator with certain inalienable rights, among which are life, liberty and the pursuit of happiness." Let it not be felt that these rights are given to us by any government. Not so. We live not because a government has given us the privilege to live; we live because God gave us life. We are free not because any government has given us our liberty—we are free not because we have received that power and that right from any human source; we are free because God made us free.

The Lord inspired the fathers of our country, our Revolutionary fathers, with this same spirit of human liberty, this right of free agency. This great struggle for liberty did not begin on this earth; it began before the foundations of it were laid. The Lord devised the plan whereby we might be liberated and made free and independent. The Lord designs that we shall be so. There was war in heaven before the foundations of this earth were laid. And what was that great conflict over? It was a struggle for the liberties of the children of God.

What is freedom? What is liberty? Does it mean license to do evil? No, indeed it does not. To be free means to liberate ourselves from the bondage of sin. We, in this country, boast of our human liberty and we have great reason to be proud of the liberty that we enjoy under our Constitution; but after all is said and done it is only a measure of civil liberty, but the greatest measure to be found among all the governments of the world. We sometimes boast of being in the land of the free, the home of the brave. Nevertheless, we are not free until we have overcome evil—until we liberate ourselves from the bondage of sin.

The Gospel of the Lord Jesus Christ is destined to make us free. It is the truth revealed from heaven that will make all men free if they will only render obedience to it. This plan of free agency was opposed by the enemies of God, foremost among whom was Lucifer, even in that primeval day when the plan of life and salvation was first promulgated among the children of God, when it was made known that they could come upon this earth and receive bodies of flesh and bones and live this earth life, in the exercise of their free agency.

> *To love and to be free,*
> *To worship God alone,*
> *As conscience guideth me,*
> *As my own heart is prone.*
> *These are rights God-given;*
> *He gave them all to me.*
> *They emanate from heaven—*
> *E'en life and liberty.*

There is none in all the world who feels more deeply than we do the import of our popular national hymn:

Our fathers' God! to thee,
Author of liberty,
To thee we sing;
Long may our land be bright
With freedom's holy light,
Protect us by thy might,
Great God, our King!

What a blessed boon is liberty. The free agency of man! The right to live upon the earth with a knowledge of good and evil. Blessed are we if we choose the good and reject the evil, provided, of course, we do so of our own volition, in the exercise of our free agency. Many there were even in the very beginning who opposed this plan. We are told in holy writ that one-third of the hosts of heaven followed Lucifer in his rebellion against God and were cast out of heaven. That war begun in heaven, is continued here on earth. To follow the enemies of God means to follow them into slavery, but to serve God means freedom, and we are under necessity of choosing whom we will serve—God or the adversary of our souls, the archenemy of God. Many there have been in all ages who have endeavored to enslave mankind—to dominate the minds and conscience of men. All such are enemies of God. They have instituted despotic governments and have ruled with an iron hand. They have established state religions and punished non-conformists as heretics and even burned them at the stake. All enemies of God are they who seek to destroy the free agency of man or to deprive them of their inherent—their inalienable rights of life and liberty, the right to worship God according to the dictates of their own consciences. The establishment of a state religion is an abomination in the sight of God. Think of poor afflicted Russia now under Soviet rule. How they have suffered in the past under the despotic rule of the Czar, and dominated by a corrupt hierarchy—an established state church, enslaving and oppressing them!

The people of that land had good reason to rise up against such conditions and all sympathy should be extended to them in their struggle for liberty; but no sooner have they liberated themselves from this condition of thralldom till the Soviet seeks to plunge them into the still more deadly slavery of atheism. These Soviet masters are still greater oppressors and tyrants than any who have ever preceded them, for they have even undertaken to prevent them from serving God in any form whatever, and when men cease to serve God, at that moment they begin to serve the devil, which means slavery. Such rulers have no conception of human rights. What they need is a Thomas Jefferson to write into their constitution a provision like this: The Soviet shall make no law respecting the establishment of any religion, nor prohibiting the free exercise thereof. They have surely broken down the establishment of a state religion, but they have also undertaken to prevent the free exercise of any religion—to deprive their people of their inherent rights. Tread lightly, ye powers that be, for this is holy ground. Even in our own land there are some who seem to think that our Constitution is unfriendly to religion. On the contrary, it is intended to encourage and protect all religions. It simply means "equal rights to all, but special privileges to none,"—no state religion, but no interference with any. This is holy ground. To congress it says "hands off."

How grateful we ought to be for those champions of human liberty that have arisen in our own land—for George Washington, "the father of his country," who led our forces in establishing this free republic, founded upon the principles of human liberty; for Abraham Lincoln, the great emancipator, who under the inspiration of the Almighty, carried on the fight to preserve unto us these sacred rights that they might not perish from the earth; for Woodrow Wilson, who led the American forces in the greatest struggle of history for human liberty, and that these principles that we love so dearly shall be extended to all mankind. The influence of these great champions of human liberty will be felt by the inhabitants of this world throughout the ages which are to come.

Let us, then, as Latter-day Saints, rejoice in the precious boon of liberty secured unto us by that great palladium of our inherent rights, the Constitution, and manifest our loyalty to it by obedience to it and the laws which have been enacted in carrying out its provisions. Let us also rejoice in the free agency of man which permeates the Gospel of Jesus Christ and manifest our appreciation of it by our obedience to that Gospel which is the "Truth that will make us free." This I pray in the name of Jesus Christ. Amen.

Levi Edgar Young

Levi Young was born February 2, 1874, in Salt Lake City, Utah. He studied at Harvard and Columbia. He was ordained a member of the Seventy in 1897 and was later called to the Presidency of the Seventy on January 23, 1910. In his conference talk in 1937, Elder Young teaches that the American Constitutional order provides an ideal for the entire world. We must be on guard, however, against tampering with the Constitution, even in minute ways or in the name of "progress," lest we open the door to a despotism while preserving only the name of the republic.

General Conference, Salt Lake City, April, 1937
Of the First Council of the Seventy

A hundred and fifty years ago, the founders of our Republic announced the sublime truth that men are free and equal. A century and a half have rolled away since then, and the history of the world has no chapter to compare with the accomplishments of America in that time. Standing on Saxon foundations, and inspired by Latin example, we have done what no race or nation or age has ever accomplished. The American people have founded a Republic on the un-limited suffrage of the millions of souls that inhabit this land. They have worked out the problem that a man, as God created him, may be entrusted with self-government.

Our forebears had a virgin continent to conquer. The fundamental problems they met with hard work and a faith in themselves. They had inher-ited from their fathers the ideals of home-life, freedom of religion, the free state, the public school, and the lands of the vast continent to till, on which they built their homes.

No nation has ever had a freer people, and no other nation of history has given its citizens the powers of happiness as our Government has done. Great wealth has been produced, but that wealth has been used to build industries and institutions of learning; it has been the power in the hands of men to build humble homes and beautiful churches, and with it all, the ideals of the founders of the Republic have been preserved, and America has wor-shipped at the shrine of its great men.

Our Government was "conceived in liberty, and dedicated to the propo-sition that all men are created equal." America has upheld this ideal before the world, and has opened its gates to all peoples of the world. Religion has been a forceful factor in our growth, and today some two hundred or more Christian sects are attempting to keep alive the divine message of the Savior of the world. The light on the hills of Judea became our light, and we have had faith in the vision of a prophet of ancient Israel:

> *The secret things belong unto the Lord our God: but those things which are revealed belong unto us and to our children for ever, that we may do all the words of this law.*

Our Government started out blessed with the rich inheritance of the ages. Its future lay before it, and that justice should rule the hearts of all its people, the Constitution of the United States was written. The influence of our Government has been felt time and time again among the nations of Europe, for they have looked to America for the solution of their problems.

A few years ago, at Independence Hall in Philadelphia, a great event took place. In that simple and dignified room, where the Declaration of Independence was written and the Constitution of our country was adopted, no fewer than twelve nations, through their representatives, assembled to make their own solemn declaration of common aims. In that sacred room, those nations made public confession of a faith which linked them in friendship with this nation. What a solemn occasion! The nations of Europe lighting their national fires at the altar of American liberty.

The peoples of the world entered our gates, and have found here a new life and happiness. Never had they been so well card for; never had they the chance to live and to look up to their God in hallowed feeling as they were given in this land. No nation of history has given homes to its people as has this our Country. Never has the wealth of land been so equitably distributed; never in all time, have so many people owned their own homes. With individual opportunity, there has gone quite naturally inequality. Inequality is a law of all social life, and to try to do away with inequality among men is to substitute tyranny for liberty.

The quality of democracy in America is that it seeks to protect and preserve that sovereign right of all people to come to a knowledge of their own better selves, and to live their own natural lives. Democracy teaches us that it is not wealth that makes happiness, but the wealth of the spirit, brought about by the opportunity to work on land and in factory, and to enjoy the blessings of church and school. Men may exploit honest labor, but such a thing is foreign to American principles. It is the wealth of America in the hands of men of vision that has built industries, and made it possible for all people to have honest labor, and to live honestly before their God. The schools of America, the churches, the institutions of higher learning have been closed to no one, and the statement of a noted writer on economics that the glory of America is that every head of a family is given an opportunity to own his home, is true. The peasants of Europe, who lived on bread and wine, have found asylum in this land, and the comforts of the humble fireside.

This is an age of change. Innovation is the idol of the times. "In this age of novelty, many things are made better, and many things are made worse. Old errors are discarded, and new errors are embraced." Governments feel the same effects in this craze for change. "But the experience of all ages," said Daniel Webster on one occasion, "will bear us out in saying that alterations of political systems are always attended with great danger, for if the Constitution is to be changed, an alteration in one part will work an alteration in another."

Nor are great and striking alterations alone to be shunned. A succession of small changes, a perpetual tampering with minute parts, steal away the breath, though they leave the body; for it is true that a Government may lose all its real character; its genius and its temper; without losing its appearance. So if we are not careful—very careful—we may find our government changed to a despotism, and yet called a Republic. It may have all the essential modes of freedom, and yet nothing of the essence, the vitality of freedom in it. The form may be left, but the spirit and the life will be gone.

To perpetuate our government, we must cherish and love it. We must preserve a correct and energetic tone of morals. After all, liberty consists more in the habits of the people, than in anything else. There are always men wicked enough to go any length in the pursuit of power, if they can find people enough to support them. Ambition of men to become dictators must be restrained by the public morality. When such men arise, they must find themselves standing alone.

America will have to suffer the hate and envy of the unappreciative. It is a law of life that we only appreciate that which we are ourselves. Millions of citizens have never risen to the appreciation of the glory of our nation, and therefore they become the fighters and destroyers of right. Wrong rules the day, and in time a wrong is felt to be right. It all means that education is the only way to reach the ideal in our souls of what our Government really means. Did the fathers reach it? They did, but it was through the faith they had in Almighty God. Such faith is the great help to true education.

We are the trustees of a sacred trust. We have been given by Providence this Government with all its potentiality, with all its accomplishment, with all its promise. The question should be to every American: How am I discharging this trusteeship? What am I doing to preserve, protect, and perpetuate the ideals of the government in which we have such implicit faith? We have a solemn obligation before us.

Every American should read the Declaration of Independence, the Constitution of the United States, Lincoln's Address at Gettysburg, and see for himself whether the American policy has been a selfish program. It has been a program to serve humanity.

Only the application of the standards of moral excellence can save our fundamental ideals. As we look into the future, will it be progress or decline? Let us pray God that it may be progress. But progress will never be unless we sacredly preserve our Constitution and hold it as the surest vision for liberty and freedom.

Albert E. Bowen

Elder Albert E. Bowen was born on October 31, 1875. He was the seventh child born to a pioneer farming family in southern Idaho. Despite hardships early in his life, he attended Brigham Young College at Logan, Utah, at the age of 20. He eventually graduated and went on to law school at the University of Chicago. Elder Bowen completed a mission and married twice, losing his first wife during childbirth. He was called as an apostle on April 8, 1937. The following excepts are first from a radio address then from a conference talk.

The Constitution
Charter of Our Liberties
Radio address given over KSL, Sunday July 4, 1937, at 8:30 P.M.

The liberty we celebrate was not born in 1776, but was prepared by 180 years practice of the art of self-government and secured by the Constitution, which accomplished at once a centralization and a decentralization of power. The Constitution, a law supreme above the powers of government, and including the process provided for effecting changes in it, was inspired of God.

One hundred sixty-one years ago today the American colonies crossed the Rubicon. On that day they declared that all-political connection between them and the State of Great Britain was dissolved, and that they were "and of Right ought to be Free and Independent States." They had to fight a war to make good the declaration.

We commemorate the day as the birthday of our nation. It is becoming that we should do so. The custom of mankind is, by fitting observance, to keep alive for the benefit of successive generations the memory of great course-determining, history-shaping events.

But all our memorials will be idle, fruitless, ceremonials unless they have the effect of focusing our attention upon the value of our institutions which were established to perpetuate the liberties for which the Revolutionary Patriots fought and died, and of inspiring us with the will to preserve them.

The Colonies emerged from the war thirteen separate States, each with its own independent government. They had won political independence, but a firm Union among them had not been established. While foreign troops were on their soil the common danger served as a sufficient bond of Union. That cohesive force was dissolved with the cessation of the armed conflict. Their first national government had failed for want of adequate powers. Internal dissension, jealousy, distrust, loomed as enemies of almost more threatening import than had been the armies of the foreign foe. The victory they had achieved at such cruel cost threatened to elude them because of the lack of institutions necessary to its protection and perpetuity, for in human society the benefits of liberty can be realized only through established law. They had a surprisingly accurate knowledge of the course of all governments within the period of recorded history and had learned that power once bestowed tends ever towards its own expansion; that the very instruments created for the guaranteeing of liberty might have in them the seeds of its destruction. They feared the possible tyranny of a strong government and dreaded the chaos, which threatened from want of one.

A DIFFICULT TASK

"In framing a government," wrote Hamilton, "which is to be administered by men over men, the great difficulty lies in this: you must first enable the government to control the governed; and in the next place oblige it to control itself."

Such was the task our Fathers had before them. They knew of the centuries of struggle and warfare, which had been waged to break down the absolutism of the crown. They had had more than one hundred years of first hand experience with the oppression of a legislature of unlimited authority. They were determined that there should be no such concentration of either executive or legislative power as would make possible the strangling of individual liberties. It was in this atmosphere that the Constitution of the United States was framed. The avowed purpose of the framers of it was to secure the blessings of liberty to themselves and their posterity. They believed they had done it by the device of making a law supreme over the government itself out of which the powers of government flowed and by which those powers were limited. The people created the Constitution; the Constitution created the government and delineated its powers. It had no others. It recognized the people as the ultimate source of all power and reconciled the need of a centralized distrust of such a government by providing for its operation concurrently with the functioning of the local state governments, each limited in the powers possessed and with the residuum of all power retained in the hands of the people. This was America's political gift to the world.

The desire for liberty was not born in the American Colonies in 1776, neither is the concept of freedom indigenous to this land. Both are age-old. The Colonists were Englishmen and had suckled the love of liberty with their mothers' milk. Their great contribution to liberty consisted in the form of government they created to preserve and protect it—a government which itself must bow before a supreme law.

A CENTRALIZATION

"Never before," says Warren, "in the world's history had there been a federal form of a Republic, in which the States should remain as sovereigns acting with limited powers upon their own citizens, but in which a central government of the States should have Executive, Legislative and Judicial authority to enforce its own limited sovereign powers directly upon the citizens of the States."

The Constitution accomplished at once a centralization and a decentralization of power. It gave to the Federal Government control over such affairs as concerned all the states alike—that is to say, those powers necessary to the existence of the Union. Regulation of affairs of purely local concern it left to the states, but the latter were expressly forbidden to do certain enumerated things. To insure against the extension of the power of either beyond the prescribed limits, it was written into the Constitution that "the powers not delegated to the United States by the Constitution, nor prohibited by it to the States, is received to the States respectively or to the people." Thus everything was done that could be done to provide against usurpation by the Government, or any department thereof, of powers not granted to it.

FRANKLIN VIEW

Contrary to an apparently prevalent opinion, the Founders understood very well that they were not framing a charter of government for the thirteen states alone. They had long known that a great western expansion was the country's inevitable destiny. Way back in prerevolutionary days Franklin had looked with favor upon the suggestion that the Colonies compromise their differences with Britain by accepting proportional representation in the British Parliament. Writing from England he supported the idea upon the theory that growth to the west would soon result in a preponderance of the population's being here with the consequent result that the seat of government would finally be moved to America.

They were providing a government for a country of ultimate wide extent, and they knew it. The principle of decentralizing national power by localizing control of local affairs in local concurrent governments, first given to the world in the Constitution of the United States of America, is a principle since adopted by the other most progressive democracies of the world. It has been adopted by the great Dominions of Canada and Australia and by the British Isles themselves. As pointed out by Mr. Walter Lippman, the great British Empire has become since the war a commonwealth of nations founded upon our own federal principle. So profoundly impressed is this keen student by the efficacy of it that he dares to predict that it is the only principle upon which "large populations, with diverse interests, can keep their independence and attain the benefits of union." That is something for Americans to think about in this day when it is being proclaimed that this principle embodied in our Constitution must give way before the wide expanse of our territory concurrently with the close knitting together and interlocking of the common interests.

At the same time he ascribes to the men who evolved the principle "a prophetic insight into the future problems of democratic government."

INSPIRED MEN

In this estimate we agree with him. The Latter-day Saints have always believed, and the Church has ever taught that God rules in the affairs of men and that the Revolutionary Fathers, the framers of the Declaration of Independence, and of the Constitution of the United States, were inspired by the wisdom of the Omnipotent. That the Constitution wholly suited none of them, and resulted from compromise of divergent views does not in the least disparage the claim. The compromises related to incidentals. The deep-seated basic underlying principles were not affected. The instrument was the product of the experiences of 180 years in the practice of the art of self-government and of the experience of centuries in the struggle of man for freedom. To hold that the founders were heaven-guided does not signify, neither do I believe, that the Constitution was written by the finger of God, nor that it sprang full grown either from the forehead of Jove or Jehovah. That is not my understanding of the way in which God works with me. It is the eternal law of life that human beings can progress only by their own effort, but under guidance.

It is so of peoples and of nations. Working through imperfect man, He does not reach down with His omnipotent power and set up a completed perfected order from which there may be no change. He respects the great eternal law of human liberty upon which alone men or nations may ameliorate their conditions and ultimately reach the goal of an ordered tranquility.

HEAVENLY GUIDANCE

In freedom, men are permitted to make mistakes and to correct their own errors. But God planted in them the impulse to struggle upward and by His guiding inspiration leads them in the way.

In nothing, I believe, did the Fathers more fully evidence the guidance of Divine Wisdom than in the process they provided for effecting change in the law they made. It necessitates the passage of time and gives opportunity for the sobering effect of reflection upon the impulse to change bred under the passing moods of passion or distress or demagogic appeal. The government has only the powers granted. Only the people may enlarge the grant. Even they may do it only after opportunity for calm reflection. By this device they provided not only against usurpation by government, but protected themselves against their own folly. God grant that the process may never become easier.

It is peculiarly suitable, therefore, that the Church should devote this period of its worship to honoring the men and memorializing the event which gave to this goodly land the great charter of its liberties. Seventeen eighty-seven flowed naturally out of 1776, the former being the consummation of the latter. The Constitution is rightly called the "charter of our liberties" which must signify that without it our liberties could neither be safeguarded nor preserved. It is the charter of our liberties because it sets up a law supreme above men and above the powers of government itself. So long as respected it guarantees to the humblest individual the inalienable rights of protection in his life, in his liberty of action and of conscience, and in his enjoyment of his own property. Each department of authority created by it is equally sacred with every other department. To teach disrespect for one must inexorably lead to the breaking down of respect for all. To indulge the practice is to sow the wind, the harvest whereof has ever been the whirlwind.

April 3, 1938

Freedom is an achievement that requires moral self-government. This freedom is threatened by the principles of modernistic despotism which now clamor for admission to our own land.

The very essence of the theology of the Latter-day Saints, is flatly denied by the totalitarian whose chief exponent has said that the ideal of happiness and indefinite progress is a "myth," and the inevitable consequence of whose teaching is the exaltation of the barbarities of paganism over the humane precepts of the Son of Man.

The people of America have been the freest people on earth precisely because more of the activities of life have here been left to self-direction than has been the case anywhere else and the domain occupied by government has been correspondingly more circumscribed. It is an historical certainty that the express purpose of the framers of the Constitution of the United States was to establish under it a government for the protection of their newly won liberties. Its highest sanctions are free speech, free press, free elections, a free legislature, a free judiciary and a definite limitation upon the powers of government over the lives of men. All these the modernistic despotisms—under whatever name—deny.

Latter-day Saints believe that these are divine principles and that the men who formulated them into a system of government were acting under the inspiration of the Almighty, in the majesty of whose name every man who comes into office under it binds himself by oath that he will preserve and defend it.

Freedom signifies more than a release from outward restraint. It is an essence, a quality of the spirit whose rarest blossoms, in an atmosphere of oppression, wither and die.

In our conception, the whole purpose and object of life is to achieve individual perfection through the unfolding of individual potentialities and the ripening of all the virtues. Learning, extension of horizons, expansion of vision, poise of character, serenity of soul—these coveted fruits of the spirit—are the consequence of voluntary free acts. In the foul and noisome air of despotism they may neither quicken nor flower. They are outside the power of human bestowal or coercion; they are in the realm of freedom. As these transcend physical acquisitions in value, so the principle of freedom transcends the power of force or compulsion.

Freedom is not bestowed; it is achieved. It is not a gift, but a conquest. It does not abide; it must be preserved.

Self-government involves self-control, self-discipline, an acceptance of and the most unremitting obedience to correct principles. Its demands are commensurate with its high privileges. Duties are the inseparable companions of rights. No other form of government requires so high a degree of individual morality. "It is ordained in the eternal constitution of things," said Burke, "that men of intemperate minds cannot be free." It is one of the missions of the Church to foster in men those virtues, without which there can be no self-government, and the alternative to which is the mentally and spiritually sterilizing scourge of tyranny.

Before we import despotic principles into our own land, which are so raucously clamoring for admission, we would better count the costs.

Thank God for Liberty!

May we and all the generations to come be as heroic in its preservation as were the Fathers in its establishment, that in our land freedom may abide forever.

David O. McKay

David O. McKay was President of the Church of Jesus Christ of Latter-Day Saints from April 1951 to his death in January of 1970, having served as an Apostle since 1906. Born September 8, 1873, President McKay grew up in Huntsville, Utah, eventually graduating from the University of Utah and becoming a professional educator. President McKay frequently proclaimed the principle of agency and warned against ideologies that threaten it. The first item presented here, a speech given when Elder McKay was serving as Second Counselor to President Grant, urges defenders of the freedoms protected by our inspired Constitution to be alert to the threat of European "isms" which had in the previous year contributed to the subjugation of two hundred and fifty million people. The second item is an official Church statement concerning the evils of Communism.

General Conference, Salt Lake City, October 6, 1940

UPHOLDING THE CONSTITUTION

Finally, if we would make the world better, let us foster a keener appreciation of the freedom and liberty guaranteed by the government of the United States as framed by the founders of this nation. Here again self-proclaimed progressives cry that such old-time adherence is out of date. But there are some fundamental principles of this Republic which, like eternal truths, never get out of date, and which are applicable at all times to liberty-loving peoples. Such are the underlying principles of the Constituion, a document framed by patriotic, freedom-loving men, who Latter-day Saints declare were inspired by the Lord.

This date, October 6, has been set apart by churches as "Loyalty Day." It is highly fitting, therefore, as a means of making the world better, not only to urge loyalty to the Consitution and to threatened fundamentals of the United States government, but to warn the people that there is evidence in the United States of disloyalty to tried and true fundamentals in government. There are unsound economic theories: there are European "isms," which, termite-like, secretly and, recently, quite openly and defiantly, are threatening to undermine our democratic institutions.

Today, as never before, the issue is clearly defined—liberty and freedom of choice, or oppression and subjugation for the individual and for nations.

As we contemplate the deplorable fact that within the brief space of one year, TEN European nations have lost their independence, that over TWO HUNDRED AND FIFTY MILLION people have surrendered all guarantees of personal liberty, deeper should be our gratitude, more intense our appreciation of the Constitution, and more strengthened our determination to resist at all costs any and all attempts to curtail our liberties, or to change the underlying system of our government.

April 9, 1966

Statement concerning the position of the Church on Communism made by President David O. McKay at the general priesthood session of the 136th Annual Conference of the Church, held in the Salt Lake Tabernacle, Saturday, April 9, 1966, at 7:00 p.m., read by Robert R. McKay.

In order that there may be no misunderstandings by bishops, stake presidents, and others regarding member of the Church participating in non-church meetings to study and become informed on the Constitution of the United States, Communism, etc., I wish to make the following statements that I have been sending out from my office for some time and that have come under question by some stake authorities, bishoprics, and others.

MEMBERS ARE FREE

Church members are at perfect liberty to act according to their own consciences in the matter of safeguarding our way of life. They are, of course, encouraged to honor the highest standards of the gospel and to work to preserve their own freedoms. They are free to participate in nonchurch meetings that are held to warn people of the threat of Communism or any other theory or principle that will deprive us of our free agency or individual liberties vouchsafed by the Constitution of the United States.

CHURCH IS POLITICALLY NEUTRAL

The Church, out of respect for the rights of all its members to have their political views and loyalties, *must maintain the strictest possible neutrality*. We have no intention of trying to interfere with the fullest and freest exercise of the political franchise of our members under and within our Constitution, which the Lord declared he established "by the hands of wise men whom [he] raised up unto this very purpose" (D&C 101:80) and which, as to the principles thereof, the Prophet Joseph Smith, dedicating the Kirtland Temple, prayed should be "established forever." (D&C 109:54.) The Church does not yield any of its devotion to or convictions about safeguarding the American principles and the establishments of government under federal and state constitutions and the civil rights of men safeguarded by these.

COMMUNISM GREATEST THREAT TO PEACE AND THE SPREAD OF GOD'S WORD TO MEN

The position of this Church on the subject of Communism has never changed. We consider it the greatest satanical threat to peace, prosperity, and the spread of God's word among men that exists on the face of the earth.

In this connection, we are continually being asked to give our opinion concerning various patriotic groups or individuals who are fighting Communism and speaking up for freedom. Our immediate concern, however, is not with parties, groups, or persons, but with principles. We therefore commend and encourage every person and every group who is sincerely seeking to study Constitutional principles and awaken a sleeping and apathetic people to the alarming conditions that are rapidly advancing about us. We wish all of our citizens throughout the land were participating in some type of organized self-education in order that they could better appreciate what is happening and know what they can do about it.

CITIZENS SHOULD EDUCATE THEMSELVES

Supporting the FBI, the police, and the congressional committees investigating Communism and various organizations that are attempting to awaken the people through educational means is a policy we warmly endorse for all our people.

COMMUNISM'S ATHEISM AND HATE

The entire concept and philosophy of Communism is diametrically opposed to everything for which the Church stands—*belief in Deity, belief in the dignity and eternal nature of man, and the application of the gospel to efforts for peace in the world.* Communism is militantly atheistic and is committed to the destruction of faith wherever it may be found.

The Russian Commissar of Education wrote: "We must hate Christians and Christianity. Even the best of them must be considered our worst enemies. Christian love is an obstacle to the development of the revolution. Down with love for one's neighbor. What we want is hate. Only then shall we conquer the universe."

On the other hand, the gospel teaches the existence of God as our Eternal and Heavenly Father and declares: ". . . him only shalt thou serve." (Matt. 4:10.)

COMMUNISM DEBASES AND DESTROYS

Communism debases the individual and makes him the enslaved tool of the state, to which he must look for sustenance and religion. Communism destroys man's God-given free agency.

No member of this Church can be true to his faith, nor can any American be loyal to his trust, while lending aid, encouragement, or sympathy to any of these false philosophies; for if he does, they will prove snares to his feet.

J. Reuben Clark, Jr.

J. Reuben Clark, Jr., was born in 1871 in Grantsville, Utah. He attended the University of Utah and Columbia Law School. As a lawyer he served in many positions within the State Department and was considered an expert on international law. He was called as a member of the First Presidency in 1933 under President Grant and continued in that capacity under both George Albert Smith and David O. McKay, until he died in 1961.

November 16, 1938

The powers of evil today strive throughout the world to set up the State as God; we have no choice but to join the battle on the side of liberty. The new State, professing love for the people, subverts freedom in the economic field, in the field of government and law, and even in the fields of family relations and religion. The Fathers of the Constitution, with divinely bestowed wisdom, established a government of limited and delegated powers. In so doing they drew upon an Anglo-Saxon tradition of common law and rejected the idea of sovereignty developed in the Roman Civil Law tradition. The maintenance of liberty depends upon a degree of virtue in the people and their representatives. Recent innovations in the taxing power and executive power portend the approach of tyranny. The Constitution is divinely inspired. Some changes are necessary to meet new circumstances, but the great fundamentals must not be changed.

Constitutional Government
Our Birthright Threatened
By J. Reuben Clark, Jr., former Under-Secretary of State of the United States.
Chairman of Executive Committee, Foreign Bondholders Protective Council,
Inc., New York, N.Y. Before the second general session of the annual
convention of the American Bankers Association at Houston, Texas.

In the economic field, this earth-wide conflict has taken the form of seizing without compensation from the man who has and giving to the man who has not, of taking without price from the worker the fruits of his work, and giving to the idler who does no work. It has from its very nature become an economic, uncompensated leveling downward, not upward, of the whole mass. This is the result in every country in which it has been tried. That this result may in one country be reached by confiscatory taxation, and in another by direct seizure, is a mere matter of method. The result is the same. In some countries outright seizure and confiscation are already openly and shamelessly practiced. All is done in the name of the State, as if it were Deity—as if the State, not God, gave all.

In the field of government, self-perpetuating governing groups are setting themselves up, either through a revolution, an overturning of the old system and the setting up of a new one, or by a perversion and prostituting of the old system into a new one. Here again the matter is merely one of method. Of what use is an election free in outward form if the government shall name the candidates?

In the new state of the world, laws and courts have lost their wonted places. Secret police, the curse of peoples, arrest, sentence, and punish as their unhampered whim, prejudice, or hate may desire. Public justice has fled the State.

Even into the field of family relationship, which, next to man's relationship to God, is the most precious and dearest of all relationships, this modern State is thrusting its polluting hand. In some lands this new State is robbing the parents of the custody of their children on the Sabbath, it is forbidding the parents to teach and admonish the children in the ways of righteous living, it is teaching the children that officers of State, not God, shall be looked to for a guide as to standards of life. The pending amendment to the Constitution of the United States is of such scope and character, that it may be easily wrenched to the same ends—a fact, which at least some of its proponents know and approve.

Into the field of religion, the holy of holies of the soul of man, this modern world State also enters, to dethrone God and exalt the State into God's place. This is the archest treason of them all. For man robbed of God becomes a brute. This sin must be felt, not told, for words cannot measure the height and breadth of this iniquity; nor can human mind encompass the punishment of those who shall commit this sin.

All over the world, this new State comes into all these fields in the disguise of a protesting love and friendship for the people, whose property it means to confiscate, whose liberties it means to steal, and whose religion it means to destroy. Thus in all the history of the world has tyranny come to the people. Tyranny has always been a hypocrite, a thief, and a seducer. It has always been a demon dethroning the true God, for it knows that unless it can touch the souls of men, it must itself die.

In their wisdom, divinely bestowed, the Fathers set up in America a government of limited and delegated powers. The government has only such powers as the people have expressly and explicitly given to it. So jealous have all branches of government been of this principle that for the century and a half of our existence it has been the settled, and heretofore undisturbed, constitutional principle that even the great clauses of the Preamble to the Constitution, which declare the very objects and purposes of our central government, have been denied the power to confer any jurisdiction upon the government. Nor has the other constitutional clause which states that Congress shall have power "to make all laws which shall be necessary and proper for carrying into execution the foregoing powers, and all other powers vested by this Constitution in the Government of the United States, or in any department or officer thereof," been interpreted as enlarging Federal jurisdiction. The powers of the Federal Government are to be found in the explicit grants made in the instrument and in them only.

Furthermore, the Ninth Amendment to the Constitution declares: "The enumeration in the Constitution of certain rights, shall not be construed to deny or disparage others retained by the people;" and the Tenth Amendment further declares:

"The powers not delegated to the United States by the Constitution, nor prohibited by it to the States, are reserved to the States respectively, or to the people."

Thus the people have told the government the things it may do; the residuum of power rests with the people.

In setting up a government on this principle the founders deliberately, and with a wisely fixed motive, kept away from government the right and power to legislate regarding, or to control the citizenry in, many matters affecting the individual liberty of the citizen. Those commonly mentioned are freedom of speech, freedom of the press, and freedom of religion, but there are many others. These things are put wholly beyond the reach of law and governmental control. The Federal Executive and the Congress may not touch them, nor may the State governmental agencies touch them, except the people of the State specifically empower them so to do.

This principle is the very genius of the Anglo-Saxon system of law as developed in this country. The people specifically grant to their governments the powers and authorities which they wish their government to have. When any power is exercised that is not granted, it is usurpation. No despotism can ever be set up when these principles operate.

The underlying theory of the Roman Civil Law, which is in force in non-Anglo-Saxon countries, is quite otherwise. There the rights and authorities of the people are granted to them by the sovereign—a Justinian or a Napoleon. The people have such rights only as they are granted. The residuum of power is in the sovereign, who may enact any measures, either against or for the people, which suits his sovereign will. Obviously, under such a system despotism may thrive.

To speak in broad generalities:

Under the Anglo-Saxon system—our constitutional system—the people look into the law to see what they may not do, for they may do everything which their government, under the specific grant of powers, has not forbidden them to do. Under the civil law, the people look into the law to see what they may do, for they may do nothing which their sovereign has not expressly or impliedly permitted them to do.

This civil law theory is so convenient to executives, impatient of the restraint of law, that it is not a matter of wonder it should be finding favor among State and national authorities. But it will lead to great usurpations of power under the Anglo-Saxon system of government.

Knowing by experience the tendency of the central power to absorb all other powers, national and local, the fathers set up a dual system of government, and left to the local unit all governing powers not necessary for the carrying on of the central government, with prime reference to its international relationships. There was to be the largest possible measure of local self-government. The fathers did not assume that any appreciable number of the electorate would ever slip so far away from the actualities as to believe that a government thousands of miles away would know better what the locality needed than the locality itself. This was the very issue of the Revolution. The fathers did not assume that any part of the electorate would ever believe that John Doe, a mediocre or worse man in his own community, would, when transferred to a government job in Washington, be thereby endowed with supernatural wisdom, enabling him to tell the home folks how best to do things he himself had never been able to do at all when he lived amongst them. This was a fallacy they thought no foolishness could reach. The fathers did not assume that any great part of the electorate would ever fail to understand that while their franchise gave power, it could not and did not bestow wisdom.

The experience of the ages tells only one story: that Liberty lives only where there is local self-government; and that she lives best and fullest where there is the largest measure of such governments.

Our constitutional fathers, experienced in the deceit and practices of tyranny, knew the ways of this approach. Knowing that tyranny must have gold to further its purposes, they placed the power to raise money in the hands of the direct representatives of the people, and provided that "All bills for raising revenues shall originate in the House of Representatives." Lodging this power in the House, they assumed that the people would never send as their representatives mere puppets of the Executive branch of the government—puppets who would levy taxes and lay burdens as the Executive might wish; nor did they assume that some of the electorate would ever fall so low in civic integrity that such puppetry could be successfully proclaimed as a virtue entitling its possessor to the franchise of the people.

Aware that a combination of legislative, executive and judicial power in one person or body was destructive of all freedom and justice, they established a government in which these three branches were distinct and wholly independent the one from the other. The fathers provided this so that no one scheming and ambitious branch of the government could absorb the others, either with or against their will. They did not contemplate that by subterfuge, cajolery, and gratuities any large part of the electorate could be brought to believe that a combination of all of these branches into one, or a domination of one over all, would be a blessing.

Conscious that long terms of office serve to entrench and solidify individuals and parties into a power that tends towards tyranny; realizing that the changing views and interests of the people required a frequent opportunity for expression through their chosen representatives, the fathers provided short terms of office for all national legislative and executive officers. The Father of His Country gave body and substance to this principle by refusing to prolong indefinitely his own tenure in public office.

The fathers did not assume that any considerable part of the electorate could ever sink to the level where their continued support could be actually purchased by the flagrant use of gratuities made available by the people's own representatives contrary to the spirit and genius of our free institutions.

Knowing that the liberties of the people, the safety of their property, and the protection of their lives, depended upon the making of laws which conformed to the Constitution and upon the due and just administration of such laws, the fathers set up a judiciary that was not only independent of the other branches of Government, and free from political domination, but beyond their reach by any direct and legal interference. They did not assume that the time would ever come when either of the other branches of government would attempt by subterfuge and indirection to do what they could not do directly and so attempt to dictate the course and character of justice in the interest of any political theory or tenet. The fathers assumed an integrity and honesty in the public servants of the nation, which would guarantee the people against indirect subversion of their institutions.

The fathers were schooled in attempts to control what they wrote and spoke in criticism of government; they knew how tyranny and oppression smart, and even slough away under publicity; they understood how "little" men in office resent disapproving comment on their acts and how they try to punish those who make the comment. So they provided that Congress should make no law "abridging the freedom of speech or of the press." But the fathers never caught the picture of a regulatory power over means of communication and publicity that could forestall all but favorable expressions regarding government. The fathers felt that when they protected freedom of speech and of the press against governmental interference they had effectively guaranteed the citizens' freedom to talk and write as they felt and thought about their own government.

The fathers based our whole system upon the equality of all men before the law. They had evolved from their experience the principle expressed in the dictum of the Declaration: "We hold these truths to be self-evident; that all men are created equal; that they are endowed by their Creator with certain inalienable rights; that among these are life, liberty, and the pursuit of happiness." The Constitution itself contains no word (save as it refers to slaves) that provides or suggests or even intimates that all laws are not to be uniformly and impartially administered.

The courts have from the beginning declared class legislation to be unconstitutional. The great immunities of the Bill of Rights ran in favor of every citizen; none were denied the blessings of liberty. The Fourteenth Amendment specifically provided that no State shall "deny to any person within its jurisdiction the equal protection of the laws," and the patriot will say that the same inhibition does not in spirit run in favor of the citizen against the United States. The fathers were careful to provide that the Chief Executive should solemnly covenant that he would "faithfully execute the office of President of the United States and would to the best of his ability preserve, protect, and defend the Constitution of the United States." The Constitution expressly prescribes that the Chief Executive "shall take care that the laws be faithfully executed." This fundamental principle of equal justice and equity is basic to any system of free government among men.

Conscious of the inherent power for oppression and abuse of the taxing power—the evils of the taxing power lay at the base of the causes of the Revolution—aware of the principle afterwards announced by the great Chief Justice that "the power to tax is the power to destroy," the fathers carefully guarded the taxing power of the Federal government and expressly denied the right of the Federal government to levy direct taxes against the individual. They saw clearly that the power to tax the individual gave the power to control him, so they left this power in the states to be handled under local self-government, where the restraints of neighborhood and acquaintanceship might be operative. Later statesmen, through the Fourteenth Amendment, protected the citizens against their own state governments in the matter of "equal protection of the laws."

Then came the time, a quarter of a century ago, when the urgency for more revenue for government expenditure, disguised by the plea of better equalizing the tax burden, led to the amendment authorizing the income tax. This tax was at first light, but it grew by leaps and bounds. Always and ever, the more you feed a government, any government, the hungrier it gets, and the more it eats. Citizens who had worked through many frugal years of hardship and sacrifice, to a competence, saw in their ripening years the government come in and take a generous part of the fruits of their life-long labor, to carry on highfalutin' plans and schemes, and to build projects in which the government had no business to engage. This led men to try to evade this government wastage of the money they had so laboriously earned, and the government itself encouraged the effort by admitting that men were justified in finding ways of taking themselves outside the purview of the law. This is a way and spirit destructive of all integrity in the citizenry.

Under an executive ordinance power recognized by the courts, but outside I feel sure of the purview of the fathers, rules and regulations have been laid down, covering the payment of income taxes, that have varied as the need for more revenue has mounted. Sometimes these regulations have been made retroactive and citizens, who paid an honest tax at the time it was due, have been forced to pay further tax years afterward, under the impact of a threat of vicious penalties if they failed.

Inheritance taxes have also come into the field.

All this has created a situation in our tax life that would enable any administration so minded to lay a heavy and unequal hand on the citizenry of the country. An administration so minded could investigate or refrain from investigating, it could make further levy or let the old levy stand, as suited its will and convenience, and in making a further levy with penalties, it could bring ruin. An administration so minded could thus bring to the citizenry a reign of terror, it could silence criticism, and it could crush all opposition. So comes tyranny in its blackest form.

Nor would the end be yet. For the governmental maw, not satiated with eating the mere incomes of the citizenry, would demand more of their goods and the next move would be a capital levy in some form. Make no mistake about this. Such has been the consistent way of all governments embarking on this course. The move to take the capital the citizens have saved will be disguised as a means of alleviating the needs of the poor, of equalizing the burdens of government, of sharing the wealth. When that comes, the conquest of the citizens will be complete; tyranny will be enthroned and rule till liberty is again brought back across many bloody fields of battle. Thus will history again repeat itself.

Our fathers knew all these approaches of tyranny. They could hear its muffled tread afar off. They left us signs and warnings to quicken our ears; they set up for us bulwarks across his path. So well did they do their work that for scores of years tyranny did not leave its lair. Human freedom, happiness, and prosperity filled the land and joy abode in the hearts of the people. We forgot that tyranny lived. Then it left its den in the night, and began stalking our liberties even as a wild beast creeps silently, through the darkness upon its victim.

The Constitution is our sole shield against this crouching beast; it is our sole weapon of defense against tyranny's freedom-destroying spring.

You men of money, you captains of industry, you employers of every kind, you keepers of the people's savings, you leaders in whatever walk of life, do not cling in the rear like slackers, justifying your act and place by the convenient and comforting assertion that by so doing you are best serving those who look to you for protection. This is false; to some it will look all too much like cowardice. No war was ever won by cravens who skulked in the rear.

I love the Constitution of the United States, and the free institutions it creates; I love the freedom and liberties it bestows upon me. I cherish the guarantees that it has given to me and that my children shall possess after me, if I shall not throw these guarantees away. From the time I stood at my mother's knee, I have been taught to reverence the Constitution as God-given. I firmly believe it is. It is the doctrine of my Church that the Lord himself has declared: "I establish the Constitution of this land by the hands of wise men whom I raised up unto this very purpose." It is also the doctrine of my Church that the Lord further declared that officers of government should exercise their authority "according to the laws and Constitution of the people, which I have suffered to be established and (which) should be maintained for the rights and protection of all flesh, according to just and holy principles." Thus the Constitution of the United States is to me and to my people as much a part of our religion as is the Decalogue given amidst the thunders of Mount Sinai or the Beatitudes spoken by the Master on the peaceful slope of the Palestinian hillside.

It is not my belief nor is it the doctrine of my Church that the Constitution is a fully-grown document. On the contrary, we believe it must grow and develop to meet the changing needs of an advancing world. We know that greed, avarice, and lust for power and dominions over men are always with us, and will be until the millennium shall come. We know that these curses of men never sleep nor die, that they alter their ways of vice to evade the control of law and order. We know that sometimes they reach such size and influence that their handling may require changes not only in legislation but on rare occasion, in the Constitution itself. But all such changes must be made to protect and preserve our liberties, not to take them from us. Greater freedom, not slavery, must follow every constitutional change.

So we do hold that in all that relates to its great fundamentals—in the division of powers and their full independence one from the other, in the equal administration of the laws, in the even-handed dispensing of justice, in the absence of all class and casts, in the freedom of the press and of speech and of religion—we believe that in all such matters as these our Constitution must not be changed. For more than a hundred years it has been our expressed and recorded belief that " . . . Governments were instituted of God for the benefit of man; that he holds men accountable for their acts in relation to them, both in making laws and administering them, for the good and safety of society."

We have declared that, "we believe that no government can exist in peace, except such laws are framed and held inviolate as will secure to each individual the free exercise of conscience, the right and control of property, and the protection of life."

As I have from infancy been taught these principles, so I have been taught that this is "a land choice above all other lands," that God has declared it shall be in his especial care so that out of it these great principles of constitutional government with its free institutions and liberties, shall flow over the earth to the blessing of the peoples of the nations, God's children all, and that nothing but the iniquity of this nation itself shall rob it of this divine destiny.

And so the same fervor and devotion that I give to the other of God's declared purposes, I give to this exalted mission and destiny of my country.

Gentlemen, do you not catch a vision of this glory of America, not the glory of a conquest bought with our blood, of a conquest over a torn, maimed, and hating foe, of a conquest that however it may seem, yet nevertheless always leaves the world poorer and more wretched, with more of woe and misery and sin and despair and hate and damnation than before it came—not these conquests.

But the conquest of peace and joy, the conquest of bringing more to eat and more to wear, of bringing more comfort, more education, more culture, the conquest of liberty over tyranny that all men may know and have the free institutions which are ours, the conquest of caste and legalized privilege and of all social inequalities, the conquest of want and misery, of hunger, and nakedness, a conquest of war itself so that peace and "righteousness shall cover the earth as the waters cover the mighty deep," a conquest that shall bring a true millennium. And this is not an idle dream of the conquest of righteousness, for it lies within our reach if we shall not forfeit it by our own iniquity.

God grant we shall not sell this glory, our national birthright, for a mess of pottage! God grant we shall not by our own sin rob ourselves of this divine destiny and the world of its divine heritage.

April 6, 1957

The Constitution is no more outmoded than the Ten Commandments, contrary to the claims of a new despotism. Without benefit of any prior blueprint, but prepared under God's guidance through study and experience, the remarkable body of men who framed the Constitution established certain fundamental principles: Three independent branches, no encroachment of one branch upon another, and no delegation of powers from one to another. Such a structure excluded kingship and provided for a national executive without war powers, who would carry out the laws passed by Congress. Under these principles the people remain sovereign, unlike the Civil Law tradition that governs Continental Europe. This Constitution is part of my religion; it is our duty to uphold it.

Our Constitution—Divinely Inspired
Address at the General Conference of
the Church of Jesus Christ of Latter-day Saints,
The Tabernacle, Salt Lake City

My brothers and sisters, contrary to my usual custom and practice, I intend to read what I have to say today. I assure you I have tried to prepare it under the influence of our Heavenly Father, and I humbly pray that it will carry the message which I have hoped for.

I plan to say something today about the Constitution of the United States of America—its Framers and some of its essential principles—America, the land choice above all other lands—for our great and priceless liberties, including the security of our homes and property, our freedom of speech and of the press, freedom of religion and the free exercise thereof, indeed freedom itself and its liberties, as our fathers knew and enjoyed, as also ourselves, depend upon its preservation. As there is much detail and as I wish to be as accurate as I may be, I have written out what I wish to say.

It seems wise to remind ourselves of these matters because some people belittle that great document and its fundamental principles, sometimes to the point of derision. Sometimes we forget the Constitution.

CONSTITUTION "OUTMODED"

These defamers say that the Constitution, and our government under it, are outmoded; not responsive to present-day conditions of life and living; not sufficient to meet and solve present-day problems; and that we need a modern, up-to-date system of government. They let us know what should be done to meet their ideas and plans, which seem always to run to despotism.

I have observed that numbers of these defamers take advantage to the utmost of every liberty and freedom created and protected by the Constitution in order to destroy it and its guarantees, so to make easy the setting up of a tyranny that would deprive the common man of his freedom and liberties under it, so permitting these defamers to set up a government that would give place, power, and privilege to them in a despotism to be imposed upon the mass of mankind. We have witnessed this very despotism. There would be a Kremlin in every country on the globe, all under the super-Kremlin in Moscow.

TEN COMMANDMENTS "OUTMODED"

One class of these defamers are the same persons who declare the Ten Commandments, the basic law of the civilized world, to be outmoded....

NO POLITICAL "BLUEPRINT" AVAILABLE

The amazing thing is that there was not in all the world's history a government organization even among confederacies, that could be taken by the Framers as a preliminary blueprint for building the political structure they were to build. Franklin declared:

"We have gone back to ancient history for models of Government, and examined the different forms of those Republics which having been formed with the seeds of their own dissolution now no longer exist. And we have viewed Modern States all round Europe, but find none of their Constitutions suitable to our circumstances."

They had been in session for about a month (June 26, 1787) when Madison declared:

". . . as it was more than probable we were now digesting a plan which in its operation wd. decide forever the fate of Republican Govt. we ought not only to provide every guard to liberty that its preservation cd. require, but be equally careful to supply the defects which our own experience had particularly pointed out."

WHO THE FRAMERS WERE

A little further detail about the thirty-nine Framers who actually signed the document will be useful.

Of those thirty-nine signers, twenty-six had seen service in the Continental Congress. They knew legislative processes and problems. Thirteen had served both in the Continental Congress and in the Army. What a wealth of experience they had obtained in both legislative and executive duties! Of the nineteen who served in the Army, seventeen had served as officers—they knew the problems of armed forces in the field; and of these seventeen, four had served on Washington's staff. . . .

What a group of men of surpassing abilities, attainments, experience, and achievements! *There has not been another such group of men in all the one hundred seventy years of our history, no group that even challenged the supremacy of this group.* Gladstone solemnly declared:

"The American Constitution is the most wornderful work ever struck off at a given time by the brain and purpose of man."

PREPARATION OF FRAMERS

No more clearly does it appear that Moses was so trained in the royal Egyptian courts that he could lead ancient Israel out of bondage, or that Brother Brigham was so trained, in directing the exodus of the Saints from Missouri to Nauvoo, that he could lead modern Israel from the mobbings and persecutions of the East to the freedom of the mountain fastnesses of the West; neither one was more clearly trained for his work than these Framers were trained for theirs—rich in intellectual endowment and ripened in experience. They were equally as the others in God's hands; he guided them in their epoch-making deliberations in Independence Hall.

The Framers were deeply read in the facts of history; they were learned in the forms and practices and systems of the governments of the world, past and present; they were, in matters political, equally at home in Rome, in Athens, in Paris, and in London; they had a long, varied, and intense experience in the work of governing their various Colonies: they were among the leaders of a weak and poor people that had successfully fought a revolution against one of the great Powers of the earth; there were among them some of the ablest, most experienced and seasoned military leaders of the world.

As to all matters under consideration by the Convention, the history of the world was combed for applicable experiences and precedents.

The whole training and experiences of the colonists had been in the Common Law, with its freedoms and liberties even under their kings. They knew the functions of legislative, executive, and judicial arms of government.

SOME CONSTITUTIONAL PRINCIPLES

Time is not available now to consider in detail the work of the Convention nor the Constitution that was framed. A very few principles only, and they among the basic ones, may be mentioned. You all know them; they are now merely recalled to your minds. Sometimes we miss the import of them.

THREE INDEPENDENT BRANCHES

First—the Constitution provided for three departments of government—the legislative, the executive, and the judicial.

These departments are mutually independent the one from the other.

Each department was endowed with all the powers and authority that the people through the Constitution conferred upon that branch of government—the legislative, the executive, and the judicial, respectively.

NO ENCROACHMENT BY ONE BRANCH UPON ANOTHER

No branch of the government might encroach upon the powers conferred upon another branch of government. In order to forestall foreseeable encroachments, the Convention provided in the Constitution itself for a very few invasions by one or the other, into one of the other departments, to make sure that one department should not absorb the functions of the other or encroach thereon, or gain an overbalancing power and authority against the other. These have been termed "checks and balances."

NON-DELEGATION OF POWERS

A third principle that was inherent in all the provisions of the Constitution was that none of the departments could delegate its powers to the others. The courts of the country have from the first insisted upon the operation of this principle. There have been some fancy near-approaches to such an attempted delegation, particularly in recent years, and some unique justifying reasoning therefor, but the courts have consistently insisted upon the basic principle, which is still operative.

An examination of the records of the Convention will show how anxiously earnest the Framers were to set up these and other principles of free government.

NO KINGS IN AMERICA

The Convention seems to have experienced no really serious difficulty in setting up a judiciary department, nor, in certain aspects, the legislative department with its powers, until it came to those powers which dealt with matters that in some governments had been regarded as belonging to the executive. You will recollect that practically all of these Framers had suffered under George III and his Minister, Lord North. So they abandoned the British model, for, as Randolph said, ". . . the fixt genius of the people of America required a different form of Government." This ruled out royalty.

It might be noted that Washington, as the Revolution closed, had definitively scotched at Newburgh, the kingship idea.

KINGS AND AMERICA

Of course, the Framers did not know (no living mortal then knew) that centuries before a prophet of the Lord had declared as to America:

"Behold, this is a choice land, and whatsoever nation shall possess it shall be free from bondage, and from captivity, and from all other nations under heaven, if they will but serve the God of the land, who is Jesus Christ, who hath been manifested by the things which we have written." (Ether 2:12.)

Nor did the Framers know (again, no living mortal then knew) that centuries after this prophecy, but still centuries before the Framers met, another prophet had declared:

"And this land shall be a land of liberty unto the Gentiles, and there shall be no kings upon the land, who shall raise up unto the Gentiles." (2 Nephi 10:11.)

The unhappy, short-lived experiences of the Dom Pedros in Brazil and of Maximilian in Mexico seem the exceptions that prove the rule. The Spirit of the Lord was leading.

THE NATIONAL EXECUTIVE

In providing for the executive department, there was considerable discussion as to whether the executive department should be one person or several. Commenting upon a proposal for three, Randolph said their unity would be "as the foetus of monarchy."

Who should choose, elect, or appoint (the terms were used almost interchangeably) the Chief Executive was exhaustively debated; so was the problem of the length of his term, from one year, to Hamilton's during "good behaviour," including the question whether he should be ineligible for re-election, and whether he should be subject to impeachment.

POWER TO DECLARE WAR

But one of their most searching examinations related to the war powers of government, including the power to declare war. It became clear very early in the debates that as Chief Executive, the President should execute the laws passed by Congress. But he was also made Commander in Chief of the Army and Navy of the United States and of the State Militia when called into the service of the United States. The delegates were fearfully anxious over this function of government. There was one suggestion that the Commander in Chief should not personally go into the field with the troops, so fearful were they of his power.

WHERE WAR POWERS REST

But in whom should rest the so-called war powers? This was the urgent problem. It soon became clear that the Convention was unalterably opposed to endowing the President with these war powers; it was conceded he should have the power to repel invasions, but not to commence war, which meant he could not declare war.

CHIEF EXECUTIVES CONCEIVED
AS PLAIN HUMAN BEINGS

Some of the arguments made in this connection, involving the possibility of a military usurper, remind one of the potential calamities pictured by Lincoln in his prophetic Lyceum Address, where he sketched what an ambitious, fame-and-power-seeking executive might do.

Various other potential actions by the executive were explored. Future Presidents of the Republic were conceived as including men capable of doing the things that ambitious men in power had done over the ages. Men were still human, had the same urges and ambitions. The earnest effort was to make as nearly impossible as could be, the malfeasances of the past by men in high executive office in the future; and seemingly perhaps beyond everything else as a practical matter, *to prevent the President from taking us into war of his own volition.* The Framers therefore provided that the war powers, including the declaration of war, should rest exclusively in the Congress, both by express provisions, and, as the record shows, by the conscious intent of the Framers.

THE NET POSITION OF THE NATIONAL EXECUTIVE

The net result may be stated thus: as Chief Executive, the President was to enforce the laws passed by Congress, including those passed by Congress in the exercise of the war powers that were explicitly and exclusively possessed by Congress; as Commander in Chief of the Army and Navy of the United States and of the Militia of the States when called into the actual service of the United States, he was to direct the military operations thereof in the field, with the powers incident thereto.

These principles should never be forgotten by any free, liberty-loving American, the kind of American the Constitution and the Bill of Rights make of us, and in which they were designed to protect us.

THE PEOPLE ARE SOVEREIGN

Furthermore, under our form of government, we the people of the United States, as the Preamble to the Constitution declares, formed this government. We alone are sovereign. We are wholly free to exercise our sovereign will in the way we prescribe. The sovereignty is not personal, as under the Civil Law. The Constitution expressly provides the only way in which we may change our Constitution.

We may well repeat again: We the people have all the powers we have not delegated away to our government, and the institutions of government have such powers and those only as we have given to them. The total residuum of powers, including all rights and liberties not given up by us to Federal or State Governments, is still in us, to remain so till we constitutionally provide otherwise. Under the Civil Law that basically governs Continental Europe, the people have only such rights as a personal sovereign or his equivalent bestows, the residuum remaining in him or them. Wherever and whenever powers are exercised by any person or branch of our government that are not granted by the Constitution, such powers are to that extent usurpations.

THE CONSTITUTION AND OURSELVES

Will not each of you ask yourself this question: What would probably have happened if Joseph Smith had been born and had attempted to carry on his work of the Restoration of the Gospel and the Holy Priesthood, if he had been born and had sought to go forward in any other country in the world?

Must we go far to seek why God set up this people and their government, the only government on the face of the earth, since the Master was here, that God has formally declared was set up at the hands of men whom he raised up for that very purpose, and the fundamental principles of which he has expressly approved?

CONSTITUTION IS PART OF MY RELIGION

Having in mind what the Lord has said about the Constitution and its Framers, that the Constitution should be "established, and should be maintained for the rights and protection of all flesh," that it was for the protection of the moral agency, free agency, God gave us, that its "principle of freedom in maintaining rights and privileges, belongs to all mankind," all of which point to the destiny of the free government our Constitution provides, unless thrown away by the nations—having in mind all this, with its implications, speaking for myself, I declare that the divine sanction thus repeatedly given by the Lord himself to the Constitution of the United States as it came from the hands of the Framers with its coterminous Bill of Rights, makes of the principles of that document an integral part of my religious faith. It is a revelation from the Lord. I believe and reverence its God-inspired provisions. My faith, my knowledge, my testimony of the Restored Gospel, based on the divine principle of continuous revelation, compel me so to believe. Thus has the Lord approved of our political system, an approval, so far as I know, such as he has given to no other political system of any other people in the world since the time of Jesus.

The Constitution, as approved by the Lord, is still the same great vanguard of liberty and freedom in human government that it was the day it was written. No other human system of government, affording equal protection for human life, liberty, and the pursuit of happiness, has yet been devised or vouchsafed to man. Its great principles are as applicable, efficient, and sufficient to bring today the greatest good to the greatest number, as they were the day the Constitution was signed. Our Constitution and our Government under it, were designed by God as an instrumentality for righteousness through peace, not war.

OUR CONSTITUTIONAL DESTINY

Speaking of the destiny that the Lord has offered to mankind in his declarations regarding the scope and efficacy of the Constitution and its principles, we may note that already the Lord has moved upon many nations of the earth so to go forward. The Latin American countries have followed our lead and adopted our constitutional form of government, adapted to their legal concepts, without compulsion or restraint from us. Likewise, the people of Canada in the British North America Act have embodied great principles that are basic to our Constitution. The people of Australia have likewise followed along our governmental footpath. In Canada and in Australia, the great constitutional decisions of John Marshall and his associates are quoted in their courts and followed in their adjudications. I repeat, none of this has come because of force of arms. The Constitution will never reach its destiny through force. God's principles are taken by men because they are eternal and true, and touch the divine spirit in men. This is the only true way to permanent world peace, the aspiration of men since the beginning. God never planted his Spirit, his truth, in the hearts of men from the point of a bayonet.

The Framers had their dark days in their work. There were discouragements, there were hours of near hopelessness for some. Yet, as they were engaged in God's work, and he was at the helm, we know it was as certain as the day dawns, that Satan would be there also, with his thwarting designs.

But I see in their diverse views, their different concepts, even the promotion of their different local interests, not the confusion which challenged Franklin, but a searching, almost meticulous study and examination of the fundamental principles involved, and the final adoption of the wisest and best of it all—I see the winnowing of the wheat, the blowing away of the chaff.

MY WITNESS

Out of more years, but of far, far less wisdom and experience, I echo Franklin's testimony "that God governs in the affairs of men," and that without his concurring aid we shall build in vain, and "our projects will be confounded, and we ourselves shall become a reproach and bye word down to future ages."

I bear my testimony that without God's aid, we shall not preserve our political heritage neither to our own blessing, nor to the blessing of our posterity, nor to the blessing of the downtrodden peoples of the world.

In broad outline, the Lord has declared through our Constitution his form for human government. Our own prophets have declared in our day the responsibility of the Elders of Zion in the preservation of the Constitution. We cannot, guiltless, escape that responsibility. We cannot be laggards, nor can we be deserters.

Ezra Taft Benson

Ezra Taft Benson was called to be an apostle in 1943 and became the 13th President of the Church in 1985. He was born on August 4, 1899, in Whitney, Idaho. After a mission in Great Britain from 1921–1923 he attended Brigham Young University in 1926 and studied agriculture, eventually receiving his Master's degree from Iowa State College in 1927. As an apostle, President Benson was active in public affairs. He was the European Mission President after the Second World War, helping to lead humanitarian efforts on the continent. From 1952–1960 Elder Benson served as the Secretary of Agriculture in the Eisenhower administration. He was unequivocal in his support for Constitutional principles whether it was as a public servant or as a representative of the Church around the world.

October, 1961

The Inspired Constitution was part of a Divine plan to raise up the first free people in modern times. It was also prophesied that this freedom would be threatened by wickedness and secret combinations. We now face such a threat in the form of socialistic-communism, whose program is essentially a war against God and the plan of salvation. We must shake off complacency and join the battle against this world-wide conspiracy by becoming informed, by using our influence in the political party of our choice, and by strengthening our homes.

The American Heritage of Freedom—A Plan of God
Conference Address
General Conference, Salt Lake City

My theme is directed particularly to the men of America and more especially to those in the Church of Jesus Christ of Latter-day Saints, who hold the Holy Priesthood of God.

Every member of the priesthood should understand the divine plan designed by the Lord to raise up the first free people in modern times. Here is how scripture says it was achieved:

First: Prophecy is abundant that God deliberately kept the American continent hidden until after the Holy Roman Empire had been broken up and the various nations had established themselves as independent kingdoms, Keeping America hidden until this time was no accident. (Book of Mormon, 2 Nephi 1:6, 8.)

Second: At the proper time, God inspired Columbus to overcome almost insurmountable odds to discover America and bring this rich new land to the attention of the gentiles in Europe. (Book of Mormon, 1 Nephi, 13:12; Dr. Samuel Eliot Morison, *Admiral of the Ocean Sea*, pp. 46–47.)

Third: God revealed to his ancient American prophets that shortly after the discovery of America there would be peoples in Europe who would desire to escape the persecution and tyranny of the Old World and flee to America. (Book of Mormon, I Nephi 13:13–16.)

Fourth: God told his prophets that the kingdoms in Europe would try to exercise dominion over the people who had fled to America, but that in the wars for independence the American settlers would win. (This is a remarkable prophecy in that 2,300 years before the Revolutionary War was fought, God through his prophets predicted who would win it.) (*Ibid.*, 16–19.)

Fifth: The prophets were told that in the latter days when the gentiles came to America they would establish it as a land of liberty on which there would be no kings. The Lord declared that he would protect the land and whosoever would try to establish kings either from within or without should perish. (Book of Mormon, 2 Nephi, 10:8–14.)

Sixth: Having declared America to be a land of liberty, God undertook to raise up a band of inspired and intelligent leaders who could write a constitution of liberty and establish the first free people in modern times. The hand of God in this undertaking is clearly indicated by the Lord, himself, in a revelation to the Prophet Joseph Smith in these words:

". . . I established the Constitution of this land, by the hands of wise men whom I raised up unto this very purpose, . . ." (Doctrine & Covenants 101:80.)

Seventh: God declared that the United States Constitution was divinely inspired for the specific purpose of eliminating bondage and the violation of the rights and protection which belong to "all flesh." (*Ibid.*, 77–80.)

Eighth: God placed a mandate upon his people to befriend and defend the constitutional laws of the land and see that the rights and privileges of all mankind are protected. He verified the declaration of the founding fathers that God created all men free. He also warned against those who would enact laws encroaching upon the sacred rights and privileges of free men. He urged the election of honest and wise leaders and said that evil men and laws were of Satan. (*Ibid.*, 98:5–10.)

Ninth: God predicted through his prophets that this great Gentile nation, raised upon the American continent in the last days, would become the richest and most powerful on the face of the earth; even above all other nations." (Book of Mormon, 1 Nephi, 18:15, 30; Ether 2:12.)

Tenth: Concerning the United States, the Lord revealed to his prophets that its greatest threat would be a vast, world-wide "secret combination" which would not only threaten the United States but seek to "overthrow the freedom of all lands, nations, and countries." (Book of Mormon, Ether 8:25.)

Eleventh: In connection with the attack on the United States, the Lord told the Prophet Joseph Smith there would be an attempt to overthrow the country by destroying the Constitution. Joseph Smith predicted that the time would come when the Constitution would hang as it were by a thread, and at that time, "this people will step forth and save it from the threatened destruction." (*Journal History*, July 4, 1854.)

It is my conviction that the elders of Israel, widely spread over the nation, will, at the crucial time, successfully rally the righteous of our country and provide the necessary balance of strength to save the institutions of constitutional government.

Twelfth: The Lord revealed to the Prophet Nephi that he established the Gentiles on this land to be a free people forever, that if they were a righteous nation and overcame the wickedness and secret abominations which would arise in their midst, they could inherit the land forever. (Book of Mormon, 14:1–2.)

Thirteenth: But on the other hand, if the Gentiles on this land reject the word of God and conspire to overthrow the liberty and the Constitution, then their doom is fixed, and they "shall be cut off from among my people who are of the covenant." (Book of Mormon, 3 Nephi, 21:11, 14, 21; 1 Nephi, 14:6; D&C 84:114, 115, 117.)

Fourteenth: The great destructive force which was to be turned loose on the earth and which the prophets for centuries have been calling the "abomination of desolation" is vividly described by those who saw it in vision. Ours is the first generation to realize how literally these prophecies can be fulfilled now that God, through science, has unlocked the secret to thermonuclear reaction.

In the light of these prophecies there should be no doubt in the mind of any priesthood holder that the human family is headed for trouble. There are rugged days ahead. It is time for every man who wishes to do his duty to get himself prepared—physically, spiritually, and psychologically—for the task which may come at any time, as suddenly as the whirlwind.

Where do we stand today? All over the world the light of freedom is being diminished. Across whole continents of the earth freedom is being totally obliterated.

Never in recorded history has any movement spread its power so far and so fast as has socialistic-communism in the last three decades. The facts are not pleasant to review. Communist leaders are jubilant with their success. They are driving freedom back on almost every front.

It is time, therefore, that every American, and especially every member of the priesthood became informed about the aims, tactics, and schemes of socialistic-communism. This becomes particularly important when it is realized that communism is turning out to be the earthly image of the plan which Satan presented in the pre-existence. The whole program of socialistic-communism is essentially a war against God and the plan of salvation—the very plan which we fought to uphold during "the war in heaven."

Up to now some members of the Church have stood aloof, feeling that the fight against socialistic-communism is "controversial" and unrelated to the mission of the Church or the work of the Lord. But the President of the Church in our day has made it clear that the fight against atheistic communism is a major challenge to the Church and every member of it. . . .

The fight against godless communism is a very real part of every man's duty who holds the priesthood. It is the fight against slavery, immorality, atheism, terrorism, cruelty, barbarism, deceit, and the destruction of human life through a kind of tyranny unsurpassed by anything in human history. Here is a struggle against the evil, satanical priestcraft of Lucifer. Truly it can be called, "a continuation of the war in heaven."

In the war in heaven the devil advocated absolute eternal security at the sacrifice of our freedom. Although there is nothing more desirable to a Latter-day Saint than eternal security in God's presence, and although God knew, as did we, that some of us would not achieve this security if we were allowed our freedom—yet the very God of heaven, who has more mercy than us all, still decreed no guaranteed security except by a man's own freedom of choice and individual initiative.

Today the devil as a wolf in a supposedly new suit of sheep's clothing is enticing some men, both in and out of the Church, to parrot his line by advocating planned government guaranteed security programs at the expense of our liberties. Latter-day Saints should be reminded how and why they voted as they did in heaven. If some have decided to change their vote they should repent—throw their support on the side of freedom—and cease promoting this subversion.

When all of the trappings of propaganda and pretense have been pulled aside, the exposed hard-core structure of modern communism is amazingly similar to the ancient Book of Mormon record of secret societies such as the Gadiantons. In the ancient American civilization there was no word which struck greater terror in the hearts of the people than the name of the Gadiantons. It was a secret political party which operated as a murder cult. Its object was to infiltrate legitimate government, plant its officers in high places, and then seize power and live off the spoils appropriated from the people. (It would start out as a small group of "dissenters" and by using secret oaths with the threat of death for defectors it would gradually gain a choke hold on the political and economic life of whole civilizations.) . . .

What is the official position of the Church on communism? In 1936 the First Presidency made an official declaration on communism which has never been abrogated. I quote the concluding paragraph:

"We call upon all Church members completely to eschew communism. The safety of our divinely inspired constitutional government and the welfare of our Church imperatively demand that communism shall have no place in America."

We must ever keep in mind that collectivized socialism is part of the communist strategy. Communism is fundamentally socialism.

Communism and socialism, closely related, must be defeated on principle.

It is significant that 118 years ago the Prophet Joseph Smith, after attending lectures on socialism, made this official entry in Church history: "I said I did not believe the doctrine." (*History of the Church*, Vol. 6, p. 33.)

No true Latter-day Saint and no true American can be a socialist or a communist or support programs leading in that direction. These evil philosophies are incompatible with Mormonism, the true gospel of Jesus Christ.

What can priesthood holders do? There are many things we can do to meet the challenge of the adversary in our day.

We should know why paternalism, collectivism, or unnecessary federal supervision will hold our standard of living down and reduce productivity just as it has in every country where it has been tried. We should also know why the communist leaders consider socialism the highroad to communism.

Second, we should accept the command of the Lord and treat socialistic-communism as the tool of Satan. We should follow the counsel of the President of the Church and resist the influence and policies of the socialistic-communist conspiracy wherever they are found—in the schools, in the churches, in government, in unions, in businesses, in agriculture.

Third, we should help those who have been deceived or who are misinformed to find the truth. Unless each person who knows the truth will "stand up and speak up" it is difficult for the deceived or confused citizen to find his way back.

Fourth, we should not make the mistake of calling people "communists" just because they happen to be helping the communist cause. Thousands of patriotic Americans, including a few Latter-day Saints, have helped the communists without realizing it. Others have knowingly helped without joining the party. The remedy is to avoid name-calling, but point out clearly and persuasively how they are helping the communists.

Fifth,, each priesthood holder should use his influence in the community to resist the erosion which is taking place in our political and economic life. He should use the political party of his choice to express his evaluation of important issues. He should see that his party is working to preserve freedom, not destroy it. He should join responsible local groups interested in promoting freedom and free competitive enterprise, in studying political issues, appraising the voting records and proposed programs, and writing to members of Congress, promoting good men in public office and scrutinizing local, state, and federal agencies to see that the will of the people is being carried out. He should not wait for the Lord's servants to give instruction for every detail once they have announced the direction in which the priesthood should go. Each member should exercise prayerful judgment and then act.

Sixth, and most important of all, each member of the priesthood should set his own house in order. . . .

The Constitution—A Heavenly Banner
September 16, 1986

The Constitution was inspired by God. Its basic principles include agency, the limitation of government to the securing of the rights and freedoms of individual citizens, the recognition of God as the author of rights, and the superiority of people to governments. This Constitution, framed by wise men raised up by God, consists of seven articles, including the following major provisions: sovereignty of the people, separation of powers, limited powers of government, representation, and the necessity of a moral and righteous people. Unfortunately, for the past two centuries our constitutional freedoms have been chipped away at; now we must study the constitution and uphold it.

On the seventeenth day of September 1987, we commemorate the two-hundredth birthday of the Constitutional Convention, which gave birth to the document that Gladstone said is "the most wonderful work ever struck off at a given time by the brain and purpose of man" (*William Ewart Gladstone: Life and Public Services,* ed. Thomas W. Handford [Chicago: The Dominion Co., 1899], p. 323).

I heartily endorse this assessment, and today I would like to pay honor—honor to the document itself, honor to the men who framed it, and honor to the God who inspired it and made possible its coming forth.

SOME BASIC PRINCIPLES

To understand the significance of the Constitution, we must first understand some basic, eternal principles. These principles have their beginning in the premortal councils of heaven.

THE PRINCIPLE OF AGENCY

The first basic principle is agency. The central issue in the premortal council was: Shall the children of God have untrammeled agency to choose the course they should follow, whether good or evil, or shall they be coerced and forced to be obedient? Christ and all who followed him stood for the former proposition—freedom of choice; Satan stood for the latter—coercion and force. The war that began in heaven over this issue is not yet over. The conflict continues on the battlefield of mortality. And one of Lucifer's primary strategies has been to restrict our agency through the power of earthly governments.

Look back in retrospect on almost six thousand years of human history! Freedom's moments have been infrequent and exceptional. We must appreciate that we live in one of history's most exceptional moments—in a nation and a time of unprecedented freedom. Freedom as we know it has been experienced by perhaps less than one percent of the human family.

THE PROPER ROLE OF GOVERNMENT

The second basic principle concerns the function and proper role of government. These are the principles that, in my opinion, proclaim the proper role of government in the domestic affairs of the nation.

> *[I] believe that governments were instituted of God for the benefit of man; and that he holds men accountable for their acts in relation to them. . . .*
>
> *[I] believe that no government can exist in peace, except such laws are framed and held inviolate as will secure to each individual the free exercise of conscience, the right and control of property, and the protection of life. . . .*
>
> *[I] believe that all men are bound to sustain and uphold the respective governments in which they reside, while protected in their inherent and inalienable rights by the laws of such governments. [D&C 134:1–2, 5]*
>
> *In other words, the most important single function of government is to secure the rights and freedoms of individual citizens.*

THE SOURCE OF HUMAN RIGHTS

The third important principle pertains to the source of basic human rights. Rights are either God-given as part of the divine plan, or they are granted by government as part of the political plan. If we accept the premise that human rights are granted by government, then we must be willing to accept the corollary that they can be denied by government. I, for one, shall never accept that premise. We must ever keep in mind the inspired words of Thomas Jefferson, as found in the Declaration of Independence:

> *We hold these truths to be self-evident, that all men are created equal, that they are endowed by their Creator with certain unalienable Rights, that among these are Life, Liberty, and the pursuit of Happiness.*
>
> *That to secure these rights, Governments are instituted among Men, deriving their just powers from the consent of the governed.*

PEOPLE ARE SUPERIOR TO GOVERNMENTS

The fourth basic principle we must understand is that people are superior to the governments they form. Since God created people with certain inalienable rights, and they, in turn, created government to help secure and safeguard those rights, it follows that the people are superior to the creature they created.

GOVERNMENTS SHOULD HAVE LIMITED POWERS

The fifth and final principle that is basic to our understanding of the Constitution is that governments should have only limited powers. The important thing to keep in mind is that the people who have created their government can give to that government only such powers as they, themselves, have in the first place. Obviously, they cannot give that which they do not possess.

By deriving its just powers from the governed, government becomes primarily a mechanism for defense against bodily harm, theft, and involuntary servitude. It cannot claim the power to redistribute money or property nor to force reluctant citizens to perform acts of charity against their will. Government is created by the people. No individual possesses the power to take another's wealth or to force others to do good, so no government has the right to do such things either. The creature cannot exceed the creator.

THE CONSTITUTION AND ITS COMING FORTH

With these basic principles firmly in mind, let us now turn to a discussion of the inspired document we call the Constitution. My purpose is not to recite the events that led to the American Revolution—we are all familiar with these. But I would say this: History is not an accident. Events are foreknown to God. His superintending influence is behind the actions of his righteous children. Long before America was even discovered, the Lord was moving and shaping events that would lead to the coming forth of the remarkable form of government established by the Constitution. America had to be free and independent to fulfill this destiny. I commend to you as excellent reading on this subject Elder Mark E. Petersen's book *The Great Prologue* (Salt Lake City: Deseret Book Co., 1975). As expressed so eloquently by John Adams before the signing of the Declaration, "There's a Divinity which shapes our ends" (quoted in *The Works of Daniel Webster*, vol. 1 (Boston: Charles C. Little and James Brown, 1851), p. 133). Though mortal eyes and minds cannot fathom the end from the beginning, God does.

GOD RAISED UP WISE MEN TO
CREATE THE CONSTITUTION

In a revelation to the Prophet Joseph Smith, the Savior declared, "I established the Constitution of this land, by the hands of wise men whom I raised up unto this very purpose" (D&C 101:80). These were not ordinary men, but men chosen and held in reserve by the Lord for this very purpose.

Shortly after President Kimball became President of the Church, he assigned me to go into the vault of the St. George Temple and check the early records. As I did so, I realized the fulfillment of a dream I had had ever since learning of the visit of the Founding Fathers to the St. George Temple. I saw with my own eyes the records of the work that was done for the Founding Fathers of this great nation, beginning with George Washington. Think of it, the Founding Fathers of this nation, those great men, appeared within those sacred walls and had their vicarious work done for them. President Wilford Woodruff spoke of it in these words:

> Before I left St. George, the spirits of the dead gathered around me, wanting to know why we did not redeem them. Said they, "You have had the use of the Endowment House for a number of years, and yet nothing has ever been done for us. We laid the foundation of the government you now enjoy, and we never apostatized from it, but we remained true to it and were faithful to God."
>
> These were the signers of the Declaration of Independence, and they waited on me for two days and two nights. . . .
>
> I straightway went into the baptismal font and called upon Brother McCallister to baptize me for the signers of the Declaration of Independence, and fifty other eminent men. [Discourses of Wilford Woodruff, sel. G. Homer Durham (Salt Lake City: Bookcraft, 1946), pp. 160–61]

These noble spirits came there with divine permission—evidence that this work of salvation goes forward on both sides of the veil.

At a later conference, in April 1898, after he became President of the Church, President Woodruff declared that "those men who laid the foundation of this American government and signed the Declaration of Independence were the best spirits the God of heaven could find on the face of the earth. They were choice spirits . . . [and] were inspired of the Lord" (CR, April 1898, p. 89). We honor those men today. We are the grateful beneficiaries of their noble work.

THE LORD APPROVED THE CONSTITUTION

But we honor more than those who brought forth the Constitution. We honor the Lord who revealed it. God himself has borne witness to the fact that he is pleased with the final product of the work of these great patriots. In a revelation to the Prophet Joseph Smith on August 6, 1833, the Savior admonished: "I, the Lord, justify you, and your brethren of my church, in befriending that law which is the constitutional law of the land" (D&C 98:6).

In the Kirtland Temple dedicatory prayer, given on March 27, 1836, the Lord directed the Prophet Joseph to say: "May those principles, which were so honorably and nobly defended, namely, the Constitution of our land, by our fathers, be established forever" (D&C 109:54).

A few years later, Joseph Smith, while unjustly incarcerated in a cold and depressing cell of Liberty Jail at Clay County, Missouri, frequently bore his testimony of the document's divinity: "The Constitution of the United States is a glorious standard; it is founded in the wisdom of God. It is a heavenly banner" (HC 3:304)

How this document accomplished all of this merits our further consideration.

THE DOCUMENT ITSELF

The Constitution consists of seven separate articles. The first three establish the three branches of our government—the legislative, the executive, and the judicial. The fourth article describes matters pertaining to states, most significantly the guarantee of a republican form of government to every state of the Union. Article 5 defines the amendment procedure of the document, a deliberately difficult process that should be clearly understood by every citizen. Article 6 covers several miscellaneous items, including a definition of the supreme law of the land, namely, the Constitution itself. Article 7, the last, explains how the Constitution is to be ratified. After ratification of the document, ten amendments were added and designated as our Bill of Rights.

Now to look at some of the major provisions of the document itself. Many principles could be examined, but I mention five as being crucial to the preservation of our freedom. If we understand the workability of these, we have taken the first step in defending our freedoms.

MAJOR PROVISIONS OF THE DOCUMENT

The major provisions of the Constitution are as follows.

Sovereignty of the People

First: Sovereignty lies in the people themselves. Every governmental system has a sovereign, one or several who possess all the executive, legislative, and judicial powers. That sovereign may be an individual, a group, or the people themselves. The Founding Fathers believed in common law, which holds that true sovereignty rests with the people. Believing this to be in accord with truth, they inserted this imperative in the Declaration of Independence: "To secure these rights [life, liberty, and the pursuit of happiness], Governments are instituted among Men, deriving their just powers from the consent of the governed."

Separation of Powers

Second: To safeguard these rights, the Founding Fathers provided for the separation of powers among the three branches of government—the legislative, the executive, and the judicial. Each was to be independent of the other, yet each was to work in a unified relationship. As the great constitutionalist President J. Reuben Clark noted:

> It is [the] union of independence and dependence of these branches—legislative, executive and judicial—and of the governmental functions possessed by each of them, that constitutes the marvelous genius of this unrivaled document. . . . It was here that the divine inspiration came. It was truly a miracle. [Church News, November 29, 1952, p. 12]

The use of checks and balances was deliberately designed, first, to make it difficult for a minority of the people to control the government, and, second, to place restraint on the government itself.

Limited Powers of Government

Third: The powers the people granted to the three branches of government were specifically limited. The Founding Fathers well understood human nature and its tendency to exercise unrighteous dominion when given authority. A constitution was therefore designed to limit government to certain enumerated functions, beyond which was tyranny.

The Principle of Representation

Fourth: Our constitutional government is based on the principle of representation. The principle of representation means that we have delegated to an elected official the power to represent us. The Constitution provides for both direct representation and indirect representation. Both forms of representation provide a tempering influence on pure democracy. The intent was to protect the individual's and the minority's rights to life, liberty, and the fruits of their labors—property. These rights were not to be subject to majority vote.

A Moral and Righteous People

Fifth: The Constitution was designed to work with only a moral and righteous people. "Our constitution," said John Adams (first vice-president and second president of the United States), "was made only for a moral and religious people. It is wholly inadequate to the government of any other" (John R. Howe, Jr., *The Changing Political Thought of John Adams,* Princeton University Press, 1966, p. 185).

The Crisis of Our Constitution

This, then, is the ingenious and inspired document created by these good and wise men for the benefit and blessing of future generations. It is now two hundred years since the Constitution was written. Have we been wise beneficiaries of the gift entrusted to us? Have we valued and protected the principles laid down by this great document?

At this bicentennial celebration we must, with sadness, say that we have not been wise in keeping the trust of our Founding Fathers. For the past two centuries, those who do not prize freedom have chipped away at every major clause of our Constitution until today we face a crisis of great dimensions.

The Prophecy of Joseph Smith

We are fast approaching that moment prophesied by Joseph Smith when he said:

> *Even this Nation will be on the very verge of crumbling to pieces and tumbling to the ground and when the constitution is upon the brink of ruin this people will be the Staff up[on] which the Nation shall lean and they shall bear the constitution away from the very verge of destruction.* [In Howard and Martha Coray Notebook, July 19, 1840, quoted by Andrew F. Ehat and Lyndon W. Cook, comps. and eds., *The Words of Joseph Smith* (Provo, Utah: Religious Studies Center, Brigham Young University, 1980), p. 416.]

The Need to Prepare

Will we be prepared? Will we be among those who will "bear the Constitution away from the very verge of destruction"? If we desire to be numbered among those who will, here are some things we must do:

1. We must be righteous and moral. We must live the gospel principles—all of them. We have no right to expect a higher degree of morality from those who represent us than what we ourselves are. To live a higher law means we will not seek to receive what we have not earned by our own labor. It means we will remember that government owes us nothing. It means we will keep the laws of the land. It means we will look to God as our Lawgiver and the source of our liberty.

2. We must learn the principles of the Constitution and then abide by its precepts. Have we read the Constitution and pondered it? Are we aware of its principles? Could we defend it? Can we recognize when a law is constitutionally unsound? The Church will not tell us how to do this, but we are admonished to do it. I quote Abraham Lincoln:

> Let [the Constitution] be taught in schools, in seminaries, and in colleges; let it be written in primers, spelling-books, and in almanacs; let it be preached from the pulpit, proclaimed in legislative halls, and enforced in courts of justice. And, in short, let it become the political religion of the nation. [*Complete Works of Abraham Lincoln*, ed. John G. Nicolay and John Hay, vol. 1 (New York: Francis D. Tandy Co., 1905), p. 43.]

3. We must become involved in civic affairs. As citizens of this republic, we cannot do our duty and be idle spectators. It is vital that we follow this counsel from the Lord: "Honest men and wise men should be sought for diligently, and good men and wise men ye should observe to uphold; otherwise whatsoever is less than these cometh of evil" (D&C 98:10). Note the qualities that the Lord demands in those who are to represent us. They must be good, wise, and honest. We must be concerted in our desires and efforts to see men and women represent us who possess all three of these qualities.

4. We must make our influence felt by our vote, our letters, and our advice. We must be wisely informed and let others know how we feel. We must take part in local precinct meetings and select delegates who will truly represent our feelings. I have faith that the Constitution will be saved as prophesied by Joseph Smith. But it will not be saved in Washington. It will be saved by the citizens of this nation who love and cherish freedom. It will be saved by enlightened members of this Church—men and women who will subscribe to and abide by the principles of the Constitution.

The Constitution Requires Our Loyalty and Support

I reverence the Constitution of the United States as a sacred document. To me its words are akin to the revelations of God, for God has placed his stamp of approval on the Constitution of this land. I testify that the God of heaven sent some of his choicest spirits to lay the foundation of this government, and he has sent other choice spirits—even you who hear my words this day—to preserve it.

We, the blessed beneficiaries, face difficult days in this beloved land, "a land which is choice above all other lands" (Ether 2:10). It may also cost us blood before we are through. It is my conviction, however, that when the Lord comes, the Stars and Stripes will be floating on the breeze over this people. May it be so, and may God give us the faith and the courage exhibited by those patriots who pledged their lives and fortunes that we might be free, in the name of Jesus Christ. Amen.

Hugh B. Brown

Hugh B. Brown was born on October 24, 1883, at Granger, Salt Lake City, Utah. He was ordained an apostle April 10, 1958 at the age of 74. At the time of this statement he was serving as First Counselor under President David O. McKay. The Statement on Civil Rights states that there is no doctrine, belief, or practice of the Church intended to deny the right to the enjoyment of full civil rights to all, regardless of race, color, or creed. On the contrary, President Brown calls upon all members to commit themselves to the establishment of full civil equality for all of God's children.

October 7, 1963
Salt Lake Tribune

"During recent months, both in Salt Lake City and across the nation, considerable interest has been expressed in the position of the Church of Jesus Christ of Latter-day Saints in the matter of civil rights."

"We would like it to be known that there is in this Church no doctrine, belief or practice that is intended to deny the enjoyment of full civil rights by any person regardless of race, color or creed."

"We say again, as we have said many times before, that we believe that all men are the children of the same God, and that it is a moral evil for any person to deny any human being the right to gainful employment, to full educational opportunity and to every privilege of citizenship, just as it is a moral evil to deny him the right to worship according to the dictates of this own conscience."

"We have consistently and persistently upheld the Constitution of the United States, and as far as we are concerned this means upholding the constitutional rights of every citizen of the United States."

"We call upon all men everywhere, both within and outside the Church, to commit themselves to the establishment of full civil equality for all of God's children. Anything less than this defeats our high ideal of the brotherhood of man."

PART THREE

Current Church Authorities

L. Tom Perry

L. Tom Perry was born in Logan, Utah on August 5, 1922. He served in World War Two as a Marine in the Pacific. Later, Elder Perry graduated from Utah State University in finance. He eventually became the Vice President and Treasurer of a department store chain in Boston, Massachusetts. Elder Perry was ordained an apostle on April 11, 1974. In the following conversation with the editor of the Ensign, *Elder Perry explains that the strength and goodness of America remains essential to the expansion of a world wide church. He repeats the distinct message of the Church regarding the inspired character of the American founding. The central message of the Church in connection with the U. S. Bicentennial is that the Lord blesses a righteous people.*

1976
The Church and the U.S. Bicentennial—A Conversation

Elder L. Tom Perry was appointed in 1974 as chairman of the Church Bicentennial Committee. *Ensign* Managing Editor Jay M. Todd this month discussed the general topic of the Church and the Bicentennial with Elder Perry.

Ensign: *Why is the Church—the earthly institution of a worldwide ecclesiastical government—so significantly involved in a national celebration, in this instance, the U.S. bicentennial?*

Elder Perry: For many reasons. The United States represents the major source of human and financial resources that go into the expansion of the Lord's work throughout the world. It is very essential that America remain strong in order that the Church can continue to support the Lord's work in all corners of the earth. It's true that Saints in other nations are beginning to come to the point where they can be "independent" in the sense that they can supply their own leadership and resources—but there are few nations in the world where the Saints are of sufficient numbers and have available means to be able to support even among themselves the expansion of the Church in a very significant manner. But as Saints in these and other lands arrive at the point where they can help in the *worldwide* expansion of the Lord's work, the Church will have moved into other new lands that will need human and financial support for a long time. To get the Saints in any nation to the point where they can stand on their own feet, so to speak, with their own leaders and supply their own financial resources represents a long nurturing process. We joyfully look to the day when more and more nations—or the Saints within them—will have arrived at that position.

But until that day comes, it is obvious that the central source of resources for the worldwide Church for the past 146 years has been America—and we think it will continue to be that way for quite some time. So we're anxious to help America be strong and good, because the American Saints are so central to supplying the needs of others throughout the world for the present.

In addition to that central idea we have a basic religious message, a unique message to tell the world—and that is that God's hand was in the founding of America. America is the cradle of the Church. We know that the great reformation of centuries ago was God-inspired. The rediscovery of America by Columbus was God-inspired. The founding of this land with a form of government that would permit the gospel to be restored and be established was God-inspired. This is a great message. A message of fulfilled prophecy. A message that God lives—that he is in our lives, that he is involved in the shaping of history in ways that many people do not know. I tell you, this is great news! The Lord himself said that he raised up "wise men" for the purpose of founding the United States' constitutional government, a form of government that has been modeled and patterned after all over the world because it provides the kind of freedom, agency, and opportunity our Father's children need in order for them to grow, mature, and develop. It should be apparent then, that the Church would want to commemorate the birth of this nation—first in thanksgiving to God for what he has done for us and for all mankind, and second, because it gives us a chance to teach the gospel, to bear witness that God lives, and to further fulfill our missionary calling to teach the gospel of Jesus Christ.

In addition to these reasons, we are also happy to have our United States members join in this celebration. We want them to be completely supportive of good programs fostered by our communities, states, and nation. We believe in being good citizens. The Church is interested in encouraging its Saints to wear the sandals of citizenship.

The bicentennial celebration is not a Church celebration. It is a national celebration. We hope our members will have become a part of their communities' activities and efforts. Certainly, in times such as these, we want to teach them to be involved with other good people seeking to do good things.

Ensign: *What are some of the things that the Church is doing to help set the tone of the nation's bicentennial?*

Elder Perry: Basically, we're trying to have the central message go out that the Lord blesses righteous people. The Lord blesses those nations that serve him.

To help convey this message, the Church is doing many things.

Ensign: *What do you hope will be the great result of all this activity?*

Elder Perry: We want our nation to hear again the words "And this is our motto—In God We Trust." We hope that our own members and all citizens throughout the nation will bow down on their knees on July 4 and thank God for his blessings and confess his goodnesses to them and all mankind. We hope it will be a time of recommitment to serving the God of this land.

Ensign: *What about the Saints in other lands—how do you hope they will respond to this bicentennial emphasis of the Church?*

Elder Perry: We hope they would thank the Lord for providing a cradle for the Restoration. It is through this nation and its human and financial resources that they have been blessed with the gospel message and its present-day program. We are not asking Saints in other lands to become bicentennially involved—only the American Saints. We think the celebration pattern we're establishing here is one that can be used whenever appropriate in other lands. In the Church, there is a bond that binds us together which knows no national boundaries. However, we of course want all members in all lands to be good citizens.

Ensign: *What has been the personal meaning to you of being chairman of the Church Bicentennial Committee?*

Elder Perry: It has forced me to study the history of this great land and to read of the faith and trust that our early Founding Fathers had in Divine Providence. I am just amazed at what they were able to accomplish. At first, I could not have named more than three or four of the signers of the Declaration of Independence. Now I feel almost personally acquainted with all of them. I love and appreciate their courage, their sacrifice.

I have gained a great appreciation for this land of America. I have received a personal witness of God's hand in its formation. I have been reassured of the blessings, which will be ours if we will only serve Him. May we always have the courage to defend that which is right.

Dallin H. Oaks

Dallin H. Oaks was born on August 12, 1932. He received his accounting degree from Brigham Young University and his law degree from the University of Chicago. Dallin Oaks has had a distinguished career in the law. He clerked for Supreme Court Justice Earl Warren, practiced and taught law in Chicago and, after serving as President of Brigham Young University, was appointed to the Utah Supreme Court. He was ordained an Apostle in April of 1984.

Freedom Festival, Provost, July 5, 1987

A review of the circumstances surrounding its framing supports Washington's remark that the U. S. Constitution (the first written constitution) was a miracle. It was inspired, but not "a fully grown document." Its "great fundamentals" include: separation of powers, a written bill of rights, federal division of powers, popular sovereignty, and the rule of law. As citizens we should study the Constitution, be law-abiding, promote morality and practice civic virtue, and be patriotic.

The Divinely Inspired Constitution

Not long after I began to teach law, an older professor asked me a challenging question about Latter-day Saints' belief in the United States Constitution. Earlier in his career he had taught at the University of Utah College of Law. There he met many Latter-day Saint law students. "They all seemed to believe that the Constitution was divinely inspired," he said, "but none of them could ever tell me what this meant or how it affected their interpretation of the Constitution." I took that challenge personally, and I have pondered it for many years.[1]

I hope I will not be thought immodest if I claim a special interest in the Constitution. As a lawyer and a law professor for more than 20 years, I have studied the United States Constitution. As legal counsel, I helped draft the bill of rights for the Illinois constitutional convention of 1970. And for three and one-half years as a justice of the Utah Supreme Court I had the sworn duty to uphold and interpret the constitutions of both the United States and the state of Utah. My conclusions draw upon those experiences and upon a lifetime of studying the scriptures and the teachings of the living prophets. My opinions on this subject are personal and do not represent a statement in behalf of The Church of Jesus Christ of Latter-day Saints.

CREATION AND RATIFICATION

The United States Constitution was the first written constitution in the world. It has served Americans well, enhancing freedom and prosperity during the changed conditions of more than 200 years. Frequently copied, it has become the United States' most important export. After two centuries, every nation in the world except six has adopted written constitutions,[2] and the U.S. Constitution was a model for all of them. No wonder modern revelation says that God established the U.S. Constitution and that it "should be maintained for the rights and protection of all flesh, according to just and holy principles" (D&C 101:77).

George Washington was perhaps the first to use the word *miracle* in describing the drafting of the U.S. Constitution. In a 1788 letter to Lafayette, he said:

It appears to me, then, little short of a miracle, that the delegates from so many different states (which states you know are also different from each other in their manners, circumstances, and prejudices) should unite in forming a system of national Government, so little liable to well-founded objections.[3]

It was a miracle. Consider the setting.

The 13 colonies and 3.5 million Americans who had won independence from the British crown a few years earlier were badly divided on many fundamental issues. Some thought the colonies should reaffiliate with the British crown. Among the majority who favored continued independence, the most divisive issue was whether the United States should have a strong central government to replace the weak "league of friendship" established by the Articles of Confederation. Under the Confederation of 1781, there was no executive or judicial authority, and the national Congress had no power to tax or to regulate commerce. The 13 states retained all their sovereignty, and the national government could do nothing without their approval. The Articles of Confederation could not be amended without the unanimous approval of all the states, and every effort to strengthen this loose confederation had failed.

Congress could not even protect itself. In July 1783, an armed mob of former Revolutionary War soldiers seeking back wages threatened to take Congress hostage at its meeting in Philadelphia. When Pennsylvania declined to provide militia to protect them, the congressmen fled. Thereafter Congress was a laughingstock, wandering from city to city.

Unless America could adopt a central government with sufficient authority to function as a nation, the 13 states would remain a group of insignificant, feuding little nations united by nothing more than geography and forever vulnerable to the impositions of aggressive foreign powers. No wonder the first purpose stated in the preamble of the new United States Constitution was "to form a more perfect union."

The Constitution had its origin in a resolution by which the relatively powerless Congress called delegates to a convention to discuss amendments to the Articles of Confederation. This convention was promoted by James Madison and Alexander Hamilton, two far-sighted young statesmen still in their 30s, who favored a strong national government. They persuaded a reluctant George Washington to attend and then used his influence in a letter-writing campaign to encourage participation by all the states. The convention was held in Philadelphia, whose population of a little over 40,000 made it the largest city in the 13 states.

As the delegates assembled, there were ominous signs of disunity. It was not until 11 days after the scheduled beginning of the convention that enough states were represented to form a quorum. New Hampshire's delegation arrived more than two months late because the state had not provided them travel money. No delegates ever came from Rhode Island.

Economically and politically, the country was alarmingly weak. The states were in a paralyzing depression. Everyone was in debt. The national treasury was empty. Inflation was rampant. The various currencies were nearly worthless. The trade deficit was staggering. Rebelling against their inclusion in New York State, prominent citizens of Vermont had already entered into negotiations to rejoin the British crown. In the Western Territory, Kentucky leaders were speaking openly about turning from the union and forming alliances with the Old World.

Instead of reacting timidly because of disunity and weakness, the delegates boldly ignored the terms of their invitation to amend the Articles of Confederation and instead set out to write an entirely new constitution. They were conscious of their place in history. For millennia the world's people had been ruled by kings or tyrants. Now a group of colonies had won independence from a king, and their unique opportunity of establishing a constitutional government Abraham Lincoln would later describe as "of the people, by the people, and for the people."

The delegates faced staggering obstacles. The leaders in the 13 states were deeply divided on the extent to which the states would cede any power to a national government. If there was to be a strong central government, there were seemingly irresolvable differences on how to allocate the ingredients of national power between large and small states. As to the nature of the national executive, some wanted to copy the British parliamentary system. At least one delegate even favored the adoption of a monarchy. Divisions over slavery could well have prevented any agreement on other issues. There were 600,000 black slaves in the 13 states, and slavery was essential in the view of some delegates and repulsive to many others.

Deeming secrecy essential to the success of their venture, the delegates spent over three months in secret sessions, faithfully observing their agreement that no one would speak outside the meeting room on the progress of their work. They were fearful that if their debates were reported to the people before the entire document was ready for submission, the opposition would unite to kill the effort before it was born. This type of proceeding would obviously be impossible today. There is irony in the fact that a constitution which protects the people's "right to know" was written under a set of ground rules that its present beneficiaries would not tolerate.

It took the delegates seven weeks of debate to resolve the question of how the large and small states would be represented in the national congress. The Great Compromise provided a senate with equal representation for each state, and a lower house in which representation was apportioned according to the whole population of free persons in the state, plus three-fifths of the slaves. The vote on this issue was five states in favor and four against; other states did not vote, either because no delegates were present or because their delegation was divided. Upon that fragile base, the delegates went forward to consider other issues, including the nature of the executive and judicial branches and whether the document should include a bill of rights.

It is remarkable that the delegates were able to put aside their narrow sectional loyalties to agree on a strong central government. Timely events were persuasive of the need: the delegates' memories of the national humiliation when Congress was chased out of Philadelphia by a mob, the recent challenge of Shay's rebellion against Massachusetts farm foreclosures, and the frightening prospect that northern and western areas would be drawn back into the orbit of European power.

The success of the convention was attributable in large part to the remarkable intelligence, wisdom, and unselfishness of the delegates. As James Madison wrote in the preface to his notes on the Constitutional Convention:

> *There never was an assembly of men, charged with a great and arduous trust, who were more pure in their motives, or more exclusively or anxiously devoted to the object committed to them.*[4]

Truly, the U.S. Constitution was established "by the hands of wise men whom [the Lord] raised up unto this very purpose" (D&C 101:80).

The drafting of the Constitution was only the beginning. By its terms it would not go into effect until ratified by conventions in nine states. But if the nation was to be united and strong, the new Constitution had to be ratified by the key states of Virginia and New York, where the opposition was particularly strong. The extent of opposition coming out of the convention is suggested by the fact that of 74 appointed delegates, only 55 participated in the convention, and only 39 of these signed the completed document.

It was nine months before nine states had ratified, and the last of the key states was not included until a month later, when the New York convention ratified by a vote of 30 to 27. To the "miracle of Philadelphia" one must therefore add "the miracle ratification."

Ratification probably could not have been secured without a commitment to add a written bill of rights. The first 10 amendments, which included the Bill of Rights, were ratified a little over three years after the Constitution itself. That the Constitution was ratified is largely attributable to the fact that the principal leaders in the states were willing to vote for a document that failed to embody every one of their preferences. For example, influential Thomas Jefferson, who was in Paris negotiating a treaty and therefore did not serve as a delegate, felt strongly that a bill of rights should have been included in the original Constitution. But Jefferson still supported the

Constitution because he felt it was the best available. Benjamin Franklin stated that view in these words:

> When you assemble a number of men to have the advantage over their joint wisdom, you inevitably assemble with those men, all their prejudices, their passions, their errors of opinion, their local interests, and their selfish views. From such an assembly can a perfect production be expected? It therefore astonishes me, Sir, to find this system approaching so near to perfection as it does. . . . The opinions I have had of its errors, I sacrifice to the public good.[5]

In other words, one should not expect perfection—one certainly should not expect all of his personal preferences—in a document that must represent a consensus. One should not sulk over a representative body's failure to attain perfection. Americans are well advised to support the best that can be obtained in the circumstances that prevail. That is sound advice not only for the drafting of a constitution but also for the adoption and administration of laws under it.

INSPIRATION

It was a miracle that the Constitution could be drafted and ratified. But what is there in the text of the Constitution that is divinely inspired?

Reverence for the United States Constitution is so great that sometimes individuals speak as if its every word and phrase had the same standing as scripture. Personally, I have never considered it necessary to defend every line of the Constitution as scriptural. For example, I find nothing scriptural in the compromise on slavery or the minimum age or years of citizenship for congressmen, senators, or the president. President J. Reuben Clark, who referred to the Constitution as "part of my religion,"[6] also said that it was not part of his belief or the doctrine of the Church that the Constitution was a "fully grown document." "On the contrary, he said, "we believe it must grow and develop to meet the changing needs of an advancing world."[7]

That was also the attitude of the Prophet Joseph Smith. He faulted the Constitution for not being "broad enough to cover the whole ground." In an obvious reference to the national government's lack of power to intervene when the state of Missouri used its militia to expel the Latter-day Saints from their lands, Joseph Smith said,

> Its sentiments are good, but it provides no means of enforcing them. . . . Under its provision, a man or a people who are able to protect themselves can get along well enough; but those who have the misfortune to be weak or unpopular are left to the merciless rage of popular fury.[8]

This omission of national power to protect citizens against state action to deprive them of constitutional rights was remedied in the Fourteenth Amendment, adopted just after the Civil War.

I see divine inspiration in what President J. Reuben Clark called the "great fundamentals" of the Constitution. In his many talks on the Constitution, he always praised three fundamentals: (a) the separation of powers into three independent branches of government in a federal system; (b) the essential freedoms of speech, press, and religion embodied in the Bill of Rights; and (c) the equality of all men before the law. I concur in these three, but I add two more. On my list there are five great fundamentals.

1. *Separation of powers.* The idea of separation of powers was at least a century old. The English Parliament achieved an initial separation of legislative and executive authority when they wrested certain powers from the king in the revolution of 1688. The concept of separation of powers became well established in the American colonies. State constitutions adopted during the Revolution distinguished between the executive, legislative, and judicial functions. Thus, a document commenting on the proposed Massachusetts Constitution of 1778 speaks familiarly of the principle

> that the legislative, judicial, and executive powers are to be lodged in different hands, that each branch is to be independent, and further, to be so balanced, and be able to exert such checks upon the others, as will preserve it from dependence on, or a union with them.[9]

Thus, we see that the inspiration on the *idea* of separation of powers came long before the U.S. Constitutional Convention. The inspiration in the convention was in its original and remarkably successful *adaptation* of the idea of separation of powers to the practical needs of a national government. The delegates found just the right combination to assure the integrity of each branch, appropriately checked and balanced with the others. As President Clark said:

> It is this union of independence and dependence of these branches—legislative, executive, and judicial—and of the governmental functions possessed by each of them, that constitutes the marvelous genius of this unrivaled document. . . . As I see it, it was here chat the divine inspiration came. It was truly a miracle.[10]

2. *A written bill of rights.* This second great fundamental came by amendment, but I think Americans all look upon the Bill of Rights as part of the inspired work of the Founding Fathers. The idea of a bill of rights was not new. Once again, the inspiration was in the brilliant, practical implementation of preexisting principles. Almost six hundred years earlier, King John had subscribed the Magna Charta, which contained a written guarantee of some rights for certain of his subjects. The English Parliament had guaranteed individual rights against royal power in the English Bill of Rights of 1689.

Even more recently, some of the charters used in establishing the American colonies had written guarantees of liberties and privileges, with which the delegates were familiar.

I have always felt that the United States Constitution's closest approach to scriptural stature is in the phrasing of our Bill of Rights. Without the free exercise of religion, America could not have served as the host nation for the restoration of the gospel, which began just three decades after the Bill of Rights was ratified. I also see scriptural stature in the concept and wording of the freedoms of speech and press, the right to be secure against unreasonable searches and seizures, the requirements that there must be probable cause for an arrest and that accused persons must have a speedy and public trial by an impartial jury, and the guarantee that a person will not be deprived of life, liberty, or property without due process of law. President Ezra Taft Benson has said, "Reason, necessity, tradition, and religious conviction all lead me to accept the divine origin of these rights."[11]

The Declaration of Independence had posited these truths to be "self-evident," that all men "are endowed by their Creator with certain unalienable Rights," and that governments are instituted "to secure these Rights." This inspired Constitution was established to provide a practical guarantee of these God-given rights (see D&C 101:77), and the language implementing that godly objective is scriptural to me.

3. *Division of powers.* Another inspired fundamental of the U.S. Constitution is its federal system, which divides government powers between the nation and the various states. Unlike the inspired adaptation mentioned earlier, this division of sovereignty was unprecedented in theory or practice. In a day when it is fashionable to assume that the government has the power and means to right every wrong, we should remember that the U.S. Constitution limits the national government to the exercise of powers expressly granted to it. The 10th Amendment provides:

"The powers not delegated to the United States by the Constitution, nor prohibited to it by the States, are reserved to the States respectively or to the people."

This principle of limited national powers, with all residuary powers reserved to the people or to the state and local governments, which are most responsive to the people, is one of the great fundamentals of the U.S. Constitution.

The particular powers that are reserved to the states are part of the inspiration. For example, the power to make laws on personal relationships is reserved to the states. Thus, laws of marriage and family rights and duties are state laws. This would have been changed by the proposed Equal Rights Amendment (ERA). When the First Presidency opposed ERA, they cited the way it would have changed various legal rules having to do with the family, a result they characterized as "a moral rather than a legal issue."[12] I would add my belief that the most fundamental legal and political objection to the proposed ERA was that it would effect a significant reallocation of law-making power from the states to the federal government.

4. *Popular sovereignty.* Perhaps the most important of the great fundamentals of the inspired Constitution is the principle of popular sovereignty: The people are the source of governmental power. Along with many religious people, Latter-day Saints affirm that God gave the power to the people, and the people consented to a constitution that delegated certain powers to the government. Sovereignty is not inherent in a state or nation just because it has the power that comes from force of arms. Sovereignty does not come from the divine right of a king, who grants his subjects such power as he pleases or is forced to concede, as in the Magna Charta. The sovereign power is in the people. I believe this is one of the great meanings in the revelation telling us that God established the Constitution of the United States,

> *That every man may act . . . according to the moral agency which I have given unto him, that every man may be accountable for his own sins in the day of judgment.*
>
> *Therefore, it is not right that any man should be in bondage one to another.*
>
> *And for this purpose have I established the Constitution of this land.* (D&C 101:78–80)

In other words, the most desirable condition for the effective exercise of God-given moral agency is a condition of maximum freedom and responsibility. In this condition men are accountable for their own sins and cannot blame their political conditions or their bondage on a king or tyrant. This condition is achieved when the people are sovereign, as they are under the Constitution God established in the United States. From this it follows that the most important words in the United States Constitution are the words in the preamble: "We, the people of the United States . . . do ordain and establish this Constitution."

President Ezra Taft Benson expressed the fundamental principle of popular sovereignty when he said, "We [the people] are superior to government and should remain master over it, not the other way around."[13] The Book of Mormon explains that principle in these words:

> *An unrighteous king doth pervert the ways of all righteousness. . . .*
>
> *Therefore, choose you by the voice of this people, judges, that ye may be judged according to the laws. . . .*
>
> *Now it is not common that the voice of the people desireth anything con-*

trary to that which is right; but it is common for the lesser part of the people to desire that which is not right; therefore this shall ye observe and make it your law—to do your business by the voice of the people. (Mosiah 29:23–26)

Popular sovereignty necessarily implies popular *responsibility*. Instead of blaming their troubles on a king or other sovereign, all citizens must share the burdens and responsibilities of governing. As the Book of Mormon teaches, "The burden should come upon all the people, that every man might bear his part" (Mosiah 29:34).

President Clark's third great fundamental was the equality of all men before the law. I believe that to be a corollary of popular sovereignty. When power comes from the people, there is no legitimacy in legal castes or classes or in failing to provide all citizens the equal protection of the laws.

The delegates to the Constitutional Convention did not originate the idea of popular sovereignty, since they lived in a century when many philosophers had argued that political power originated in a social contract. But the United States Constitution provided the first implementation of this principle. After two centuries in which Americans may have taken popular sovereignty for granted, it is helpful to be reminded of the difficulties in that pioneering effort.

To begin with, a direct democracy was impractical for a country of 4,000,000 people and about 500,000 square miles. As a result, the delegates had to design the structure of a constitutional, representative democracy, what they called "a Republican Form of Government."[14]

The delegates also had to resolve whether a constitution adopted by popular sovereignty could be amended, and if so, how.

Finally, the delegates had to decide how minority rights could be protected when the government was, by definition, controlled by the majority of the sovereign people.

A government based on popular sovereignty must be responsive to the people, but it must also be stable or it cannot govern. A constitution must therefore give government the power to withstand the cries of a majority of the people in the short run, though it must obviously be subject to their direction in the long run.

Without some government stability against an outraged majority, government could not protect minority rights. As President Clark declared:

The Constitution was framed in order to protect minorities. That is the purpose of written constitutions. In order that the minorities might be protected in the matter of amendments under our Constitution, the Lord required that the amendments should be made only through the operation of very large majorities—two-thirds for action in the Senate, and three-fourths as among the states. This is the inspired, prescribed order.[15]

The delegates to the Constitutional Convention achieved the required balance between popular sovereignty and stability through a power of amendment that was ultimately available but deliberately slow. Only in this way could the government have the certainty of stability, the protection of minority rights, and the potential of change, all at the same time.

To summarize, I see divine inspiration in these four great fundamentals of the U.S. Constitution:

—the separation of powers in the three branches of government;
—the Bill of Rights;
—the division of powers between the states and the federal government; and
—the application of popular sovereignty.

5. *The rule of law and not of men.* Further, there is divine inspiration in the fundamental underlying premise of this whole constitutional order. All the blessings enjoyed under the United States Constitution are dependent upon the rule of law. That is why President J. Reuben Clark said, "Our allegiance run[s] to the Constitution and to the principles which it embodies, and not to individuals."[16] The rule of law is the basis of liberty.

As the Lord declared in modern revelation, constitutional laws are justifiable before him, "and the law also maketh you free" (D&C 98:5–8). The self-control by which citizens subject themselves to law strengthens the freedom of all citizens and honors the divinely inspired Constitution.

CITIZEN RESPONSIBILITIES

U.S. citizens have an inspired Constitution, and therefore, what? Does the belief that the U.S. Constitution is divinely inspired affect citizens' behavior toward law and government? It should and it does.

U.S. citizens should follow the First Presidency's counsel to study the Constitution.[17] They should be familiar with its great fundamentals; the separation of powers, the individual guarantees in the Bill of Rights, the structure of federalism, the sovereignty of the people, and the principles of the rule of the law. They should oppose any infringement of these inspired fundamentals.

They should be law-abiding citizens, supportive of national, state, and local governments. The 12th Article of Faith declares:

"We believe in being subject to kings, presidents, rulers, and magistrates, in obeying, honoring, and sustaining the law."

The Church's official declaration of belief states:

We believe that governments were instituted of God for the benefit of man; and that he holds men accountable for their acts in relation to them. . . .

We believe that all men are bound to sustain and uphold the respective gov-ernments in which they reside. (D&C 134:1, 5)

Those who enjoy the blessings of liberty under a divinely inspired constitution should promote morality, and they should practice what the Founding Fathers called "civic virtue." In his address on the U.S. Constitution, President Ezra Taft Benson quoted this important observation by John Adams, second president of the United States:

"Our Constitution was made only for a moral and religious people. It is wholly inadequate to the government of any other."[18]

Similarly, James Madison, who is known as the "Father of the Constitution," stated his assumption that there had to be "sufficient virtue among men for self-government." He argued in the *Federalist Papers* that "republican government presupposes the existence of these qualities in a higher degree than any other form."[19]

It is part of our civic duty to be moral in our conduct toward all people. There is no place in responsible citizenship for dishonesty or deceit or for willful law-breaking of any kind. We believe with the author of Proverbs that "righteousness exalteth a nation: but sin is a reproach to any people" (Prov. 14:34). The personal righteousness of citizens will strengthen a nation more than the force of its arms.

Citizens should also be practitioners of civic virtue in their conduct toward government. They should be ever willing to fulfill the duties of citizenship. This includes compulsory duties like military service and the numerous voluntary actions they must take if they are to preserve the principle of limited government through citizen self-reliance. For example, since U.S. citizens value the right of trial by jury, they must be willing to serve on juries, even those involving unsavory subject matter. Citizens who favor morality cannot leave the enforcement of moral laws to jurors who oppose them.

The single word that best describes a fulfillment of the duties of civic virtue is patriotism. Citizens should be patriotic. My favorite prescription for patriotism is that of Adlai Stevenson:

What do we mean by patriotism in the context of our times? . . . A patriotism that puts country ahead of self; a patriotism which is not short, frenzied outbursts of emotion, but the tranquil and steady dedication of a lifetime.[20]

I close with a poetic prayer. It is familiar to everyone in the United States, because U.S. citizens sing it in one of their loveliest hymns. It expresses gratitude to God for liberty, and it voices a prayer that he will continue to bless them with the holy light of freedom:

Our fathers' God to thee,
Author of liberty,
To thee we sing;
Long may our land be bright
With freedom's holy light.
Protect us by thy might,
Great God, our King![21]

NOTES

1. A version of this address, given at the 1987 Freedom Festival, Provo, Utah, was printed in *Utah Forum,* Fall/Winter 1989, pp. 1–11.
2. See "The Constitution," *Wilson Quarterly,* Spring 1987, pp. 97, 126.
3. Letter from Washington to Lafayette, 7 Feb. 1788, quoted in Catherine Drinker Bowen, *Miracle at Philadelphia* (Boston: Little, Brown and Company, 1966), p. xvii.
4. Quoted in William O. Nelson, *The Charter of Liberty* (Salt Lake City, Utah: Deseret Book Company, 1987), p. 44.
5. *Notes of the Debates in the Federal Convention of 1787 Reported by James Madison,* p. 653, quoted in Nelson, The Charter of Liberty, (Ibid.) p. 57.
6. J. Reuben Clark, Jr., *Stand Fast by Our Constitution* (Salt Lake City, Utah: Deseret Book Company, 1973), pp. 7, 172.
7. J. Reuben Clark, Jr., quoted in Martin B. Hickman, "J. Reuben Clark, Jr.: the Constitution and the Great Fundamentals," in Ray C. Hillam, ed. *By the Hands of Wise Men* (Provo, Utah: Brigham Young University Press, 1979), p. 53.
8. *History of The Church of Jesus Christ of Latter-day Saints,* vol. 6, B. H. Roberts, editor (Salt Lake City, Utah: Deseret Book Company, 1963), p. 57.
9. Quoted in Gerhard Casper, "Constitutionalism," *Occasional Papers from the Law School* (Chicago: University of Chicago Press), no. 22 (1987).
10. *LDS Church News,* (Salt Lake City, Utah, 29 November 1952), p. 12, quoted in Hillam, op. cit., p. 48.
11. Ezra Taft Benson, *The Constitution, a Heavenly Banner* (Salt Lake City, Utah: Deseret Book Company, 1986), p. 6.
12. Letter from the LDS First Presidency, 12 Oct. 1978.
13. Benson, *The Constitution, a Heavenly Banner,* p. 7.
14. U.S. Constitution, Art. IV, Sec. 4.
15. *J. Reuben Clark: Selected Papers on Religion, Education, and Youth,* David H. Yarn, Jr., editor (Provo, Utah: Brigham Young University Press, 1984), p. 163.
16. Ibid., p. 43.
17. Letter issued by the LDS Church First Presidency, 15 Jan. 1987.
18. Benson, *The Constitution, a Heavenly Banner,* p. 23.

19. *The Federalist,* no. 55.
20. Adlai Stevenson, speech given in New York City, 27 August 1952, quoted in John Bartlett, *Familiar Quotations,* Boston: Little, Brown and Co., 1955, p. 986.
21. "My Country, 'Tis of Thee," *Hymns,* The Church of Jesus Christ of Latter-day Saints (Salt Lake City, Utah, 1985), no. 339.

Some moral absolutes must be at the foundation of any system of law. A shift to moral relativism is producing a shift of emphasis from responsibilities to rights. What passes for "neutrality" is often a hostility to religion. Religion is a legitimate source of the values underlying public policy, and churches and church leaders are as entitled as anyone to participate in public debates, but they must expect to be exposed to the same broad latitude of discussion that applies to other's views, and they should exhibit openness and tolerance.

February 29, 1992
Religious Values and Public Policy
From an Address Given to the Brigham Young University Management Society,
Washington, D.C.

Fundamental to the role of religion in public policy is this most important question: Are there moral absolutes? Speaking to our BYU students earlier this year, President Rex E. Lee said:

"I cannot think of anything more important than for each of you to build a firm, personal testimony that there are in this life some absolutes, things that never change, regardless of time, place, or circumstances. They are eternal truths, eternal principles and, as Paul tells us, they are and will be the same yesterday, today, and forever."[1]

Unfortunately, other educators deny the existence of God or deem God irrelevant to the human condition. Persons who accept this view deny the existence of moral absolutes. They maintain that right and wrong are relative concepts, and morality is merely a matter of personal choice or expediency. For example, a university professor reported that her students lacked what she called "moral common sense." She said they believed that "there was no such thing as right or wrong, just good or bad arguments."[2] In that view, even the most fundamental moral questions have at least two sides, and every assertion of right or wrong is open to debate.

I believe that these contrasting approaches underlie the whole discussion of religious values in public policy. Many differences of opinion over the role of religion in public life simply mirror a difference of opinion over whether there are moral absolutes. But this underlying difference is rarely made explicit. It is as if those who assume that all values are relative have established their assumption by law or tradition and have rendered illegitimate the fundamental belief of those who hold that some values are absolute.

One of the consequences of shifting from *moral absolutes* to *moral relativism* in public policy is that this produces a corresponding shift of emphasis from *responsibilities* to *rights*. Responsibilities originate in moral absolutes. In contrast, rights find their origin in legal principles, which are easily manipulated by moral relativism. Sooner or later the substance of rights must depend on either the voluntary fulfillment of responsibilities or the legal enforcement of duties. When our laws or our public leaders question the existence of absolute moral values, they undercut the basis for the voluntary fulfillment of responsibilities, which is economical, and compel our society to rely more and more on the legal enforcement of rights, which is expensive.

Some moral absolutes or convictions must be at the foundation of any system of law. This does not mean that all laws are so based. Many laws and administrative actions are simply a matter of wisdom or expediency. But many laws and administrative actions are based upon the moral standards of our society. If most of us believe that it is wrong to kill or steal or lie, our laws will include punishment for those acts. If most of us believe that it is right to care for the poor and needy, our laws will accomplish or facilitate those activities. Society continually legislates morality. The only question is whose morality and what legislation.

In the United States, the moral absolutes are the ones derived from what we refer to as the Judeo-Christian tradition, as set forth in the Bible—Old Testament and New Testament.

Despite ample evidence of majority adherence to moral absolutes, some still question the legitimacy of a moral foundation for our laws and public policy. To avoid any suggestion of adopting or contradicting any particular religious absolute, some secularists argue that our laws must be entirely neutral, with no discernible relation to any particular religious tradition. Such proposed neutrality is unrealistic, unless we are willing to cut away the entire idea that there are moral absolutes.

Of course, not all moral absolutes are based on traditional religion. A substantial segment of society has subscribed to the environmental movement, which Robert Nisbet, a distinguished American sociologist, has characterized as a "national religion," with a "universalized social, economic, and political agenda."[3] So far as I am aware, there has been no responsible public challenge to the legitimacy of laws based on the environmentalists' set of values. I don't think there should be. My point is that religious values are just as legitimate as those based on any other comprehensive set of beliefs.

RELIGION AND THE PUBLIC SECTOR

Let us apply these thoughts to the role of religions, churches, and church leaders in the public sector.

Some reject the infusion of religious-based values in public policy by urging that much of the violence and social divisiveness of the modern world is attributable to religious controversies. But all should remember that the most horrible moral atrocities of the twentieth century in terms of death and human misery have been committed by regimes that are unambiguously secular, not religious.

Even though we cannot reject religious values in law-making on the basis of their bad record by comparison with other values, there are examples of hostility to religious values in the public sector. For example, less than a decade ago, the United States Department of Justice challenged a federal judge's right to sit on a case involving the Equal Rights Amendment on the ground that his religious views would prejudice him. The judge was Marion Callister. The religious views were LDS. In that same decade, the American Civil Liberties Union took the position that any pro-life abortion law was illegitimate because it must necessarily be founded on religious belief.[4]

A few years ago some Protestant and Jewish clergymen challenged a federally financed program to promote abstinence from sexual activity among teenage youngsters. The grant recipients included BYU and some Catholic charities in Virginia and Michigan. The ACLU attorney who filed this challenge declared that "the 'chastity law' is unconstitutional because it violates the requirement for separation of church and state" because taxpayer dollars "are going to religious institutions, which use the funds to teach religious doctrines opposing teen-age sex and abortion."[5] In the meantime, the "value" judgments that permit public schools to distribute birth control devices to teenagers supposedly violate no constitutional prohibition because the doctrine that *opposes* chastity is secular.

During this same period, Professor Henry Steele Commager criticized the Moral Majority and the Roman Catholic Church for "inject[ing] religion into politics more wantonly than at any time since the Know-Nothing crusade of the 1850's." Writing in a *New York Times* column, this distinguished scholar asserted that "what the Framers [of the U.S. Constitution] had in mind was more than separating church and state: it was separating religion from politics." While conceding that no one could question the right to preach "morality and religion," Commager argued that church-men of all denominations crossed an impermissible line "when they connect morality with a particular brand of religious faith and this, in turn, with political policies."[6]

Apparently, churchmen can preach morality and religion as long as they do not suggest that their particular brand of religion has any connection with morality or that the resulting morality has any connection with political policies. Stated otherwise, religious preaching is okay so long as it has no practical impact on the listeners' day-to-day behavior, especially any behavior that has anything to do with political activity or public policy.

As we know, the idea that there is an absolute right and wrong comes from religion, and the absolute values that have influenced law and public policy are most commonly rooted in religion. In contrast, the values that generally prevail in today's academic community are relative values.

I have read serious academic arguments to the effect that religious people can participate in public debate only if they conceal the religious origin of their values by translating them into secular dialect. In a nation committed to pluralism, this kind of hostility to religion should be legally illegitimate and morally unacceptable. It is also irrational and unworkable, for reasons explained by BYU law professor Frederick Mark Gedicks:

"Secularism has not *solved* the problem posed by religion in public life so much as it has *buried* it. By placing religion on the far side of the boundary marking the limit of the real world, secularism prevents public life from taking religion seriously. Secularism does not teach us to live with those who are religious; rather, it demands that we ignore them and their views. Such a 'solution' can remain stable only as long as those who are ignored acquiesce in their social situation."[7]

Fortunately, the Supreme Court has never held that citizens could not join together to translate their moral beliefs into laws or public policies even when those beliefs are derived from religious doctrine. Indeed, there are many sophisticated and articulate spokesmen for the proposition that the separation of church and state never intended to exclude religiously grounded values from the public square. For example, I offer the words of Richard John Neuhaus:

"In a democracy that is free and robust, an opinion is no more disqualified for being 'religious' than for being atheistic, or psychoanalytic, or Marxist, or just plain dumb. There is no legal or constitutional question about the admission of religion to the public square; there is only a question about the free and equal participation of citizens in our public business. Religion is not a reified 'thing' that threatens to intrude upon our common life. Religion in public is but the public opinion of those citizens who are religious.

"As with individual citizens, so also with the associations that citizens form to advance their opinions. Religious institutions may understand themselves to be brought into being by God, but for the purposes of this democratic polity they are free associations of citizens. As such, they are guaranteed the same access to the public square as are the citizens who comprise them."[8]

No person with values based on religious beliefs should apologize for taking those values into the public square. Religious persons need to be skillful in how they do so, but they need not yield to an adversary's assumption that the whole effort is illegitimate. We should remind others of the important instances in which the efforts of churches and clergy in the political arena have influenced American public policies in great historical controversies whose outcome is virtually unquestioned today. The slavery controversy was seen as a great moral issue and became the major political issue of the nineteenth century because of the preaching of clergy and the political action of churches. A century later, churches played an indispensable role in the civil rights movement, and, a decade later. clergymen and churches of various denominations were an influential part of the antiwar movement that contributed to the end of the war in Vietnam.

Many sincere religious people believe there should be no limitations on religious arguments on political issues so long as the speaker genuinely believes those issues can be resolved as a matter of right or wrong.

I believe that questions of right and wrong, whether based on religious principles or any other source of values, are legitimate in any debate over laws or public policy. Is there anything more important to debate than what is right or wrong? And those arguments should be open across the entire political spectrum. There is no logical way to contend that religious arguments or lobbying are legitimate on the question of abstinence from nuclear war by nations but not on the question of abstinence from sexual relations by teenagers.

CHURCH PARTICIPATION IN POLITICAL DEBATE

What limitations should churches and their leaders observe when they choose to participate in public debate on political issues?

I emphasize at the outset that I am discussing limits to guide all churches across a broad spectrum of circumstances. I am not seeking to define or defend a Mormon position. As a matter of prudence, our church has confined its own political participation within a far smaller range than is required by the law or the Constitution. Other churches have chosen to assert the full latitude of their constitutional privileges and, in the opinion of some, have even exceeded them.

Where should we draw the line between what is and is not permissible for church and church-leader participation in public policy making?

At one extreme, we hear shrill complaints about political participation by any persons whose political views are attributable to religious beliefs or the teachings of their church. The words "blind obedience" are usually included in such complaints. Complaints there are, but I am not aware of any serious or rational position that would ban religious believers from participation in the political process. The serious challenges concern the participation of churches and church leaders.

Perhaps the root fear of those who object to official church participation in political debates is power: They fear that believers will choose to follow the directions or counsel of their religious leaders. Those who have this fear should remember the celebrated maxim of Jefferson: "Error of opinion may be tolerated where reason is left free to combat it."[9] Some may believe that reason is not free when religious leaders have spoken, but I doubt that any religious leader in twentieth-century America has such a grip on followers that they cannot make a reasoned choice in the privacy of the voting booth. In fact, I have a hard time believing that the teachings of religions or churches deprive their adherents of any more autonomy in exerting the rights of citizenship than the teachings and practices of Labor unions, civil rights groups, environmental organizations, political parties, or any other membership group in our society.

I submit that religious leaders should have at least as many privileges as any other leaders, and that churches should stand on at least as strong a footing as any other corporation when they enter the public square to participate in public policy debates. The precious constitutional right of petition does not exclude any individual or any group. The same is true of freedom of speech and the press. When religion has a special constitutional right to its free exercise, religious leaders and churches should have *more* freedom than other persons and organizations not less.

If churches and church leaders should have full rights to participate in public policy debates, should there be any limits on such participation?

Of course there are limits that apply specially to churches and church officials, as manifest in the United States Constitution's prohibition against Congress's making any law respecting an establishment of religion. Some linkages between churches and governments are obviously illegitimate. It would clearly violate this prohibition if a church or church official were to exercise government power or dictate government policies or direct the action of government officials independent of legal procedures or political processes.

Fundamentally, I submit that there is no persuasive objection in law or principle to a church or church leader taking a position on any legislative matter, if it or he or she chooses to do so.

Now, relative to church participation in public debate, when churches or church leaders choose to enter the public sector to engage in debate on a matter of public policy, they should be admitted to the debate and they should expect to participate in it on the same basis as all other participants. In other words, if churches or church leaders choose to oppose or favor a particular piece of legislation, their opinions should be received on the same basis as the opinions offered by other knowledgeable organizations or persons, and they should be considered on their merits.

By the same token, churches and church leaders should expect the same broad latitude of discussion of their views that conventionally applies to everyone else's participation in public policy debates. A church can claim access to higher authority on moral questions, but its opinions on the application of those moral questions to specific legislation will inevitably be challenged by and measured against secular-based legislative or political judgments. As James E. Wood observed, "While denunciations of injustice, racism, sexism, and nationalism may be clearly rooted in one's religious faith, their political applications to legislative remedy and public policy are by no means always clear."[10]

Finally, if church leaders were also to exhibit openness and tolerance of opposing views, they would help to overcome the suspicion and resentment sometimes directed toward church or church-leader participation in public debate.

In summary, I have pointed out that many U.S. laws are based on the absolute moral values most Americans affirm, and I have suggested that it cannot be otherwise. I have contended that religious-based values are just as legitimate a basis for political action as any other values. And I have argued that churches and church leaders should be able to participate in public policy debates on the same basis as other persons and organizations, favoring or opposing specific legislative proposals or candidates if they choose to do so.

Politicians sometimes seek to use religion for political purposes, and they sometimes even seek to manipulate churches or church leaders. Ultimately this is always self-defeating. Whenever a church (or a church leader) becomes a pawn or servant of government or a political leader, it loses its status and the credibility it needs to perform its religious mission.

Churches or their leaders can also be the aggressors in the pursuit of intimacy with government. The probable results of this excess have been ably described as "the seduction of the churches to political arrogance and political innocence or even the politicizing of moral absolutes."[11]

The relationship in the world between church and state and between church leaders and politicians should be respectful and distant, as befits two parties who need one another but share the realization that a relationship too close can deprive a pluralistic government of its legitimacy and a divine church of its spiritual mission. Despite that desirable distance, government need not be hostile to religion or pretend to ignore God.

NOTES

1. Rex E. Lee. "Things That Change and Things That Don't," BYU Winter Devotional, 14 Jan. 1992.

2. Professor Christina Hoff Sommers of Clark University, as quoted in *Insight*, 23 Dec. 1991, p. 18.

3. Quoted by Allan Carlson in "The 'Green' Alternative and the Death Watch for Industrial Society, *Persuasion at Work*, Sept. 1984, p. 1.

4. Both of these examples are cited by Russell Kirk in "We Cannot Separate Christian Morals and the Rule of Law," *Imprimis*, 4 Apr. 1983

5. Quoted in Robert Pear, "Treating the Nation's Epidemic of Teen-Age Pregnancy," *New York Times*, 3 June 1984, p. E–5.

6. Henry Steele Commager, "Public Morality, Not Religion," *New York Times*, 16 Sept. 1984, Section 4, p. 23, col. 2.

7. Frederick Mark Gedicks, "The Religious, the Secular, and the Antithetical," *Capital U.L. Rev* 20 (1991): 191, note 9.113, 139.

8. Richard John Neuhaus, "A New Order of Religious Freedom," *First Things*, Feb. 1992, p. 13. Also see Richard John Neuhaus, *The Naked Public Square*, 1984.

9. Thomas Jefferson, First Inaugural Address, quoted in Bartlett's *Familiar Quotations*, 13th ed., 1955, p. 374.

10. Reported in James E. Wood, Jr. "Church Lobbying and Public Policy," *Journal of Church and State* 28 (1986):183.

11. Ibid.

M. Russell Ballard

M. Russell Ballard has been an Apostle in the Church since October 1985. Prior to his calling to the Council of Twelve Apostles he was a member of the First Quorum of Seventy for approximately ten years. Elder Ballard was born on October 8, 1928, and attended the University of Utah. In this 1992 speech Elder Ballard discusses the relationship between government and religion. He argues that modern secularism and relativism have obscured the meaning of divinely inspired Constitutional guarantees and rights. It is up to responsible individuals to stand up for moral and religious freedom.

July 5, 1992
Religion in a Free Society
From a talk Given at the Freedom Festival in Provo, Utah

Recently a group of religious and political leaders and scholars from all around the world met in Budapest, Hungary, to discuss the practical challenges faced by the former communist nations that are moving toward some form of religious liberty. The concept of religious freedom is revolutionary for many countries, and they are struggling with many potentially divisive issues: To what extent should public schools recognize and teach religion? How much should the state regulate a church's charitable activities? Should churches be exempted from general laws? To what degree should church and state be separated? Should there be an official state church?

Do those issues sound familiar? They should. The Founding Fathers of the United States wrestled with them more than two hundred years ago, and they continue to be serious topics of discussion and debate to this very day.

The principles and philosophies upon which the U.S. constitutional law is based are not simply the result of the best efforts of a remarkable group of brilliant men. They were inspired by God, and the rights and privileges guaranteed in the Constitution are God-given, not man-derived. The freedom and independence afforded by the Constitution and Bill of Rights are divine rights—sacred, essential, and inalienable. In the 98th section of the Doctrine and Covenants, the Lord indicates that the "law of the land which is constitutional, supporting that principle of freedom in maintaining rights and privileges, belongs to all mankind, and is justifiable before me." (V.5.)

I focus my comments on sixteen significant words found in the First Amendment to the Constitution: "Congress shall make no law respecting an establishment of religion or prohibiting the free exercise thereof."

These words are simple and direct. Their message and meaning appear to be clear. But through the years presidents, Congress, and the courts have interpreted them in so many different ways that many people today have no sense of the perspective upon which they were based.

Believe it or not, at one time the very notion of government had less to do with politics than with virtue. According to James Madison, often referred to as the father of the Constitution: "We have staked the whole future of American civilization not upon the power of the government—far from it. We have staked the future of all of our political institutions upon the capacity of each and all of us to govern ourselves according to the Ten Commandments of God." (Russ Walton, *Biblical Principles of Importance to Godly Christians,* New Hampshire: Plymouth Foundation, 1984, p. 361.)

George Washington agreed with his colleague James Madison. Said Washington: "Reason and experience both forbid us to expect that national morality can prevail in exclusion of religious principle." (James D.

Richardson, *A Compilation of the Messages and Papers of the President, 1789–1897,* U.S. Congress, 1899, vol. 1, p. 220.)

Nearly one hundred years later, Abraham Lincoln responded to a question about which side God was on during the Civil War with this profound insight: "I am not at all concerned about that, for I know that the Lord is always on the side of the right. But it is my constant anxiety and prayer that I and this nation should be on the Lord's side. (*Abraham Lincoln's Stories and Speeches,* ed. J.B. McClure, Chicago: Rhodes and McClure Publishing Co., 1896, pp. 185–86.)

Madison, Washington, and Lincoln all understood that democracy cannot possibly flourish in a moral vacuum and that organized religion plays an important role in preserving and maintaining public morality. Indeed, John Adams, another of America's Founding Fathers, insisted: "We have no government armed with power capable of contending with human passions unbridled by morality and religion." (John Adams, *The Works of John Adams, Second President of the United States,* Charles F. Adams, 1854.)

Yet that is precisely the position we find ourselves in today. Our government is succumbing to pressure to distance itself from God and religion. Consequently, the government is discovering that it is incapable of contending with people who are increasingly "unbridled by morality and religion." A simple constitutional prohibition of state-sponsored church has evolved into court-ordered bans against representations of the Ten Commandments on government buildings, Christmas manger scenes on public property, and prayer at public meetings. Instead of seeking the "national morality" based on "religious principle" that Washington spoke of, many are actively seeking a blind standard of legislative amorality, with a total exclusion of the mention of God in the public square.

Such a standard of religious exclusion is absolutely and unequivocally counter to the intention of those who designed our government. Do you think that mere chance placed the freedom to worship according to individual conscience among the first freedoms specified in the Bill of Rights—freedoms that are destined to flourish together or perish separately? The Founding Fathers understood this country's spiritual heritage. They frequently declared that God's hand was upon this nation, and that He was working through them to create what Chesterton once called "a nation with the soul of a church." (Richard John Neuhaus, "A New Order for the Ages," speech delivered at the Philadelphia Conference on Religious Freedom, 30 May 1991.) While they were influenced by history and their accumulated knowledge, the single most influential reference source for their work on the Constitution was the Holy Bible. Doubtless they were familiar with the Lord's counsel to the children of Israel as they struggled to become a great nation:

"And it shall come to pass, if thou shalt hearken diligently unto the voice of the Lord thy God, to observe and to do all his commandments which I command thee this day, that the Lord thy God will set thee on high above all nations of the earth:

"And all these blessings shall come on thee, and overtake thee, if thou shalt hearken unto the voice of the Lord thy God.

"Blessed shalt thou be in the city, and blessed shalt thou be in the field.

"Blessed shall be the fruit of thy body, and the fruit of thy ground, and the fruit of thy cattle, the increase of thy kine, and the flocks of thy sheep.

"Blessed shall be thy basket and thy store.

"Blessed shalt thou be when thou comest in, and blessed shalt thou be when thou goest out.

"The Lord shall cause thine enemies that rise up against thee to be smitten before thy face: they shall come out against thee one way, and flee before thee seven ways.

"The Lord shall command the blessing upon thee in thy storehouses, and in all that thou settest thine hand unto; and he shall bless thee in the land which the Lord thy God giveth thee.

"The Lord shall establish thee an holy people until himself, as he hath sworn unto thee, if thou shalt keep the commandments of the Lord thy God, and walk in his ways." (Deut. 28:1–9.)

In other words, that nation that keeps God's commandments and walks in His ways will prosper. The framers of our Constitution knew that, and they tried to lay a solid moral foundation for a society that could be so blessed. As they did so, perhaps they thought of Roger Williams and others like him who made a heroic fight for religious freedom.

Roger Williams began his ministry in England, where his zealous work to free the church from the influence of the king brought the wrath of the government upon him. Eventually he and his young wife were forced to flee to the New World. But instead of finding himself among like-minded reformers in America, he encountered much of the same resistance and persecution until he established a new colony called Providence in Rhode Island. Here America had its first taste of true religious freedom, and the success of the Providence colony convinced many that the concept tasted good.

The Founding Fathers very likely were aware of the experiences of Roger Williams and others when they wrote in the First Amendment that the government cannot impede the free exercise of religion. They wrote that the church and the state were to be separate, independent entities, not to eliminate morality and God's law but to make sure that the power of government could never be used to silence religious expression or to persecute religious practice. Once again quoting George Washington: "If I could have entertained the slightest apprehension that the Constitution, framed in the convention where I had the honor to preside, might possibly endanger the religious rights of any ecclesiastical society, certainly I would never have placed my signature to it." (*Maxims of Washington,* New York: D. Appleton and Co., 1894, pp. 370–71)

What would Washington have thought if he could have foreseen our day? Would he have signed the document?

I believe he would have been troubled to see a time when citizens are forbidden to pray in public meetings; when people claim that you can't legislate morality, as if any law ever passed did not have at its heart some notion of right and wrong; when churches are called intruders when they speak out against public policy that is contrary to the commandments of God; when many people reject the correcting influence of churches if it infringes on daily living; when religion is accepted as a social organization but not as an integral part of national culture; when people bristle if representatives of churches speak in any forum except from the pulpit.

Indeed, some people now claim that the Founding Fathers' worst fear in connection with religion has been realized; that we have, in fact, a state-sponsored religion in America today. This new religion, adopted by many, does not have an identifiable name, but it operates just like a church. It exists in the form of doctrines and beliefs, where morality is whatever a person wants it to be, and where freedom is derived from the ideas of man and not the laws of God. Many people adhere to this concept of morality with religious zeal and fervor, and courts and legislatures tend to support it.

While you may think I am stretching the point a bit to say that amorality could be a new state-sponsored religion, I believe you would agree that we do not have to look far to find horrifying evidence of rampant immorality that is permitted if not encouraged by our laws. From the plague of pornography to the devastation caused by addiction to drugs, illicit sex, and gambling, wickedness rears its ugly head everywhere, often gaining its foothold in society by invoking the powers of constitutional privilege.

We see a sad reality of contemporary life when many of the same people who defend the right of a pornographer to distribute exploitive films and photos would deny freedom of expression to people of faith because of an alleged fear of what might happen from religious influence on government or public meetings. While much of society has allowed gambling to wash over its communities, leaving broken families and individuals in its soul-destroying wake, it reserves its harshest ridicule for those who advocate obedience to God's commandments and uniform, inspired standards of right and wrong.

As M.J. Sobran recently wrote: "A religious conviction is now a second-class conviction, expected to step deferentially to the back of the secular bus, and not to get uppity about it." (*Human Life Review,* Summer 1978, pp. 58–59.)

There are probably many reasons for the change in public attitudes toward religion. Certainly we've had too many wolves posing as shepherds, prompting a national skepticism toward any who profess to represent God. The news media, which rarely report on the good things churches are doing in the world, almost never miss an opportunity to tell people when active church members do wrong. We read about crimes that are committed by former Sunday School teachers, ministers, or missionaries. But when was the last time you read that a crime was committed by someone who hasn't stepped inside a church in forty years?

For that matter, when was the last time you saw religion or people of faith portrayed positively in any film or television program? For the most part, Hollywood's attitude toward religion is typified by the expression of cartoon character Bart Simpson, whose mealtime grace consisted of these words: "Dear God, we pay for all this stuff ourselves, so thanks for nothing." Can you imagine how embarrassed and disappointed our Founding Fathers would be to know of the blasphemous disregard many of those of the media have for God our Eternal Father. In fact, noted film critic Michael Medved accuses Hollywood of a deliberate attempt to undermine organized religion: "A war against standards leads logically and inevitably to hostility to religion, because it is religious faith that provides the ultimate basis for all standards." ("Popular Culture and the War against Standards," speech delivered at Hillsdale College, 18 Nov. 1990.)

Organized religion finds itself increasingly on the defensive. Not only are people questioning the right of the church—*any* church—to be involved in matters of public policy, but some are even beginning to wonder whether the church is entitled to exert any kind of meaningful influence on people's lives. As one churchgoer recently said on a radio talk show, "I think the world of my minister—as long as he doesn't try to tell me how to live my life."

Is it any wonder, then, that religion now finds itself under attack in legislative assemblies and in the courts? In fact, the United States Supreme Court recently discontinued the time-honored judicial standard that gave considerable legal latitude to the free exercise of religion. Allowing people of faith to practice their religion free from the burdening effects of public policy is, according to the court, "a luxury that can no longer be afforded." While the justices acknowledged that the ruling would "place at a relative disadvantage those religious practices that are not widely engaged in," they said it was "an unavoidable consequence of a democratic government." (*Oregon Employment Division* v. Smith, 1990.)

I do not promote the religious practice that was in question in that case but I am concerned with the long-term implications of the decision. Wherever religious groups are in the minority and are not considered part of the mainline religious community, the potential for state intrusion upon their religious practices is real. With legislative bodies responding most often to the will of the majority, the free exercise of religion by minority faith groups is in peril.

The Religious Freedom Restoration Act (HR 2797) is presently before Congress. This important piece of legislation is designed to restore the protections for religious freedom that existed before this recent Supreme Court decision placed those protections in jeopardy. Because the Religious Freedom Restoration Act is necessary for the preservation of the free exercise of religion, it demands our support.

The constitutional provisions relating to government and religion were not intended to control the religious rights of people. Rather, they were intended to expand them and eliminate the fear of government intrusion. These provisions were meant to separate religion and government so that religion would be independent. The experiences of Roger Williams and other reformers provided the Founding Fathers of the U.S. with important facts to help them deal with the potential risks of a state religion corrupted by politics. Consequently, they drafted an article in the Bill of Rights to guarantee religious freedom from government as opposed to government freedom from religion.

In fact, the framers of the Constitution probably assumed that religious freedom would establish religion as a watchdog over government, and believed that free churches would inevitably stand and speak against immoral and corrupt legislation. All churches not only have the right to speak out on public moral issues, but they have the solemn obligation to do so. Religion represents society's conscience, and churches must speak out when government chooses a course that is contrary to the laws of God. To remove the influence of religion from public policy simply because some are uncomfortable with any degree of moral restraint is like the passenger on a sinking ship who removes his life jacket because it is restrictive and uncomfortable.

Today, the buzz words *family values* are being incorporated in almost every politician's thirty second sound bite. But what does that phrase really mean? Whose values are we going to embrace: the values of politicians? The values the media tell us we should cherish? The values of special interest groups and organizations? The values of rank-and-file Americans, as determined by scientific survey? Obviously, it would not be politically expedient to say that the values that the Founding Fathers drew upon are eternal, unchanging values. But that is a fact. The values that made America great are, in reality, the commandments of God. They provide the foundation upon which the American republic was built. And if American democracy seems shaky today, it's only because that foundation has been eroded and weakened under the guise of separation of church and state.

Maybe Washington really was speaking of our day when he said, "If I could conceive that the general government might ever be so administered as to render the liberty of conscience insecure, no one would be more zealous than myself to establish effectual barriers against the horrors of spiritual tyranny and every species of religious persecution." (*Maxims of Washington*, p. 371.)

Samuel Adams, who is sometimes called the father of the American Revolution, wrote: "I thank God that I have lived to see my country independent and free. She may long enjoy her independence and freedom if she will. It depends upon her virtue." (Wells, *The Life of Samuel Adams*, 3:175.)

That means it depends on us. If we would maintain the independence and freedom the Founding Fathers intended, we must work to preserve and protect the moral foundation upon which they built the U.S. government. We must stand boldly for righteousness and truth, and must defend the cause of honor, decency, and personal freedom espoused by Washington, Madison, Adams, Lincoln, and other leaders who acknowledged and loved God. Otherwise, we will find ourselves in the same predicament President Lincoln observed in 1863.

Said Lincoln: "We have grown in numbers, wealth and power as no other nation has ever grown. But we have forgotten God. We have forgotten the gracious hand which preserved us in peace and multiplied and enriched and strengthened us; and we have vainly imagined, in the deceitfulness of our hearts, that all these blessings were produced by some superior wisdom and virtue of their own. Intoxicated with unbroken success, we have become too self-sufficient to feel the necessity of redeeming and preserving grace, too proud to pray to the God that made us!" (*A Proclamation "to designate and set apart a day for national prayer and humiliation."*)

Let us resolve to make our own families truly free by teaching them that God holds us all accountable. His laws are absolutes; breaking them brings misery and unhappiness; keeping them brings joy, happiness, and the blessings of heaven. Let us teach our families and others the importance of moral responsibility based on the laws of God.

The freedom we give thanks for is at stake—for ourselves and for our posterity. No nation or people that rejects God or His commandments can prosper or find happiness. History and the scriptures are filled with examples of nations that rejected God. Let us be wise and remember the source of our blessings and not be timid or apologetic in sharing this knowledge with others.

James E. Faust

James E. Faust was born on July 31, 1920 in Delta, Utah. He served in the Air Force during World War II, and as a missionary to Brazil. He attended the University of Utah, graduating with a law degree in 1948. Brother Faust then practiced law in Salt Lake City until his call to the Quorum of the Twelve on October 12, 1972. He served, at Caret, President Kennedy's Lawyer's Committee for Civil Rights and Racial Unrest. On March 12, 1995, Elder Faust was called to be a Counselor to President Gordon B. Hinckley. In this speech Elder Faust warns against the misreading of the First Amendment and the establishment of a new, secular civil religion.

July 19, 1992
A New Civil Religion
From a talk Given at a Pioneer Day fireside at
Weber State University, Ogden, Utah

We memorialize this weekend those valiant pioneers who settled Utah and the surrounding areas. They were a people persecuted and driven out of what was then the United States because of their religious beliefs. They came seeking to worship Almighty God according to the dictates of their own conscience.

Almost three centuries before, in a like manner, God-fearing believers, most notable of which were the Pilgrims, left Europe with its state religions and came to America to seek freedom of worship. As a consequence of this, the deepest taproots of the U.S. and Utah in the past have lain in the very essence of our humanity—our faith in God. Some of our coins still contain the phrase "In God We Trust." Our pledge of allegiance states that we are one nation under God, indivisible, with liberty and justice for all."

The recent controversy in Utah and the nation regarding the constitutionality of certain public prayers casts a serious cloud over the reality and meaning of the sacred in our society.

There seems to be developing a new civil religion. The civil religion I refer to is a secular religion. It has no moral absolutes. It is nondenominational. It is nontheistic. It is politically focused. It is antagonistic to religion. It rejects the historic religious traditions of America. It feels strange. If this trend continues, nonbelief will be more honored than belief. While all beliefs must be protected, are atheism, agnosticism, cynicism, and moral relativism to be more safeguarded and valued than Christianity, Judaism, and the tenets of Islam, which hold that there is a Supreme Being and that mortals are accountable to him? If so, this would, in my opinion, place America in great moral jeopardy.

For those who believe in God, this new civil religion fosters some of the same concerns as the state religions that prompted our forefathers to escape to the New World. Nonbelief is becoming more sponsored in the body politic than belief. History teaches well the lesson that there must be a unity in some moral absolutes in all societies for them to endure and progress. Indeed, without a national morality they disintegrate. In Proverbs, we are reminded that "righteousness exalteth a nation; but sin is a reproach to any people." (Prov. 14:34.) The long history and tradition of America, which had its roots in petitions for divine guidance, is being challenged.

The new civil religion is different from that envisioned by Benjamin Franklin, who seems to have first used the term "civil religion." (M. Marty, *Pilgrims in Their Own Land*, 1984, pp. 155–66.) Franklin's "civil religion," as I understand it, was envisioned to replace the state religions of Europe, with their forced taxation and oppression. Franklin no doubt envisioned that this vacuum would be filled with a patriotism reflected by national symbolism, pride, ethics, values, and purpose. His eloquent statement concerning divine intervention in the Constitutional Convention clearly indicated he was not opposed to religiosity.

FREE EXERCISE CLAUSE

The new civil religion isn't really a religion as you and I would use that term to describe a faith or a church or a synagogue of people that worship Almighty God and espouse a code of moral conduct. This new civil religion teaches a sectarian philosophy that is hostile to traditional religion. It has its own orthodoxy. It could even end up in an ironic violation of the U.S. Constitution that says that there shall be no religious basis for office. (Article IV, U.S. Constitution.) Will irreligion become a test for office? May I share with you several examples that illustrate this?

Every American has been taught that the "freedom of religion" is the "first freedom" guaranteed by the Bill of Rights. The First Amendment to the Constitution recognizes the "free exercise of religion" as the preeminent position among constitutional rights as intended by the Founding Fathers.

Most Americans are unaware, however, that two years ago this most fundamental right was substantially eroded. For decades, whenever government tried to pass a law that interfered with any right guaranteed under the Constitution, the law was given careful scrutiny by the courts. Government was required to show that first, it had a "compelling governmental interest" that justified the interference with a constitutional right, and second, that this "compelling governmental interest" could not be achieved through some other, less intrusive means. This strict scrutiny of law was applied even to rights that have been created by the courts, though they are not specifically found in the Constitution—such as the right to privacy, which is the basis for the legalization of abortion.

In the case of *Oregon Employment Division v. Smith* (110 Supreme Ct., 1595, 1990), however, this strict scrutiny and the burden on government to demonstrate a "compelling interest" was abandoned in cases involving the free exercise of religion. According to the court, religious exclusions to public policy are "a luxury we can no longer afford."

As a result, an government (federal, state, or local) can now pass any law that infringes upon individual religious liberty as long as the law applies generally to everyone.

ESTABLISHMENT CAUSE

The civil secular religion also teaches that the establishment clause of the First Amendment—companion to the "free exercise" clause—should be applied to prevent religious organizations from working cooperatively with the government to bring about worthwhile public policy. There are many laudatory public purposes, such as education, literary, public health, welfare, and assistance to the poor where charitable institutions, including churches, can and should work with government assistance programs for the public good.

There are numerous examples, however, where governments have tried to provide accommodation to religious institutions which provide public service through tax incentives, grants of educational materials, or other commodities—only to be challenged in court for fostering religion in violation of the establishment clause.

I have chosen to emphasize this subject because the twin religious clauses of the Bill of Rights—"Congress shall make no law respecting an establishment of religion nor prohibit the free exercise thereof" (First Amendment, U.S. Constitution)—are golden threads which in the past have permitted those who believe in God to publicly affirm that there is a higher power that "rules in the affairs of men." These religious clauses have fostered the creative impulses and the vitality of religion in an open heterogeneous society. They have freed this country from the terrible religious violence that has existed in Europe over the centuries and from which our forefathers in this country sought to escape. One author described these religious clauses in the Constitution as "the Articles of Peace." (Father J. Murray, *We Hold These Truths*, 1960, p. 45.)

The establishment and free exercise clauses should be read together to harmonize the importance of religious liberty with freedom from government regulation. Rather, today in our nation the establishment clause is being used to restrict religious institutions from playing a role in civic issues, and the free exercise clause denies to individuals their religious liberty. It does not accord the equivalent to what the Constitution accords to secularism—the new civil religion.

One basic deference between Franklin's concept of a civil religion and the new secular religion is that the new secular religion rejects in large measure the basic concept of Anglo-Saxon-American jurisprudence. Our traditional jurisprudence has held that God is the source of all of our basic rights, and that the principal function of government is only to secure those rights for its citizenry. May I quote from the Declaration of Independence: "We hold these truths to be self-evident, that all men are created equal; that they are endowed by their Creator with certain inalienable rights;. . . that to secure these rights, governments are instituted among men."

In contrast, the new civil religion I speak of finds its source of rights by invoking the power of the state. It seems to have little purpose, few common values for morality except self-interest. Most recently that power was invoked by the Supreme Court in a case known in legal circles as *Lee v. Weisman*. This is the case that resulted in the Supreme Court's banning ceremonial prayer at public school exercises. Commenting on the case, Edwin Yoder, distinguished columnist for the *Washington Post*, observed that "the decision is more than a natural extension of the original school prayer decision of 1962. It more closely resembles a promotion of secularity in the public forum—a result which some of the framers of the First Amendment establishment clause probably did not so much as dream of."

Yoder further states: "Religion has a legitimate public ceremonial and community function which may be stunted by such decisions. It is far from clear why children, even of tender years, need to be protected from religion, even on special ceremonial occasions." There are natural safeguards in a God-fearing people that promote respect for law and order, decency, and public civility. That restraining influence is the belief that the citizenry will be accountable to their Creator for their conduct under a high moral law. This respect for and adherence to moral law transcends the constraints of the civil and criminal codes. In a people who are not God-fearing however, these characteristics are notably absent.

When recently viewing residents of Los Angeles lawlessly looting business establishments and happily carrying out stolen goods, when viewing the daily television fare, and when confronted with the overwhelming social ills of this country, we can hardly say that our citizenry have been overexposed to moral teachings. One of the responsibilities of government under their police powers is to protect the health, safety, and morals of the citizenry. Our governments have not succeeded well in this duty of protecting morals, especially to the coming generation.

The new civil religion is, in my opinion, coming dangerously close to become a *de facto* state religion of secularism. Litigation—and the fear of litigation—have made school boards and local governments reluctant to publicly defend moral principles. As a consequence, fewer public institutions are willing to take the stand in defense of moral values.

With the public religion now turning increasingly toward the secular, I wonder how this nation will preserve its values. In my view, there is a substantial governmental interest within the limits of the religious clauses of the Constitution in public prayer and expressions of all faiths which acknowledge the existence of deity. Such prayer and expressions accommodate the abiding values shared by a great majority of our citizenry. They give meaning to a transcendent spiritual reality and idealism which, in the past at least, were quite firmly held by the people of our society. The very essence of our concern for human welfare and alleviation of human suffering lies in our spiritual feelings and expressions.

So now we find ourselves in a situation where, unlike the Pilgrims, the Mormon pioneers, and others, there is nowhere to go to escape a new civil *de facto* secular state religion that continually limits public religious expression and fosters instead the secular values and expressions. How do we preserve the essence of our humanity?

Surely we must begin in our homes. We must teach our children and grandchildren. The moral teachings of all our churches must have an honored place in our society. The general decline in the moral fabric of the citizenry places a greater responsibility on homes and churches to teach values—morality, decency, respect for others, patriotism, and honoring and sustaining the law.

We can exercise our right, with all other citizens, to vote for men and women who reflect our own values. We can also express our views as all other citizens have a right to do in the legislative process of both the state and the nation. With all others, we can claim our rights of free expression. We can petition for the redress of grievances.

We must hold to our beliefs and do what we can, for there is no desert to flee to in order to have full freedom. There is no place across the waters for the Pilgrims.

Neal A. Maxwell

Born on July 6, 1926, Elder Neal A. Maxwell has spent much of his life as an educator. He earned both his Bachelor's and Master's degrees at the University of Utah, where he eventually became an Executive Vice President. He served as the Church Commissioner for Education and was called as a member of the First Quorum of the Seventy in 1976. He was ordained an Apostle on July 23, 1981. In this speech Elder Maxwell uses the song "America the Beautiful" as a standard against which to measure serious flaws in contemporary society. While our inspired Constitution is designed to protects us from excesses in governmental power, it cannot protect us from our own excessive appetites or from indifference to basic principles.

July 4, 1993
America: "God Mend Thine Every Flaw"

Usually, and rightfully, we celebrate that dimension of patriotism which honors Americans who have fought militarily in defense of our freedoms—even going abroad to rescue the unfree and to make safe the distant shore.

Being privileged, almost within the month, to visit the 122-acre cemetery in France overlooking Omaha Beach, with its more than nine thousand sobering graves, was a moving experience. Families strolled the peaceful Omaha Beach that day. Gulls looped and swooped in serene flight. What a contrast to the thundering sounds of intense battle on that beach and on its overlooking bluffs, where, next June, it will be fifty years since D-Day at Normandy! What an unselfish thing it was for so many to give their lives so far from home and in behalf of so many others—whom they never even knew, but who nevertheless yearned for freedom!

Earlier that have also been, for me, tender and sobering visits back to Okinawa, where I participated briefly as an infantry-man in that World War II campaign, and heard, firsthand, what General MacArthur called "the strange, mournful mutter of the battlefield." (Army General Douglas MacArthur. Address accepting Sylvanus Thayer Award, West Point, 12 May 1962.) For me, therefore, this traditional dimension of patriotism is particularly and understandably touching and impressive. Yet it is only one important dimension of patriotism, for there are other expressions of patriotism that beckon us.

No attempt will be made tonight to exaggerate the virtues of America's past or to exaggerate the flaws of its present. Even so, reflecting on that special patriotic hymn, "America the Beautiful," provides so much to ponder! Given America's present circumstances, certain of the hymn's lyric phrases are actually haunting.

As we sing, for instance, of a "patriot dream that sees beyond the years," it reminds us of the special perspective that patriotism possesses. True patriotism takes a long view of this nation's needs. For instance, what does this reminding lyric tell us about our consistent and collective refusal, regardless of party, to face America's mounting national debt and our destabilizing budget deficits? The national debt increases one *billion* dollars every 24 hours— or in other words, during the few minutes I occupy this pulpit, America's national debt will grow by $694,444 *per minute*—approximately $21 million dollars! By this persistent lack of national resolve in our time we are robbing our children and grandchildren, however silently, of their economic freedom and future. We cannot seem to see beyond the political moment, let alone "beyond the years." Indeed, if certain conditions remain uncorrected in a lasting way, the "patriots' dream" may be replaced by some nightmares!

So it is that, whenever we talk about patriotism, the risks are that we will define it too narrowly. Moreover, no dimension of true patriotism is unworthy. Rather, no one portion comprises the whole of full patriotism. For instance, we would all quickly agree that patriotism is more than paying taxes. It is likewise more than voting. Yet it includes these—along with all the other unglamorous chores of citizenship. Patriotism requires public perspiration as well as an educated public . . . who can see "beyond the years."

Besides, the perspective of patriotism is vital because democracy and memory are not automatic partners, as Tocqueville observed: "Not only does democracy make every man forget his ancestors, but it hides his descendants and separates his contemporaries from him; it throws him back forever upon himself alone and threatens in the end to confine him entirely within the solitude of his own heart." (Alexis de Tocqueville, *Democracy in America*, as quoted in Andrew M. Scott, *Political Thought in America*, Rinehart & Co., Inc., 1959, p. 225.) Such loneliness an isolation can increase selfishness.

By contrast, James Wilson, one of America's founding fathers, urged delegates to the Constitutional Convention of 1787 to look beyond their own time and constituencies to the needs of generations yet unborn. They did, and all succeeding generations were blessed! Patriotism that sees "beyond the years" leaves legacies to rising generations instead of debt. It leaves clean turf, not the debris-strewn fields of a selfish society. Tolkien wisely counseled: "It is not our part to master all the tides of the world, but to do what is in us for the succour of those years wherein we are set, uprooting the evil in the fields that we know, so that those who live after may have clean earth to till. What weather they shall have is not ours to rule." (Gandolf in *The Return of the King*, by J.R.R. Tolkien. New York: Ballantine Books, 1965, p. 190.)

How are we doing with "those years wherein we are set"?

As we sing the words "confirm thy soul in self-control," what of our society's increasing lack of impulse control? So many people "act out" their impulses in so many inappropriate and destructive ways, including the neglect of families and children. More than we realize, our whole society really rests on the capacity of its citizens to give "obedience to the unenforceable." We do this by complying willingly with the law and behaving voluntarily according to time-tested standards. Such citizenship expresses a high form of volunteerism. In contrast, widespread and sustained lack of self control, however, will bring either several external controls or anarchy. America's founders were determined to avoid both of those awful alternatives.

The lack of self-control collectively and individually adds to our debt, to America's devastating drug problem, and to our growing crime. The quality of self-control is best grown in healthy family gardens, yet so many families are failing. Healthy families are the first places in which we learn how to balance rights and responsibilities.

In "America the Beautiful" we also sing about establishing a "thoroughfare of freedom." Many of our streets, instead of being a "thoroughfare of freedom," are unsafe. Ironically, drugs and pornography often have staked out their own well-worn "thoroughfares" or corridors, and "free" zones. Surely it is one of the first duties of government to protect its citizens. Nevertheless, however beefed up, law enforcement cannot realistically be expected to compensate fully for widespread lack of individual self-control.

We rightly sing about how a "good" America should be crowned "with brotherhood." But instead of increasing brotherhood there is increasing separatism. There is even rising racism. Among our citizens there is also decreasing respect for each other. Engulfing gangs remind us soberingly of failing families and neighborhoods.

We sing, too, about how our "alabaster cities gleam, undimmed by human tears." Yet our cities don't gleam. Many are decaying, covered with graffiti. They are dimmed with human tears of desperation by those who feel left out of the American dream.

The challenges of urban decay actually threaten to overwhelm America. Thomas Jefferson was especially farseeing when he said that once people were piled upon people in big cities in America, then, as in Europe, America would have serious problems. We do!

Sorely needed, therefore, are wise expressions of patriotism that will improve the quality of life in our decaying cities.

We plead for God to "mend" America's "every flaw." But can we both acknowledge our flaws productively and believe in the Mender? God's blessings will depend upon our behavior. We can be "free from bondage, and from captivity," if we serve God (see Ether 2:12).

Being worthy of America's past and deserving God's blessings in the future are vital not only for America but also for the world. More hinges on what happens in America than we realize. It was so in the beginning as the Declaration of Independence was one of the special acts in human history. It not only affected the people of America but also spurred much of mankind. In an address in Independence Hall on February 22, 1861, Abraham Lincoln so noted, saying:

> *I have often pondered over the dangers which were incurred by the men who assembled here and framed and adopted that Declaration. I have pondered over the toils that were endured by the officers and soldiers of the army who achieved that independence. I have often inquired of myself what great principle or idea it was that kept this Confederacy so long together. It was not the mere matter of separation of the colonies from the motherland, but that sentiment in the Declaration of Independence which* gave liberty not alone to the people of this country, but hope to all the world, for all future time. *It was that which gave promise that in due*

time the weights would be lifted from the shoulders of all men, and that all should have an equal chance. *This is the sentiment embodied in the Declaration of Independence. (Emphasis added.)*

America, with all its problems, is still a beacon. This beacon needs to shine more brightly today for the sake of all mankind in order to give, in Lincoln's words, "hope to all the world."

Whatever the dimension of patriotism, it requires that America have and maintain a spiritual core in order that our hopes are not in vain. Without this spiritual core, our liberties, our cities, our fiscal policies, and our brotherhood will finally falter and fail.

Virtue must, therefore, reside in the people as well as in the leaders. John Adams so cautioned: "Our constitution was made only for a moral and religious people. It is wholly inadequate to the government of any other." (In John R. Howe, Jr., *The Changing Thought of John Adams* [Princeton: Princeton University Press, 1966], p. 185.)

Unexciting as a prescription, nevertheless the best single way to improve the quality of life in America is to improve the quality of our own individual lives and our own neighborhoods. Otherwise, citizen failures to respect property or chastity—with all the consequences of those failures—cannot be corrected by mere legislation. Similarly, our neglect of the poor or of our civic duties cannot be corrected merely by Executive Orders.

· Our inspired Constitution is wisely designed to protect us from our excess of power, but it can do little to protect us from excesses of appetite or from our indifference to great principles or institutions.

Any significant unraveling of the moral fiber of the American people, therefore, finally imperils the Constitution. The moral fabric of this society can become dangerously and relentlessly frayed as too few strands strain to hold us together. Hence shared patriotic, spiritual, and moral commitments within this nation's borders are as vital as defending those borders!

Therefore, while great leaders are needed, so also are informed and wise followers. John Stuart Mill counseled as follows:

> *A people may prefer a free government, but if, from indolence, or carelessness, or cowardice, or want of public spirit, they are unequal to the exertions necessary for preserving it; if they will not fight for it when it is directly attacked; if they can be deluded by the artifices used to cheat them out of it; if by momentary discouragement, or temporary panic, or a fit of enthusiasm for an individual, they can be induced to lay their liberties at the feet even of a great man, or trust him with powers which enable him to subvert their institutions, in all these cases they are more or less unfit for liberty: and though it may be for their good to have had it even for a short time, they are unlikely long to enjoy it. (Considerations on*

Representative Government *[London: Parker, Son, and Bourn, West Strand., 1861], p. 6).*

Aaron Wildavsky observed of the interaction of people and their leaders:

Surely it would be surprising if the vices of politicians stemmed from the virtues of the people. What the people do to their leaders must be at least as important as what the leaders do to them.

Citizenship and leadership are thus intertwined. So are individual morality and constitutional viability. So are rights and responsibilities.

Our various Constitutional freedoms are likewise irrevocably intertwined. For instance, President Rex Lee has observed of the interplay of certain freedoms: "Like the speech, press, and assembly guarantees, the free-exercise-of-religion clause deals directly with the protection of individual liberties, whereas the establishment clause is a structural provision, regulating institutional relationships between church and state. Moreover, speech and assembly are central to most religious activity." (Rex E. Lee, *A Lawyer Looks at the Constitution* [Provo: Brigham Young University Press, 1981], p. 135.)

As I move to the concluding portions, let us part the curtains of American history briefly. Doing so can permit our rich past to inspire our troubled present. This nation had an inspired and breathtakingly close passage in its founding. The initial success in founding this nation was not accidental; it was inspirational!

Catherine Drinker Bowen's book about the Constitutional Convention was appropriately called *Miracle at Philadelphia.* She wrote: "Miracles do not occur at random, nor was it the author of this book who said there was a miracle at Philadelphia in the year 1787. George Washington said it, and James Madison. They used the word in writing to their friends: Washington to Lafayette, Madison to Thomas Jefferson." (Catherine Drinker Bowen, *Miracle at Philadelphia* [Boston: Little, Brown, and Company, 1986], p. xi.)

Historian Barbara Tuchman called our founding fathers "the most remarkable generation of public men in the history of the United States or perhaps of any other nation" (Barbara W. Tuchman, *The March of Folly,* [New York: Alfred A. Knopf, 1984], p. 381). Tuchman said "it would be invaluable if we could know what produced this burst of talent from a base of only two and a half million inhabitants" (Tuchman, p. 383).

Some of us believe there was divine design associated with that "burst of talent," involving "wise men whom [God] raised up unto this very purpose" (D&C 101:80).

Of one of these, Washington, his prize-winning biographer, Flexner, has written: "In all history few men who possessed unassailable power have used that power so gently and self-effacingly for what their best instincts told them was the welfare of their neighbors and all mankind" (James Thomas Flexner, *Washington The Indispensable Man* [New York: Plume, 1984], p. xvi).

Power is most safe with those, like Washington, who are not in love with it.

The miracle of constitution writing at Philadelphia was soon followed by a second miracle, the miracle of Constitution ratification that ensued for ten months. Most of the same individuals "raised up" to write the Constitution also labored to help secure its ratification. But not all. Fighting ratification were prestigious and influential patriots like Samuel Adams, James Winthrop, George Mason, James Monroe—later to be the fifth president— and Patrick Henry!

In Pennsylvania, anti-federalists tried to stay away from the meeting in order to prevent the formation of the required quorum for ratification. Finally, two of the recalcitrant, anti-federalist assemblymen were dragged in and held in their seats until the business was successfully concluded. In December, after Pennsylvania ratified the Constitution, a mob attacked and beat James Wilson, the distinguished founding father quoted from earlier. Rhode Island did not even ratify until after the new government was functioning.

New Hampshire narrowly approved by 57 to 46, Virginia approved by a margin of only 10 out of 168. New York approved by the narrowest margin of 30 to 27.

Over two hundred years have passed since the twin miracles of writing and ratifying the Constitution. Surely America has not come thus far only to squander our precious liberties in license or our economic strengths in national indulgence!

In a real way, each generation of Americans has its chance to re-ratify the Constitution. We can do this by abiding by its principles and by leaving our own legacy to posterity; likewise, by both preserving our rights and filling our responsibilities. Otherwise, expressions of patriotism are no more than verbal veneration without actual emulation! Re-ratification will require statesmanship among both people and leaders. Statesmanship does not treat symptoms, but cures the underlying diseases. our founding fathers did statesman-like work in 1776 and 1787. In our time, sadly, we seem preoccupied with treating symptoms, with quick fixes, and with getting by a little longer.

Yes, our Constitution has a marvelous system of checks and balances. But if uninspired individuals lack their own checks and balances, the inspired Constitution cannot correct that imbalance.

More remedies for our nation's ills are to be found in individual restraint than in restraining orders. More remedies are to be found inside our souls than inside our courts. Or, in families than in legislative bodies! There is more need for neighborly affection than for litigation in resolving local disputes.

Yes, courts can adjudicate between citizens, but courts cannot supply one citizen with esteem for his fellow citizens.

Washington in his "Farewell Address" counseled: "Of all the dispositions and habits which lead to political prosperity, religion and morality are indispensable supports. In vain would that man claim the tribute of patriotism who should labor to subvert these great pillars of human happiness—the firmest props of the duties of men and citizens. The mere politician, equally with the pious man, ought to respect and cherish them. A volume could not trace all their connections with private and public felicity."

Earlier, in his first inaugural, Washington said: "There exists in the economy and course of nature an indissoluble union between virtue and happiness . . . we ought to be no less persuaded that the propitious smiles of Heaven can never be expected on a nation that disregards the eternal rules of order and right which Heaven itself has ordained."

Significantly, the Senate replied to Washington's Inaugural, saying: "We feel, sir, the force and acknowledge the justness of the observation that the foundations of our national policy should be lain in private morality. If individuals be not influenced by moral principles, it is in vain to look for public virtue." (Thomas G. West, "The Rule of Law in the Federalist," in *Saving the Revolution: The Federalist Papers and the American Founding*, ed. Charles R. Kesler [New York: The Free Press, 1987], 166–67.)

May I presume to speak for all of us as if to Washington on this July Fourth night, 1993, and say, with those senators, "We feel, Sir, the force and acknowledge the justness of your observations."

God bless America by helping us to mend our flaws! God bless all of you, in the name of Jesus Christ. Amen.

Jeffrey R. Holland

Jeffrey R. Holland was born in St. George, Utah on December 3, 1940. He earned both his Bachelor's and Master's degrees from Brigham Young University. He then continued his education at Yale University, where he earned another Master's degree and a Doctorate in American Studies. He has served as the Church Commissioner of Education and as a member of the First Quorum of Seventy. He was called and ordained a member of the Quorum of the Twelve June 23, 1994. In this 1996 address, Elder Holland affirms that the Constitution is dependant largely upon the virtue of the people, rather than merely on a structural system of checks and balances.

June 30, 1996
"Except the Lord Build the House"

Dear friends and neighbors, brothers and sisters. Thank you for the invitation to be with you tonight on a campus I dearly love in a community we long called home. I also thank you for the privilege of being involved in what has become a magnificent Fourth of July tradition in this state. I pay tribute to those who do so much to make this annual Freedom Festival all that it has become and all that it will again be this week.

I have loved the Fourth of July for as long as I can remember. In St. George, during my growing up years virtually every young boy in town slept out of doors on the night of the third of July, carefully positioned in a sleeping bag out on his front lawn. That way he would not miss any of the fireworks and rocketry that my father and other civic leaders helped introduce and perpetuate in what was then a quiet and sleepy southern Utah community.

Actually the front lawn at the Holland home seemed to attract more than its share of boys on the night of the third because on the morning of the Fourth each would find under his pillow a bottle of homemade, hand-bottled, nigh-unto-exploding bottle of root beer they could enjoy at their leisure right at sunrise. That was when the six-piece senior citizen band would ride through town playing with all the zeal (if not quite the precision or tonality) of a John Philip Sousa contingent. Such a patriotic arousal on the morning of the Fourth, followed by Alice Holland's waffles for as many boys as were there to eat them, is one of the sweet and permanent memories of my youth. Thanks again to our Freedom Festival team for providing a younger generation of girls and boys with new memories of what Independence Day in Provo will always mean to them.

Today, however, I have memories of a different kind—and not quite so joyful. They are reflections on my experience of just a few days ago. Last Sunday I addressed the members of The Church of Jesus Christ of Latter-day Saints gathered in Budapest, Hungary, in a large building not far from the beautiful Hungarian Statue of Liberty that overlooks that city, so war-torn and devastated for so much of this century. Just the Tuesday before that I had met with a counterpart group of Latter-day Saints in Prague, the capital of the Czech Republic, a beautiful land that has lived with tyranny and despotism and occupation for nearly three-fourths of this century.

In between those two wonderful experiences in these marvelously renewed nations now bustling with freedom, and loving it, I traveled down between the now-fateful nations of Croatia and Serbia to go into the devastating interior of Bosnia in order to meet with and try to give inspiration to our LDS military troops who are deployed there in a difficult and demanding peacekeeping assignment.

I will leave all the emotion and details of that sobering experience for another day, but suffice it to say I literally wept as I stood on a windswept hill overlooking Sarajevo and saw the scarred remains of what no one would have believed could happen in the enlightened and freedom-granting days of the 1990s. This had been the site of the 1984 Winter Olympics, one of the loveliest little mountain cities in all Europe. And now it appeared like a scene out of the Apocalypse.

These lines from the book of Revelation were riveted in my mind: "And I looked, and behold a pale horse and his name that sat on him was Death, and Hell followed with him. And power was given unto them over the fourth part of the earth, to kill with sword, and with hunger, and with death, and with the beasts of the earth."[1] After a very long and demanding trip, with such scenes as those in Bosnia indelibly impressed on my mind and heart forever, I found myself coming home with renewed appreciation for the lines of Henry Van Dyke I had heard in my youth:

> So it's home again, and home again, America for me!
> My heart is turning home again, and there I long to be
> In the land of youth and freedom beyond the ocean bars,
> Where the air is full of sunlight and the flag is full of stars.[2]

By and large this is not a time of war for Americans generally, and we feel wonderfully safe in these valleys of the mountains. But I come to you today having just seen war, and war of the worst kind, a kind that can be sobering for us even in the sweet splendor of these summer Utah days. For in this tragedy that was once Yugoslavia I saw *not* the battle lines of large nations or differences that were entire continents apart. No, this was not the stuff of G.I. Joe movies I had seen as a boy in the old Dixie Theater in St. George. What I saw was the tragic, telling, catastrophic effects of a war *between neighbors,* a war between people living on the same street, a war among families clustered in groups of houses exactly like those in which you and I live.

What I saw was not a war of despotism and tyrants—though there have been some of those in this conflict—but it was rather a war of venom and malice and villainy in the human hearts—hatred embedded in human beings who were together very much like you and I live together in Provo and Orem and Pleasant Grove and Santaquin and Payson and anywhere else we might come from tonight. I was brought up short by the stark scenes before me that war is not something always waged by an Adolf Hitler or a Joseph Stalin, those personifications of evil from days of my boyhood. No, in this worst-case example the ruthless and relentless were Adolf who lived across the street and Joseph who owned the home just next door. This tragic Yugoslavian war is horrible most of all because it has been neighbor against neighbor, and although peace has been imposed, fear and disbelief still stare blankly from the faces of the people who have survived that war.

These sobering thoughts about the human heart and the central issue of morality and tolerance and personal character have driven me back on this Fourth of July to a consideration of the foundation of this republic. The reminder that I wish to leave with you tonight is that our special American history and our unique democratic experience in living together and prospering together declares the everlasting truth that freedom and self-government and civility and peace require something from the *people,* not just the government—people who know they must love the noble and demonstrate the moral, people who must reject the darker impulses and influences in this world, people who must practice virtue and protect the high hopes for safety and happiness that they and every one of their neighbors has the right to embrace and uphold. The key to peace and liberty—private or public, individual or national—lies within the hearts and souls of you and me. The hope of "liberty and justice for all" (to quote from our Pledge of Allegiance) is a hope that must emanate from our families, our homes, our schools, and our neighborhoods. The call to patriotism is the call to every one of us, because war of the Bosnian brand is only a neighbor away.

That is a principle upon which this marvelous nation of ours was built. Long before the Declaration of Independence and the Revolution of 1776 a common system of human values had led to that emerging sense of something that was to be called America. Since the first Pilgrims had landed on our eastern shores there had been a belief that these settlers were led by heaven and that they had before them a great mission, an important obligation to live in a certain way and reflect certain ideals. They had obligations to God and to their fellow men and women.

In 1620, while still aboard their sailing vessel on their way to America, our ancestors entered into a covenant known as the Mayflower Compact, in which they stated: "We whose names are underwritten . . . do by these Presents, solemnly and mutually in the presence of God and one another, covenant and combine ourselves together into a civil Body Politik." One legal scholar reviewing that language termed it a truly "extraordinary statement" with the realization that, in the form of what was virtually a religious covenant, these Pilgrims were voluntarily choosing to limit their personal power and their individual exercise of political force in order to have something larger, something greater, something called the common good.

Some of the clergymen among that band of colonists saw this as a new "promised land" set apart by God for a new people, a new expression of religious living, a new state, even a New Jerusalem. And that would require selfless citizens indeed. As John Winthrop, one of the greatest of all those first Puritans, stated in 1630: "We must consider that we shall be as a City upon a Hill, [where] the eyes of all people are upon us."[3] "We must be knit together in this work as one . . . we must delight in each other, make others' conditions our own, rejoice together, mourn together, labor and suffer together . . . as members of the same body."

A first generation Puritan layman praised this colonial adventure as the settlement of a new Mount Zion in the American wilderness, and during the Revolution many of the clergy used the pulpit openly and often brazenly for a call to arms, typically referring to the revolutionary troops as the "Armies of Israel." "The finger of God," said Phillip Payson in 1782 "has been so conspicuous in every stage of our glorious struggle, that it seems as if the wonders and miracles performed for Israel of old were repeated over anew for the American Israel in our day."[4]

Many would have agreed with the vision of French philosopher Alexis de Tocqueville, who later visited America in 1831. It seemed to him that this land had been "kept in reserve by the Deity,"[5] that the colonists were "not a mere party of adventurers gone forth to seek their fortune beyond [the] seas, but the germ of a great nation wafted by Providence to a predestined shore."[6] "I think I see," he wrote, "the destiny of America embodied in the first [believer] who landed on these shores, just as the whole human race was represented by the first man [Adam]."[7]

So our American fathers and mothers believed and lived. As events transpired leading to the Declaration of Independence, the American Revolution, and the adoption of a Constitution, the founders spoke more and more in terms of a "mission" for the new land they occupied, and reference to an intervening Providence appeared increasingly in their writings and their spoken word. Their sense of history and belief in God combined to engender a cautious hypothesis that Providence had placed them in this place and at this time with opportunities that had great import for all humanity for all time to come.

In the Philadelphia Convention, Benjamin Franklin reminded his colleagues that "All of us who were engaged in this struggle must have observed frequent instances of a Superintending providence in our favor. . . . The longer I live," he said, "the more convincing proofs I see of this truth—that God governs in the affairs of men."[8]

James Madison wrote in the *Federalist*, "It is impossible for the man of pious reflection not to perceive in it a finger of that Almighty hand which has been so frequently and signally extended to our relief in the critical stages of the Revolution."[9]

George Washington insisted that the "Supreme Being" had protected "the liberty and happiness of these United States. . . . The hand of Providence has been so conspicuous in all this," he said, "that he must be worse than an infidel that lacks faith, and more than wicked, that has not gratitude enough to acknowledge his obligations [in return]."[10] In his Inaugural Address, Washington stated: "No people can be found to acknowledge and adore the

Invisible Hand which conducts the affairs of men more than the people of the United States. Every step by which they have advanced to the character of an independent nation seems to have been distinguished by some token of Providential agency."

And so the theme would continue. In Thomas Jefferson's Second Inaugural Address, he acknowledged "that Being in whose hands we are, who led our forefathers as Israel of old, from their native land and planted them in a country flowing with all the necessaries and comforts of life, who has covered our infancy with his Providence and our ripe years with his wisdom and power."[11]

The responsibilities of a new nation weighed heavily upon the Founders. Given their understanding of the complexity of man, including the possibility of dark forces and feelings, they were forced to ask themselves: Is a republic even possible? Indeed, were the people of America capable of self-government? Was the "genius of the people" (which meant their total character) strong enough to support any form of democracy?

James Madison spent much of his time attempting to prove that America had been chosen by Providence for this grand experiment in testing the human capacity for self-government. "The free system of government we have established," he said, "[will] produce approbation and a desire for imitation. . . . Our country, if it does justice to itself, will be the workshop of liberty to the Civilized World, and do more than any other for the uncivilized."[12]

The times were such that Thomas Paine wrote in his *Common Sense,* "The cause of America is in great measure the cause of all mankind."[13] John Adams prophesied that if America failed in her divinely appointed mission, it would be "treason against the hopes of the world."[14] And Thomas Jefferson confirmed, "The last hope of human liberty rests on us."[15]

Still, the great question remained: were these American people in this new American nation really capable of fulfilling their personal, ethical, private as well as public responsibilities, especially as they believed them to be God-given responsibilities?

Through their knowledge of history, their commitment to the moral values and traditions in which they believed, and through their own experience, the American founding fathers knew that *a morally corrupt people could never enjoy the luxury of freedom.* Their teacher, the great English philosopher, Edmund Burke, had said it best:

"Men are qualified for civil liberty in exact proportion to their disposition to put moral chains on their own appetites. [May I repeat that: *"Men are qualified for civil liberty in exact proportion to their disposition to put moral chains on their own appetites."*] . . . Society cannot exist unless a controlling power upon the will and appetite be placed somewhere, and the less of it there is within, the more there must be without. It is ordained in the eternal constitution of things, that men of intemperate minds cannot be free Their passions forge their fetters."[16]

Among the most important terms used in this new language of the Republic were "moral sense" and "virtue." Thomas Jefferson, for example, believed that if moral sense and personal virtue had not been God-given within the human being, then the building of any republic—especially the one we enjoy today—would simply have been impossible.

According to Jefferson, "passions and appetites are parts of human nature," but so are "reason and moral sense."[17] "It would have been inconsistent [by God] in [the very act of] creation," he insisted, "to have found man for [life in a] social state, and not to have provided virtue and wisdom enough to manage the concerns of [that] society."[18] "I believe that it is instinct[ive], and innate, that the moral sense is as much a part of our [personal] constitution as that of feeling, seeing, or hearing. A wise Creator must have seen [this as] necessary in [a being] destined to live [together] in society."[19]

But men and women would not always be moral and they would not always demonstrate virtue.

As James Madison wrote in the *Federalist*, "men are not angels," and "good men will not always be at the helm,"[20] therefore "auxiliary precautions" would be necessary that is, certain checks and balances in government, which would be supportive to a people striving to be virtuous.[21]

But no system of checks and balances can withstand forever the multiplying forces of selfishness, malice, and immorality. The moral sense, though God given, can be damaged and diminished. Virtue, inherent within all, can be compromised and corrupted.

And the founding fathers warned time after time against such a possibility.

George Washington reminded us that "reason and experience both forbid us to expect that national morality can prevail in exclusion of religious principles. It is substantially true, that virtue and morality are a necessary [foundation] of popular government."[22]

At the Constitutional Convention in 1787, Benjamin Franklin voiced his concern that although the new government would likely "be well administered for a course of years," it *could* "end in despotism, as other forms have done before it, when the people have become so corrupted as to need despotic government, being incapable of any other."[23]

John Adams warned two years later: "We have no government . . . capable of contending with human passions unbridled by morality and religion."[24] At another time he wrote, "Liberty can no more exist without virtue . . . than the body can live without a soul."[25] And Samuel Adams added, although "revelation assures us that 'righteousness exalteth a nation,' . . . the public liberty will not long survive the total extinction of morals."[26] "If we are universally vicious and debauched in our manners," he warned, "though the form of our

Constitution carries the face of the most exalted freedom, we shall in reality be the most abject of slaves."[27]

In that spirit James Madison cried out: "Is there no virtue among us? If there be not, we are in a wretched situation No theoretical checks—no form of government—can render us secure. To suppose that any form of government will secure liberty or happiness without any virtue in the people, is a chimerical idea."[28]

With this understanding, a critically important realization came to bear on the minds and hearts of the founding fathers. Success in their endeavors depended not only upon virtue in the people at that time, but it also depended on the continuation of those virtues in every successive generation to come.

Clearly the key to true liberty lay in the human heart, and today that means our hearts—yours and mine and our children and our children's children—as well as those of Pilgrims, Puritans, and the original founding fathers.

As Alexander Hamilton said so beautifully: "The sacred rights of mankind are not to be rummaged for among old parchments and musty records. They are written as with a sunbeam in the whole volume of human nature, by the hand of Divinity itself, [upon the soul of man]. . . . The Supreme Being gave existence to man, together with the means of preserving and beautifying that existence. He endowed him with rational faculties, by which he could discern and pursue such things as were consistent with his duty and interest, and invested him with an inviolable right to personal liberty and personal safety."[29]

So America was founded on principles of personal virtue and private morality that would give meaning and vitality to those more technical political principles of constitutional government with its executive, legislative, and judicial branches of activity. Undergirding all of this was the commitment of the individual citizen as well as that of the elected official. From such a personal devotion would come the determination to live together in peace and liberty and safety and freedom. These are blessings we want for ourselves, our children, our neighborhoods and our world. They are very much the blessings for which this nation was settled and for which that initial War of Independence was fought.

War waged for the triumph of these blessings will still need to be fought in our time, in our day, and forever. We pray it will not be a war of weapons and bullets, but it is a war nonetheless—a daily battle of discipline and hard work and requiring help from heaven. We have to keep winning the peace in every generation by emphasizing over and over the fundamental need for virtue in the human heart. To paraphrase James Madison: "If such concepts as justice, mercy, good faith, integrity, courtesy and all the qualities which elevate the character of a nation and fulfill the ends of government—if these virtues can abide in the hearts of our people and be the objective of our civil establishments, then the cause of freedom and the rights of liberty will acquire a dignity and a luster no despot, tyrant, or warring faction can ever destroy. On the other hand, if families, or communities, or governments should in any way be blotted with the reverse of such cardinal and essential virtues—virtues which have characterized good living and good lives in every age of mankind—if we lose these virtues or pursue the opposite of them, then the great cause that we know as America will be betrayed dishonored, and finally destroyed." As Mr. Madison said, "If such an immoral and uncivil day should come [to America], then this last and fairest experiment in favor of the rights of man will be turned against him."[30]

Daniel Webster, one of the most distinguished statesmen and political orators of the nineteenth century, said: "Let us not forget the religious character of our origins. Our fathers were brought here by their high veneration for [their faith]. They journeyed by its light, and labored in its hope. They sought to incorporate its principles with the elements of their society, and to diffuse its influence through all their institutions—civil, political and literary. Let us cherish these sentiments, and extend this influence still more widely, in the full conviction that the happiest society [is the one] which partakes in the highest degree of the mild and peaceable spirit of [true Christ-like behavior]."[31]

With my renewed gratitude for the heritage and happiness that has been our history for more than two centuries I say to all, "Except the Lord build the house, they labour in vain that build it."[32] May we live in such a way that the God and Father of us all will continue to bless America, "land that we love." And may He bless all of His children everywhere—especially you and your families—forever. Have a grateful Fourth of July. Thank you and good night.

NOTES

1. Revelations 6:8.
2. Cite in *The Home Book of Quotations*, sel. Burton Stevenson (New York: Dodd, Mead & Company, 1934), p. 52.
3. John Winthrop, "A Model of Christian Charity," in Perry Miller and Thomas H. Johnson, *The Puritans* vol. 1 (New York: Harper and Row, 1963), p. 199. See also Sacvan Vercovitch, *The Puritan Origins of the American Self* (New Haven: Yale University Press, 1975.)
4. Cited in James Hitchinson Smylie's "American Clergymen and the Constitution of the United States of America, 1781–1796" (Ph.D. dissertation, Princeton Theological Seminary, Princeton, New Jersey), and quoted in

Michael Chadwick, *God's Hand in the Founding of America, As Acknowledged by the Early Clergymen of the United States* (Salt Lake City: Deseret Book Co., 1980), p. 3.

5. Alexis de Tocqueville, *Democracy in America*, trans. Henry Reeve (New York: Knopf, 1945), vol. 1, p. 302.

6. Ibid., p. 34.

7. Ibid., p. 301.

8. Max Farrand, ed., *The Records of the Federal Convention of 1787*, vol. 1, p. 451.

9. *The Federalist*, No. 20.

10. John C. Fitzpatrick, ed., *The Writings of George Washington 1745-1799* (George Washington Bicentennial Commission, 1931; reprinted at Westport, Connecticut, 1970), vol. 12, p. 343.

11. Cited in Richard Vetterli and Gary Bryner, *In Search of the Republic* (Savage, MD: Rowman & Littlefield Publishers, Inc., 1987), p. 68.

12. Adrienne Koch, *Power, Morals, and the Founding Fathers* (Ithaca, N.Y.: Cornell University Press, 1961), p. 105.

13. "There is an exaltation, an excitement, about Common Sense that conveys the very uncommon sense of adventure Americans felt as they moved toward independence. With it would come new perils, but also new opportunities, new freedoms. They knew they were on the threshold of a great experience not only for themselves but perhaps for the whole world." Edmund S. Morgan, *The Birth of the Republic* (Chicago: University of Chicago Press, 1956), p. 75.

14. L.H. Butterfield, ed., *Adams Family Correspondence* (Cambridge: Harvard University Press, 1963), pp. 30–31.

15. John Dewey, *The Living Thoughts of Thomas Jefferson* (New York: Longman's, Green, 1940), p. 56.

16. Edmund Burke, *The Works of Edmund Burke*, vol. 4 (Waltham, Mass.: Little, Brown, 1866), pp. 51–52.

17. C. F. Adams, *Writings of John Adams*, vol. 6, p. 115.

18. Lester J. Cappon, ed., *The Adams-Jefferson Letters* (Chapel Hill: University of North Carolina Press, 1959), p. 388.

19. Ibid., p. 492.

20. Willmoore Kendall and George Cary, *The Basic Symbols of the American Political Tradition* (Baton Rouge: Louisiana State University Press, 1970). See also David Epstein, *The Political Theory of the Federalist* (Chicago: University of Chicago Press, 1984).

21. *The Federalist*, No. 51.

22. George de Huszar, et al., *Basic American Documents* (Ames, Iowa: Littlefield, Adams, 1953), vol. 2, pp. 108–9.

23. Max Farrand, ed., *The Records of the Federal Convention of 1787*, vol. 2, pp. 641–42.

24. C.F. Adams, *The Works of John Adams,* vol. 9, p. 229.
25. Bernard Bailyn, "A Fear of Conspiracy against Liberty," in Robert F. Berkhofer, Jr., *The American Revolution* (Boston: Little, Brown, 1971), p. 101.
26. Letter from Samuel Adams to John Scollary of Boston, April 30, 1776; from the *Samuel Adams Papers,* Bancroft Transcripts, New York Public Library.
27. William V. Wells, *The Life and Public Services of Samuel Adams* (Boston: Little, Brown, 1865), vol. 1, p. 22–23.
28. Jonathan Elliot, ed., *The Debates in Several State Conventions on the Adoption of the Federal Constitution* (Philadelphia: Lippincott, 1890), vol. 2, p. 175.
29. Alexander Hamilton, "The Farmer Refuted," (February, 1775); John C. Hamilton, ed., *The Works of Alexander Hamilton,* vol. 2 (New York: Charles S. Francis, 1851), p. 80.
30. Gaillard Hunt, ed., *The Writings of James Madison* (New York: G. P. Putnam, 1902), vol. 1, pp. 459–60.
31. Cited in *The Treasure Chest,* ed. Charles L. Wallis [New York: Harper & Row, Publishers, 1965], p. 177.
32. Psalm 127: 1.

Gordon B. Hinckley

Gordon B. Hinckley was born June 23, 1910. He became the 15th President of the Church in 1995. He has had a long and remarkable history of Church service. He served for twenty years as the Executive Secretary of the Church's Radio, Publicity and Literature Committee. During this time he attended the University of Utah. President Hinckley was ordained an Apostle in 1961. In 1981 he was called to the First Presidency under President Kimball and was again called to serve in the Presidencies of both President Benson and President Hunter. In these 1996 remarks at the Provo Freedom Festival, President Hinckley expresses his support and love for the Constitution and laments the increasing secularization of American society, which he sees as the source of many of the social ills that afflict us. He warns against neglecting the moral basis of the inspired Constitution.

August 4, 1996
Remarks at the Provo City Community Centennial Service

Truly we are blessed in being a part of this great nation and in living in these valleys of the western mountains. We have every reason to rejoice and be grateful.

I am enthusiastic about this part of the world. I have faith in the future of this state. I have faith in the future of my beloved America.

And yet, I am deeply concerned. I am more deeply concerned about the growing moral deficit than I am about the monetary deficit. Tonight we have given a Pledge of Allegiance to the flag of the United States and to the Republic for which it stands, "One nation under God, indivisible, with liberty and justice for all."

We sang together the first verse of our national anthem. This has become customary. I wish we would sing the third verse which reads,

> *Oh, thus be it ever, when free men shall stand*
> *Between': their loved homes and the war's desolation!*
> *Blest with vict'ry and peace, may 'he heav'n rescued land*
> *Praise the Pow'r that hath made and preserved us a nation!*
> *Then conquer we must when our cause it is just,*
> *And this be our motto: "In God is our trust!" (Hymns, #340).*

There has been going on in this nation for a good while a process which I call, "secularizing America." It is of this that I wish to say a few words this evening because I feel so strongly about it and because I feel we are paying a terrible price because of it.

A few months ago Lady Margaret Thatcher, former Prime Minister of Great Britain, spoke on this campus and in other places while she was visiting Utah. She spoke of the goodness and strength of America, which was settled by people from the British Isles who, as she said, came with the English Bible and the English common law. Those early settlers from the British Isles were Christian people who came with the Judeo-Christian concepts of right and wrong, of truth and error, which they derived from reading that Bible. They were people who looked to God for strength and inspiration and expressed their gratitude to Him for every blessing.

Lady Thatcher said, "You use the name of Deity in the Declaration of Independence and in the Constitution of the United States, and yet you cannot use it in the schoolroom." Those words of hers were almost a rebuke to America. I heard her make the statement more than once, and I have not forgotten it. This is symptomatic of what I refer to as the secularizing of America. Reverence for the Almighty, gratitude for His beneficent blessings, pleadings for His guidance, are increasingly being dropped from our public discourse. I take you back to George Washington's first inaugural address, spoken April 30, 1789, in Federal Hall in New York. Said he on that occasion:

". . . It would be peculiarly improper to omit, in this first official act, my fervent supplications to that Almighty Being, who rules over the universe, who presides in the councils of nations, and whose providential aids can supply every human defect, that His benediction may consecrate to the liberties and happiness of the people of the United States a government instituted by themselves for these essential purposes. . . . In tendering this homage to the great Author of every public and private good, I assure myself that it expresses your sentiments not less than my own; nor those of my fellow citizens at large. . . . No people can be bound to acknowledge and adore the invisible hand, which conducts the affairs of men, more than the people of the United States. Every step, by which they have advanced to the character of an independent nation, seems to have been distinguished by some token of providential agency" (*Harvard Classics*, Vol. 43, p. 242).

Wonderfully significant words are these spoken 207 years ago by him whom we idolize as the Father of our Country.

Long before that, in 1620, before the Pilgrims left the Mayflower to set foot on Plymouth Rock, they signed a compact in which they "solemnly and mutually in the presence of God, and one another, covenant and combine ourselves together into a civil body politic for our better ordering and preservation and furtherance of the ends aforesaid" (*Ibid.*, p. 62).

The motto, "In God We Trust," has graced our currency and coinage for two centuries. Now some are questioning that the practice should be continued.

Oaths of office and oaths in other legal procedures have concluded with the phrase, "So help me God."

Now, the state of New Jersey has passed a law banishing the mention of God from State courtroom oaths. The *Wall Street Journal* advised the other day that following this action by the New Jersey Legislature, a county judge now has decided to ban Bibles for such oaths "because you-know-Who is mentioned inside." The *Journal* editorial continues, "It now appears that Jersey's judges can swear in jurors however they see fit. Maybe just a non-secular wave on the way into the box" (*Wall Street Journal*, July 31, 1996).

In recent years the Boy Scouts of America have been attacked because of the language in the Scout Oath: "On my honor I will do my best, to do my duty to God, and my country."

It is acknowledgment of the Almighty that gives civility and refinement to our actions. It is accountability to Him that brings discipline into our lives. It is gratitude for His gracious favors that takes from us the arrogance to which we are so prone.

I believe that one of the root causes of the terrible social illnesses that are running rampant among us is the almost total secularizing of our public attitudes. People who carry in their hearts a strong conviction concerning the living reality of the Almighty and of accountability to Him for what we do with our lives and our society, are far less likely to become enmeshed in those problems which inevitably weaken our society. Let me briefly mention some of those problems.

The Congress and the President have recently enacted and signed new legislation concerning welfare. Hopefully, substantial good will come of it. But only a new set of rules to deal with an old problem is unlikely to produce a cure. There must be a change of attitude, the taking on of a sense of accountability for one's actions. We are shutting the doors of our homes against the God of the universe. Divine law has become a meaningless phrase. What was once so commonly spoken of as sin is now referred to only as poor judgment. Transgression has been replaced by misbehavior.

Family prayer was once the norm in the homes of the people across the nation. It has largely been forgotten. Marriage was once regarded as the most sacred of institutions, to be upheld through sunshine and storm. Now, the epidemic of divorce rages on, and while parents quarrel children suffer. The very foundation of their lives—a secure and happy home—is pulled from under them.

An editorial in the Wall Street Journal speaks of a report issued by the Council on Families in America after two years of intense study. The conclusion of that report is this: "American society would be better off if more people got married and stayed married." What a remarkable conclusion that is. Any of us in this hall could have said that without a long and costly study.

In support of its conclusion, the study states "that children who don't live with both parents are more likely to grow up poor, have problems in school, and get into trouble with the law. . . . The children in fatherless homes are five times more likely to be poor than those who live with both parents. For black families, where the decline in marriage has been most acute, 57% of children in fatherless households live in poverty, while only 15% of children in intact families are poor."

The editorial in the Journal concludes: "Marriage may be an imperfect institution, but so far in human history no one has come up with a better way to nurture children in a stable society" (*Wall Street Journal*, April 25, 1995).

Marriage was once generally regarded as a sacred sacrament. Fortunately it still is with many, and most of you in this hall can testify to that. But for the people of the nation as a whole it is becoming an increasingly secular ceremony. We are losing something. We are losing something that speaks of accountability, not only to one another, but to God who is our Father and who will stand in judgment upon us.

I am deeply concerned about the children of America, speaking of them as a whole. I am particularly concerned about the millions who come into the world with handicaps, seemingly impossible to overcome, children whose lives are blighted by neglect and abuse by parents and others, children, many of whom have limitless capacity but almost no opportunity. In the long term this may well be the most serious problem facing our nation because its consequences multiply and reach forward through generations.

The report of the *Carnegie Task Force on Meeting the Needs of Young Children* paints a dismal picture. It says:

"Our nation's infants and toddlers and their families are in trouble. Compared with most other industrialized countries, the United States has a higher infant mortality rate, a higher proportion of low birth-weight babies, a smaller proportion of babies immunized against childhood diseases, and a much higher rate of babies born to adolescent mothers. Of the twelve million children under the age of three in the United States today, a staggering number are affected by one or more risk factors that undermine healthy development. One in four lives in poverty. One in four lives in a single-parent family. One in three victims of physical abuse is a baby under the age of one" (*Carnegie Report, page* xii).

It is a startling and dismal fact that 28% of the children born to white mothers in this nation are born to single women. That is more than one in four. Sixty-eight percent of children born to black mothers across the nation, and 80% in our larger cities, are born to single women. That is four out of five.

Staggering are the burdens that are placed upon society through taxes levied to meet the needs of such children and their mothers. The *Carnegie Report* indicates that "of teens who give birth, 46% will go on welfare within four years. [That is almost one out of every two.] Of unmarried teens who give birth, 73% will be on welfare within four years." [That is almost three out of every four.]

You may ask why I am speaking along these lines tonight. You say that this is not the case in Provo. And I reply, "I know that, and I am grateful." But we are not without the problem right here. Furthermore, the problem exists in your nation, and in your world, and in your generation—and you cannot close your eyes to it because you will have to bear the burden of it.

My sad observation is that what is happening in the nation is happening likewise, even if at a lower degree, in Utah and in these very communities in which we live and prize so highly.

Every young man must be made to realize that in fathering a child he takes upon himself a responsibility that will endure as long as he lives. Let every young woman know that in giving birth to a child, she places upon herself a responsibility from which she will never be entirely free. How tragic is the desolate and ever increasing picture of illegitimate birth. With each such birth comes responsibility, to the mother, to the father if he stands up to it, and, inevitably, to society at large.

The lack of self-discipline and of a sense of responsibility, in my judgment, is one of the fruits of the increasing secularization of our society. I was appalled to read the other day that in one community a proposal was made that young women be paid a dollar a day for not becoming pregnant. How stupid. Where is our sense of values?

I recently read that between 1972 and 1990 there were twenty-seven million abortion procedures performed. Think of it. What is happening to our concept of the sanctity of life? Can we doubt that there is a sickness in our society? We cannot build prisons, even here, fast enough to accommodate the need. We have in this nation more than a million people in prison. The number is constantly increasing. Why is this happening? I believe that a substantial factor in all of this is that we as a nation are forsaking the Almighty, and He is forsaking us. We are secularizing America. We are shutting the door against the God whose sons and daughters we are. We sing, "My country, 'tis of Thee, Sweet land of liberty." We need to sing again and again the fourth verse of that hymn:

> Our fathers' God, to thee,
> Author of liberty,
> To thee we sing;
> Long may our land be bright
> With freedom's holy light.
> Protect us by thy might,
> Great God, our King! (Hymns, #339).

A recent poll indicated that a majority of Americans believe that the private lives of public officials need not be considered as a factor in their eligibility for public office. How far we have come from the time of George Washington who stated in that first inaugural address the mandate "that the foundations of our national policy will be laid in the pure and immutable principles of private morality." He went on to say, "there is no truth more thoroughly established, than that there exists in the economy and course of nature an indissoluble union between virtue and happiness, between duty and advantage, between the genuine maxims of an honest and magnanimous policy, and the solid rewards of public prosperity and felicity; since we ought to be no less persuaded that the propitious smiles of heaven can never be expected on a nation that disregards the eternal rules of order and right, which heaven itself has ordained" (Op. cit., p. 243).

It was said of old, "Where the spirit of the Lord is, there is liberty" (2 Cor. 3:17).

The Psalmist wrote, "The counsel of the Lord standeth forever, the thoughts of his heart to all generations. Blessed is the nation whose God is the Lord" (Psalms 33:11–12).

There is a divine mandate which states, "Look to God and live" (Alma 37:47).

Is the situation hopeless? No. Is it too late to begin a turnaround? It is never to late to try to improve.

Lest you think that I am only a man of gloom and doom, let me assure you that there is still so much of strength in America. There is so much of goodness in so many of her people. We live under a Constitution that after more than two centuries stands as the greatest bulwark of human freedom to be found anywhere on earth. Of it, the great Gladstone said: "As the British Constitution is the most subtle organism which has proceeded from progressive history, so the American Constitution is the most wonderful work ever struck off at a given time by the brain and purpose of man" *(Gladstone, Kin Beyond the Sea; from the North American Review* [September 1878]).

This Constitution is the keystone of our national life.

It is my faith and my conviction that it came not alone of the "brain and purpose of man," but of the inspiration of the Almighty. He Himself has declared, "I established the Constitution of this land, by the hands of wise men whom I raised up unto this very purpose . . . for the rights and protection of all flesh, according to just and holy principles" (D&C 101: 80, 77).

In this Constitution, with its Bill of Rights, are the great concepts which have made of this a mighty nation, the greatest the world has ever known.

As a nation, we have passed through terrible fires, the worst of which was the Civil War. As the tide of that terrible conflict turned in favor of the Union, President Lincoln said: "With malice toward none; with charity for all; with firmness in the right, as God gives us to see the right, let us strive on to finish the work we are in; to bind up the nation's wounds, to care for him who shall have borne the battle, and for his widow, and his orphan—to do all which may achieve and cherish a just and lasting peace among ourselves and with all nations" (Op. cit., pgs. 451–52).

That war was a great test for this nation. We survived without division. We have enjoyed the blessings of the Almighty in a world that since has been engrossed in much of conflict. We have reached out and paid a terrible price to help those of other nations. The world is so much the better, I firmly believe, for the presence of the United States of America.

The other day, I walked about the American Military Cemetery on the outskirts of Manila in the Philippines. Here, row upon row, in perfect symmetry, stand marble crosses and stars of David marking the graves of 17,000 American dead. Inscribed in the marble of beautiful colonnades surrounding that hallowed ground are 35,000 additional names, the names of those who were lost in the battles of the Pacific and whose remains were never found. Out of all of the terrible sacrifices of the First World War and the Second World War, and subsequent wars, this nation has not reached out for territory to hold, but has been magnanimous in assisting those who have been impoverished by the costs of conflict. What other nation on the face of the earth has done what the American people did under the Marshall plan for the rehabilitation of Europe?

Many years ago, we had an Arab guide when we visited Jerusalem before the 1967 war when the city was a divided city. During a moment of introspection this wise old man said, "You are part of the greatest nation on earth. You have given generously of your treasure and the lives of your people, and have never retained conquered territory as a prize of war." He went on to say. "There has never been anything else like it in human history."

These impulses still beat in the hearts of the American people.

While I speak of secularizing the nation, I am mindful of the fact that 45% of the people of America sometimes attend church. I know of nothing else quite like it. There is still much of faith and goodness in this wonderful land.

I think of our own inheritance in this State of Utah. These communities in which we live are singular in their origins. I stand in reverence before the sacrifices of our forebears who came to lay the foundations of these cities "which [you and I] built not" but in which we enjoy so much of the good life (Joshua 24:13). I stand in awe at the boldness of Brigham Young and his associates in coming here, leading thousands and tens of thousands of people to those valleys where they had never before tested farming, where they had never planted a crop or harvested one, where they knew little, if anything, of the vagaries of the soil, of weather, of the seasons. They came to these valleys and were here isolated a thousand miles from the nearest settlement to the east and 700 or 800 miles to the west. I know it was not the "blind leading the blind." I know it was the inspiration of the Almighty leading a people to a place where they could worship God according to the dictates of their own conscience and where they could extend the same privilege to all others, "let them worship how, where, or what they may" (11th Article of Faith).

There followed those of other denominations—Catholics and Protestants of various persuasions, Jews and Greeks, and more recently, Muslims. I think that without exception those who came in early days were men and women who believed in and worshiped God, although their interpretation of Him may have varied. They grew strong and have built for us a tremendous inheritance because they were men and women of faith, of conviction. They had no government largess to fall upon, but looked to God in every extremity and thanked Him for every blessing.

And so, my dear friends, I share with you a great love for this land, for this state, for these communities. I draw strength and inspiration from these magnificent mountains that are about us. I draw comfort from the integrity and goodness of so many wonderful people whom I know, and who, with you, enjoy marvelous blessings as we walk across the stage of history in our time and season. I reverence and respect those of the past who have built so well for us.

My great concern, my great interest, is that we preserve for the generations to come those wondrous elements of our society and manner of living that will bequeath to them the strengths and the goodness of which we have been the beneficiaries. But I worry as I see some of the signs of sickness of which I have spoken. I believe that a significant factor in the decay we observe about us comes of a forsaking of the God whom our fathers knew, loved, worshipped, and looked to for strength. There is a plainly discernible secularization that is occurring. Its consequences are a deterioration of family life, a weakening of self-discipline, a scoffing at the thought of accountability unto the Almighty, and an unbecoming arrogance for any people who have been so richly blessed through the goodness of a generous Providence as we have been.

This evening as we celebrate the centennial of our statehood, in these most favorable precincts, on the campus of this great university, I would hope that there would come into the heads of each of us a resolution to live nearer to God and the commandments He has given us as a guide in our lives; to walk with gratitude before Him for His generous mercies; to recognize that someday each of us must give an accounting of our lives to Him; and to seek His strength, His wisdom, His inspiration, and His love as we serve in the great society of which each of us is a part.

God bless America, and may America be worthy of His blessing.

God bless this state in which we live and the communities in which we dwell. May we walk in thankfulness before Him, putting our trust in Him, recognizing Him as the source of all true wisdom and every beneficent blessing.

Such is my prayer which I invoke in the sacred name of His Son, the Lord Jesus Christ, amen.

ABOUT THE AUTHOR

Ralph C. Hancock is Professor of Political Science at Brigham Young University, where he has taught American Heritage and political philosophy classes since 1987. An alumnus of BYU, Professor Hancock received his Ph.D. from Harvard University. He is author or editor of numerous works in political philosophy, including *Calvin and the Foundations of Modern Politics* (Cornell, 1989), *The Legacy of the French Revolution* (Rowman & Littlefield, 1996), and *America, the West, and Liberal Education* (Rowman & Littlefield, 1998). He and his wife, Julie, are the parents of five children.